D1562756

Cutback management in public bureaucracies

Cutback management in public bureaucracies

Popular theories and observed outcomes in Whitehall

ANDREW DUNSIRE
University of York

CHRISTOPHER HOOD
University of Sydney

with the assistance of
MEG HUBY
University of York

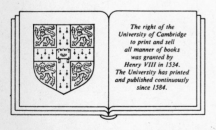

The right of the
University of Cambridge
to print and sell
all manner of books
was granted by
Henry VIII in 1534.
The University has printed
and published continuously
since 1584.

CAMBRIDGE UNIVERSITY PRESS

Cambridge

New York   Port Chester   Melbourne   Sydney

Published by the Press Syndicate of the University of Cambridge
The Pitt Building, Trumpington Street, Cambridge CB2 IRP
40th West 20th Street, New York, NY 10011, USA
10 Stamford Road, Oakleigh, Melbourne 3166, Australia

First published 1989

Printed in Great Britain at the University Press, Cambridge

British Library cataloguing in publication data

Dunsire, Andrew, 1924–
Cutback management in public bureaucracies:
popular theories and observed outcomes in
Whitehall
1. Great Britain. Civil Service. Financial
management
I. Title   II. Hood, Christopher, 1947–
III. Huby, Meg
354.410072

Library of Congress cataloguing in publication data

Dunsire, Andrew
Cutback management in public bureaucracies : popular theories and
observed outcomes in Whitehall/Andrew Dunsire, Christopher Hood,
with the assistance of Meg Huby.
        p.   cm.
Bibliography.
Includes index.
ISBN 0–521–37240–2
1. Great Britain – Officials and employees – Dismissal of.
2. Government spending policy – Great Britain.   3. Administrative
agencies – Great Britain – Management.   4. Bureaucracy – Great Britain.
5. Great Britain – Politics and government – 1979– I. Hood,
Christopher C.   II. Huby, Meg.   III. Title.
JN425.D824   1989
354.41001'84 – dc19   88–34136   CIP

ISBN 0 521 37240 2

VN

Contents

Figures

Tables

Preface

In 1976 there were nearly three-quarters of a million civil servants in the UK central government service; by 1985 there were fewer than 600,000, a drop of nearly 20 percent. This was unprecedented in modern government. We ask: how did it happen? Not *why* did it happen. Something like it is now observable in many countries, if not on quite the same scale, and with much the same ostensive justification. The spirit of the times seems to hold that people have come to expect too much of the state; bureaucracy has got out of hand; taxes are too high, and state provision does not give value for money. Even left-wing governments have embarked on cutbacks and retrenchment, voluntarily.

This is not a book about the causes or the effects of cutbacks, however, but about the process. There is no shortage of theories about what happens in times of cutback, who gets less, when, how. What has been lacking is a systematic analysis of what did happen in a specific country in a specified period. This has not come from the government. It has not even come from the cutback theorists. This is what we aim to provide: a study of the management of cutbacks which first spells out the range of theories advanced by political scientists and economists, and then tests these against what happened in Britain in the decade from the mid seventies to the mid eighties.

We are grateful, first, to the UK Economic and Social Research Council who financed the research; second, to certain officials of HM Treasury, who by convention remain anonymous but who could not have been more helpful in providing information that fell between the published and the confidential. We wish to acknowledge the great contribution to this volume of Dr Meg Huby, our resourceful Research Fellow, and to thank Professor Keith Hartley and other colleagues in the Institute for Research in the Social Sciences at the University of York, whose advice and assistance was much valued. Helpful comments on some sections of the work also came from Professor Peter Jackson and a variety of academic colleagues.

Our intellectual debt to particular scholars of the bureaucratic politics of growth and cutback, Rudolf Klein, Patrick Dunleavy, and Torben Beck Jørgensen, will become readily apparent and is gratefully acknowledged. The faults of the work are all ours.

1 The cutback management problem

Stated rationally, the 'cutback management problem' for government is how to achieve cuts in public expenditure and personnel at minimum cost to political objectives. It is not a problem that has had much rational consideration. Governments, and their advisers, have spoken of the need to rein in spending; critics have been virtually unanimous that there are too many civil servants. But there have always been many reasons why the time was not ripe for actual cuts *now*. Cutting down public bureaucracy is not easy. A great deal of academic thought has been given to explaining the problem of government *growth*, but there has been no comparable attention to explaining how the difficulties of cutting back government might best be approached, over a lengthy period of time, in a sustained campaign – until the last ten years or so.

The cutback management problem – how to wind back bureaucratic spending and staff with least damage to whatever is held dear (including one's hold on power) – can be broken up into three different kinds of problem. We can call them macro-, meso-, and micro-problems. Macro-problems concern such questions as whether to deal with imbalance by cutting expenditure or raising revenue; if to cut, whether to cut uniformly 'across the board', or cut selectively; if selectively, on what criteria; how to handle consequent unemployment; and so on. Meso-problems occur at the level of the department or agency ('organisation problems'); whether and how to 'preserve the base', whether and how to maintain existing symbiotic patterns or reorganise; whether and how to close down units (schools, wards, plant, etc.); how to maintain morale; and so on. Micro-problems affect the individual worker or small work-group: redundancies, obviously, with the family and social stresses involved; effects on promotion prospects and career choice; but also 'professional' problems, when engineers, doctors, teachers, and the like find themselves trying to maintain standards while being denied essential resources. The cumulation of these micro-effects of closures and shutdowns in a particular area affects the local economy and community health and spirit.

We are not in this book, however, going to deal with meso- and micro-level problems of cutback management, except incidentally. Nor shall we be concerned with developing a recommendatory stance on 'rational' responses to pressures towards cutbacks, much less advocating where reductions should be made. The book is basically about what actually happened in British central government in the period 1975–85 (with occasional looks back to 1921–31 for comparisons), as measured by a number of aggregate indices drawn mainly from published documentary sources. Its aim is to examine a range of theories about cutback processes, embodied both in popular expectations and in American and British academic writing on public policy and administration; and to test the plausibility of these theories by systematic study of the figures on the public record.

The UK in the 1970s is a uniquely – or at least unusually – good site for exploring ideas about cutback management in a pressure group democracy. In those years it was one of the least successful of the developed economies, in terms of growth rate, inflation, and unemployment; and one where both 'sides' of industry, management and labour, were well organised and involved in macroeconomic decision making through their 'peak' organisations and tripartite structures of neocorporatism such as the National Economic Development Council. Attempts have been made to cut back the public sector since the financial disciplines imposed by the International Monetary Fund on a Labour government in 1976; and from 1979 to the time of writing (1988), the UK has had a Conservative government which has promised the voters at three successive elections to cut back public spending and numbers of civil service bureaucrats. We thus have a suitable test site for exploring with empirical data many kinds of theory about retrenchment.

In the last section of this chapter some basic data of total cuts in staffing and spending, in 1975–85 and 1921–31, will be presented, plans being compared with outturns wherever feasible. The next chapter will set out a range of theories, or conjectures, about how cutback processes operate: how programmes and categories and agencies are chosen for selective treatment, and what strategies are adopted by potential victims. Chapters 3 to 5 analyse the data to see how far these theories were borne out; and Chapter 6 looks at the sources of staff 'savings' in British central government in the late 1970s and early to mid 1980s. The next chapter, 7, deals with the theories and facts about the dynamics of the process: what was cut first, what next, and what last. The final chapter raises some general questions about long-term consequences and secular trends.

I The cutback experience

But of course the 1970s were not the earliest decade to experience either cutbacks or theories about cutbacks. Adam Smith in his great treatise on *The Wealth of Nations* came at the very end of its five books to consider the national debt and how the public revenue might be liberated from its burdens; that liberation, he said, 'can never be brought about without either some very considerable augmentation of the public revenue, or some equally considerable reduction of the public expense' (Smith 1776/1812, 748). There then follow twelve pages on how the revenue might be augmented, by taxing Ireland and the colonies; but the only contribution concerning the reduction of the public expense is one sentence (the last in the book), that if revenue could not thus be raised, then Britain should abandon altogether the financial support of the colonies, 'and endeavour to accommodate her future views and designs to the real mediocrity of her circumstances' (Smith 1776/1812, 760).

William Ewart Gladstone dominated the public finance of the second half of the nineteenth century as Chancellor of the Exchequer and as Prime Minister in eight Liberal administrations, carrying on the 'economical reform' movement initiated by Pitt and Burke in the 1780s. He certainly kept the reduction of the public expense very much in the forefront of policy, through reform of the civil service and through better Treasury control of extravagance and waste; but he also advanced pragmatic thinking about the overall level of public expenditure, in his budget speech of 1860, by relating it to national income as indicated by the total of income tax raised:

The country may be right in the course which she is now taking, but, at all events, that course ought not to be pursued blindfold. We ought, on the contrary, to have a clear knowledge of the proportion which our wealth bears to our expenditure, in order that we may be able to take a comprehensive view of our financial position . . . I may at once venture to state frankly that I am not satisfied with the state of the public expenditure, and the rapid rate of its growth. I trust, therefore, that we mean in a great degree to retrace our steps . . . (Hansard, 10 February 1860, cols. 821–6; quoted in Bridges 1964, 221)

Gladstone returned to the theme constantly, but attempts to make severe cuts in government expenditure were defeated in Cabinet in 1874 and 1894, as were similar attempts by Conservative Chancellors (Punnett 1968, 282).

Economising Chancellors do better in what the twentieth century soon learned to call an 'economic crisis'. There was one such just after the end of the First World War, when a short boom was followed by a collapse in 1921. Unemployment rose rapidly to unprecedented levels (nearly 18 percent overall, in June 1921, with over 36 percent in the heavy engineering industries), and the 'dole' (uncovenanted unemployment benefit) was born. Distress was felt among both the poor and the rich, and the House of Commons demanded economies – abetted by a 'squandermania' campaign in the popular press (Mowat 1955, 130). The government, which had already required considerable reductions in departmental estimates for 1922/3 expenditures, appointed a committee of businessmen under Sir Eric Geddes 'To make recommendations . . . for effecting forthwith all possible reductions in the National Expenditure on Supply Services, having regard especially to the present and prospective position of the Revenue'. The Committee expressed the 'cutback management problem' in trenchant terms, thus:

We take this opportunity of explaining that we realise that some of our recommendations relate to classes of expenditure which will have many advocates. Powerful arguments can no doubt be urged for such expenditure. But in present circumstances only one overriding comment is necessary: 'Has the nation the means at the present time to continue incurring it?' To that question your remit to us is a full and complete answer. We are invited to recommend reductions in expenditure because they are absolutely necessary to keep our outgoings at a level with our income. Our remit is not how best to spend money from an overflowing Exchequer, but how, with the least harm, to bring expenditure within the limits of our income. (Preamble to *Second Report*, Cmd 1582, p.4, 1922)

A Treasury circular of May 1922 had required that expenditure on services, running at £603m for 1921/2, be reduced to £490m for 1922/3, a cutback of £113m or nearly 19 percent; the Committee were invited to aim at economies totalling £175m, or 29 percent. Departments had already revised their estimates downwards to the extent of £75m, which left £100m for the Committee to find.

· They began with the biggest spenders, because only there could money of that sort be found, and especially the 'Fighting Services' – £21m off the Navy, £20m off the Army, £5.5m off the Air Force; then, £18m from Education, £2.5m from Health, £3.3m from War Pensions, £3.6m from Old Age Pensions, and so on; this gave them over £73m towards their £100m target, which in the second and third Reports they pushed to £86.75m, leaving the balance to be found by yet further reductions in the fighting services as an outcome of treaty negotiations. 'Even the Government was aghast', as Mowat put it (1955, 130), at what their wishes for overall cutbacks looked like when translated into concrete and detailed proposals. 'Geddes' Axe' was condemned on all sides, by the Right for its attack on the sacred cows of the fighting services, by the Left for its slashing of the social services; but the government accepted cuts totalling £64m (on top of the £75m already 'offered' by departments), a reduction of 23 percent; and as we shall see shortly, those cutbacks were sustained and even deepened in the years following. Expenditure in real terms only began to climb again in 1928.

By the second post-war period, Heclo and Wildavsky could say

Economic crises and emergency cuts in government spending have recurred so often as to be a normal part of the contemporary British expenditure process. At least a dozen major cutting exercises punctuated the years 1950–70 . . . In most cases, these exercises have followed a deteriorating balance of payments situation, speculation against the pound, and international creditor pressure to 'hold back' public expenditures. (Heclo and Wildavsky 1974, 30)

But in this period the attempts were not so much to *cut* public expenditure as to check the rate of its growth. This was the period of the 'long boom'. Not until the International Monetary Fund took a hand in Britain's affairs in 1976 did cuts of the 1922 order reappear; and even then, there was no new Committee on National Expenditures to survey the whole scene from outside.

What until then received most academic and political attention was less how public expenditure can best be cut than why it should continually *grow* in such an apparently inexorable way. Peacock credits Alexis de Tocqueville ((1835) 1965, 150) with being the first to link growth in government expenditure and the spread of democracy – where the poor constitute a minimum winning voting coalition but pay relatively few taxes (Peacock 1979, 107). The classic theoretical formulation of Gladstone's hunch was Adolph Wagner's 'law' that public expenditure would always now rise faster than national output, because of the increasing complexity of modern industrial states (1877, 1890; see Musgrave and Peacock 1958) – the starting point for a considerable literature (Peacock and Wiseman 1961; Musgrave 1969; Nutter 1978). De Tocqueville's insight is taken up by the economic theory of democracy (e.g., Downs 1957; Buchanan and Tullock 1962; Buchanan 1967; Meltzer and Richard 1978), followed by other 'supply side' arguments such as the economic theory of bureaucracy (Niskanen 1971; Breton 1974). More recently debate has turned to whether there is an upper limit to public expenditure – the 'overload' thesis (see Tarschys 1975; Rose and Peters 1978; Rose 1984).

Apparently inexorable growth in public *employment* has been noted and deplored over a similar period, sometimes distinguished from growth in public expenditure as such, sometimes seen as integral to it; and explained in similar terms. De Tocqueville, again, noted that a taste for jobs and a life at the public expense was the 'great and permanent weakness' of his own nation; it was 'the combined effect of the democratic constitution of our civic society and the excessive centralisation of our government'. This, he went on, is 'the hidden illness that has gnawed away at every ancient authority, and will do the same to all others in the future' (de Tocqueville 1850, 42: quoted in Peacock 1979, 105). Bagehot in 1867 anticipated Tullock (1965) and Niskanen by about a century: 'A bureaucracy . . . overdoes the quantity of government, as well as impairs its quality' (Bagehot 1867 (1964), 197). More sophisticated analyses have shown, however, that growth in public employment has not been equal 'across the board', as these endogenous dynamics would imply, but has been 'policy-driven', as governments took on new obligations and developed new agencies to discharge them (Rose 1985). But as with public expenditure, people worry about the increasing proportion of total employment provided by public agencies (reaching 40 and 50 percent even in non-socialist countries of Europe); and there is a whole literature on debureaucratisation (see Meyer 1985; Grunow 1986).

Such 'technical' worries about the growth of public expenditure and public employment, even if largely among intellectuals rather than those who benefit from the growth, did no more than provide theoretical support for cutbacks. It would appear that the benefits that accompanied growth for the decision makers themselves (politicians and top civil servants), or the disbenefits that were perceived to accompany a cessation of growth, were sufficient to inhibit any serious moves to institute actual cuts – until *force majeure* was applied. In the only two periods in recent British history when sustained public-sector cutbacks have been attempted – the decade 1921–31, and the years after 1975 – the major stimulus was pressure from Britain's external creditors, the international bankers.

Perhaps there is, as well as an atmosphere of 'crisis', a more subtle vital ingredient in the mix: a public climate of something approaching shame over past excesses, a sense of extravagance, even decadence, such as hung over *la belle époque* in the first ('Edwardian') decade of the century, and which can be detected in public acquiescence in the current use of such rebukes as 'The party's over', at the end of *the long boom* of the fifties and sixties; or its characterisation as 'treble affluence' – simultaneous increase in Gross Domestic Product, public expenditure, and household incomes (Rose and Peters 1978). In such a climate resistance to cuts may be enervated, even where there is strong opposition to the ruling libertarian ideology of 'rolling back the state' (see below). Even then, cutting is not easy, it appears.

II   Cutting is not easy

It is a commonplace of recent writings on public expenditure that spending plans in the post-war period were predicated on continued steady growth in Gross Domestic Product (GDP). Economic growth became in the mid fifties the avowed objective of governments of all colours (and in virtually all countries). It was a Conservative Chancellor of the Exchequer who in 1954 promised to double the standard of living in the next twenty years, and a Labour theoretician who in 1956 regarded a rapid rate of growth, at least for the next ten years, as a precondition of the attainment of socialist ideals (Crosland 1956, 378; quoted in Wright 1981, 7). Governments of both parties used public expenditure as an instrument of economic management. Klein (1976, 413) shows that, despite first appearances, governments of both parties between 1953 and 1974 switched from expansion to contraction (or at least slower growth) as the situation appeared to demand. In Table 1.1 we have used Klein's formulation but, wishing to subdivide the periods further, have substituted our own data for actual government expenditure (the story remains the same). It can be seen that although the Conservatives' rate of increase seemed to be slower than Labour's (last column), the effect disappears when you break down each government into its significant periods. Chancellor Maudling's expansion was almost as great as post-devaluation Labour, and the Conservatives' post-U-turn growth was greater even than Labour's pre-devaluation. The figures would, however, fit with the stereotype explanation that Conservative Chancellors *try* to keep public expenditure down, until the pressures grow too great; while Labour Chancellors are happy enough to let public expenditure rise, until the pressures grow too great.

The pressures on Chancellors of either party, however, are similar: the heads of 'spending' departments always want to spend more, yet party managers are anxious about extra taxation, and international creditors take fright if growth in public spending gets out of line with growth in GDP. In the 1950s and 1960s, as already mentioned, 'economic crises' and emergency cuts in spending were quite frequent, if short lived: Heclo and Wildavsky (1974, 30) list the following: July 1952; July 1955; February 1956; September 1957; July 1961; October 1964; July 1965; July

Table 1.1. *Growth and party*

	Average annual % increase in central government expenditure*	
Conservative government 1953–64		1.13
1953–57 (Thorneycroft period)	0.03	
1957–60 (Amory period)	1.36	
1960–62 (Lloyd period)	−1.94	
1962–64 (Maudling period)	2.06	
Labour government 1964–70		7.38
1964–68 (pre-devaluation)	7.89	
1968–70 (post-devaluation)	2.11	
Conservative government 1970–74		5.84
1970–72 (pre-'U-turn')	−0.16	
1972–75	8.72	

Note: After Klein 1976, 413–14.
* At constant prices – 1980 = 100.
Source: Appropriation Accounts (annually).

1967; November 1967; January 1968; October 1970. Yet all the evidence suggests that such cuts were not taken very seriously. Faith in the underlying upward trend of the economy was strong, and civil servants and Ministers alike seemed to regard the necessity for cuts as being what we would now call 'presentational', a matter of window-dressing, of meeting the required reductions in the figures without actually threatening any existing programmes. For this the favoured device was reductions in *planned* expenditure, the so-called 'fairy gold'.

There were two kinds of reason why Ministers found cutting expenditure far from easy: the first a matter of bureaucratic politics, the other more technical and to do with the planning mechanism itself. Cabinet government as practised in Whitehall rests on more than collective control over the majority party in the House of Commons; in law, each Minister has separate statutory authority for (as well as conventional responsibility for) the acts of his or her department, and in political terms, a reputation to make or uphold for 'getting things done'. But the Treasury holds the purse-strings. Ministers are therefore used to 'fighting their corners' with the Treasury, only occasionally allying with other 'spending Ministers' in log-rolling tactics (insincere support from one Minister for another Minister's budget in exchange for insincere return support for his or her own budget). It is the prime mark of a 'good Minister', in the eyes of his own civil servants and of his client groups, that he or she can hold on to existing resources and if possible increase them, in the annual budget and PESC (Public Expenditure Survey Committee) exercises (see Heclo and Wildavsky 1974, chap.4). Hence making, or accepting, cuts in departmental expenditure (at least at the beginning of the period we are considering) goes quite against the grain of Cabinet government as we knew it.

Heclo and Wildavsky tell the story of one Minister who felt he ought to co-operate with the Chancellor in achieving a lower level of public expenditure. But he could not stomach the size of the cut the Chancellor proposed to him in private, and said he could only accept half of that. The Chancellor did not inform other Ministers of this agreement, and the Minister felt obliged to stick to it nevertheless; but when he failed to fight in Cabinet against the proposed cut, he had 'crippled his reputation': 'According to fellow Ministers, the chances of this man ever having a major department again were considerably reduced' (Heclo and Wildavsky 1974, 136–7).

As Hartley remarks (1981, 137), all Ministers' budgets are cut annually, in that departments habitually bid for more funds than they are eventually allocated. Certainly during this period, and to a large extent even today in a somewhat different climate, Ministers have little to gain, and much to lose, by 'giving in to the Treasury' on their allocations for next year. Sir Harold Wilson once wrote: 'The most difficult problem a Cabinet has to face is when it has . . . to make reductions in the announced programme for the year immediately ahead' (Wilson 1976, 94). It is easier to contemplate surrendering some growth for two or three years ahead, however. The real battle for those resources will only be fought next year or the year after, by which time maybe the situation will have improved.

As Wright shows (1977), the expenditure planning system lent itself to this way out. Begun in 1961, the PESC (Public Expenditure Survey Committee) system in Britain was greatly admired in other countries into the 1970s (Heclo and Wildavsky 1974, 202). Basically it brought all spending programmes into one perspective, and did so on a five-year rolling basis – years one and two more or less committed, years three to five in outline only. Once a programme was accepted at a certain volume into the PESC plan, any proposal for early change would mean reopening all the relativities. However, the farther into the future a change referred to, the more it could be absorbed into the projection uncertainties. As a consequence,

the profile of planned public expenditure in the five white papers published prior to 1977 has taken the form of a relatively high rate of growth in the early years of the Survey period, followed by a levelling off and a reduction in the growth of public expenditure towards the end of the period. This is sometimes referred to as 'the hump effect'. (Wright 1977, 153)

The situation in 1921/2 was the reverse – a period of underlying decline in demand as war expenditures fell off; but the Geddes Committee castigated similar dissembling on the part of departments. Estimates *ought* to have fallen 'automatically':

In many cases, the reductions proposed by the Departments are automatic, due to the fall in prices and wages, or to windfalls or to the cessation of special expenditure on services arising out of the war. The reductions in estimates shown in response to your circular are therefore by no means fully the result of curtailment of activity, or of economical administration, and this point cannot be too clearly brought out. (Preamble, First Report: Cmd 1581, p. 3, 1922)

And specifically with respect to 'offered' cuts of about 6.5 percent in social services: 'Disappointing as this figure must appear, it is doubly so when the fact is noted that it is actually less than the saving which will automatically accrue from the reduction in the costs of "services arising out of the war"' (Cmd 1581, p. 103).

Commitment among Ministers to 'real' cuts, as opposed to 'paper' cuts of both these kinds, was much stronger in the following years, and in the years after 1979; but even in November 1980 a Treasury proposal for spending cuts totalling £2bn was greatly watered down in Cabinet (Lee 1981, 46), and at the time of writing the pressures for increases in spending on several programmes are rising forcibly, conflicting with the commitment of the Chancellor and the Prime Minister to reductions in taxation.

Wright (1981, 11) suggests that other distinctions ought to be kept in mind when appraising 'cuts'. A decision to reduce the future rate of growth of a programme is a 'cut', but of a different order from a decision to allot fewer resources next year than this year. A 'cut' can be in volume terms or cash terms: fewer ships, or school places, or hospital beds next year than this year could conceivably mean higher spending next year than this, if public-sector pay and prices have meanwhile risen more than allowed for. Then, budget cuts do not inevitably turn out exactly as planned, in actual expenditure, which for a variety of reasons is likely to be either higher or lower than budgeted. In some years 'shortfall' (unintended undershoot of estimates in spending on particular programmes) has been greater than the intended budget cuts. Getting a spending total 'just right', for any large and complex organisation, is virtually impossible.

Other forms of 'cosmetic cuts' are instanced by commentators. Local authorities may accept cuts in central funding for a programme but maintain its level from their own resources (Midwinter and Page 1981, 63). Hood shows how a drive for reduction in the numbers of departmental 'fringe bodies' or 'quangos' was satisfied by a series of amalgamations (Hood 1981, 109). In the defence field, the cuts of the 1960s and 1970s, according to Hartley (1981, 144), were achieved by 'sacrificing' Britain's world-wide role – involving mainly old equipment while leaving intact all the prestige weapons projects. Apparent cuts in staffing can be produced by judicious reclassifications: for example, over 16 percent of the numbers 'lost' from civil service staff returns between 1980 and 1985 were accounted for by 'hiving-off' blocks of work from the department proper into separate statutory enterprises, so that the 'cuts' were essentially of a book-keeping nature. 'Creative accounting' can promise higher savings than are likely to be made in reality. The largest savings in the cutback exercise at the end of 1979 were £41m at the Ministry of Defence and £29m at the Property Services Agency, to be obtained by contracting out cleaning, catering, and maintenance work. But the savings actually made would depend upon the contract terms arrived at, rather than on the hopeful calculations of the budgeteers (Wright 1981, 17).

We should not, therefore, be too ready to take figures of spending and staffing cuts at their face value. A theme running through the cutback literature is the ingenuity of officials in presenting Ministers with the reductions in expenditure or staffing they are demanding, while not actually cutting activities. Statistical sleight-of-hand and cosmetic massaging of figures is universally suspected whenever government claims to be achieving its targets – of any sort, but especially when the targets are smaller budgets and fewer officials. Perhaps such suspicions are actually out of date: perhaps they derive from the sixties and seventies, when as we have seen 'savings' all too often *did* mean a postponement of future growth rather than less next year than this. Let us see what happened in the decade 1975–85 to total spending figures and total staffing in British central government, comparing that with the 'era of retrenchment' decade 1921–31.

III   The extent of the cuts

The Labour government that assumed power in March 1974 as a minority government did not initially have *cutbacks* in mind, but recovery. It inherited an economy in severe distress: a combination of the international oil crisis and a national coal strike had put the country on a three-day week, prices were rising, stock markets falling world-wide. The main instrument of recovery was to be the 'social contract' – an agreement with the trade unions that, in return for increased state social spending on food subsidies, housing, pensions, and so on the unions would moderate their wage demands. On top of the effect of this on public expenditure, expansionary policies to aid business were introduced. A second election within the year produced a small Labour majority overall; but the economy did not respond, unemployment was increasing as well as inflation, and the social contract simply did not work – wages showed an annual rise of 25 percent, and some claims were being settled at around 30 percent. The 1975 budget cut planned expenditure by £900m, including food and housing subsidies, and taxes were increased quite sharply. Wage rises were made subject to a limit by means of sanctions on firms who paid them, through controls on prices.

The White Paper on public expenditure issued in February 1976 (Cmnd 6393) was minatory. Popular expectations of better public services and welfare programmes, it began, had not been matched by growth in output, or by willingness to forgo private affluence; in the previous three years output had risen by less than 2 percent while public expenditure had grown by nearly 20 percent, and the ratio of public expenditure to Gross Domestic Product had gone up from 50 percent to 60 percent. There were, however, signs that the recession was bottoming out, and hopes were now pinned on an export-led recovery. The plan therefore was to stabilise public expenditure at its 1976/7 level for a number of years, so that the GDP ratio could come down again.

The money markets did not, however, favour the level of state borrowing necessary to finance even a stabilised public expenditure total, and in fact it kept on rising; by mid 1976 not even a new wage-limit agreement and high interest rates halted the slide in sterling, and the government, embracing the fashionable Chicago-school doctrines of 'monetarism', announced further cuts in public expenditure plans. Still the pound fell, and the government sought a loan of nearly $4bn from the International Monetary Fund (IMF) – the price of which was increased taxation and bigger cuts in public expenditure *now*. Cuts amounting to £3bn over the next two years were announced in December 1976.

During 1977 and 1978 a recovery did take place, aided by Britain's entry into world oil markets as a producer. Sterling was high and the rate of inflation was again within single figures. The White Paper of January 1978 (Cmnd 7049) included an addition of £1bn to the expenditure plans for 1978/9. To help improve *control* over public expenditure, 'cash limits' were introduced and more careful Treasury monitoring promised. But the government was again a minority government dependent on a pact with the Liberals; it had many other troubles, including public-service strikes over pay and problems with Scottish and Welsh devolution. It was over one of these that it was eventually defeated by one vote in the House of Commons, and at the general election there was a massive swing to the Conservatives.

The Conservative Party under Mrs Margaret Thatcher took office pledged to reverse current trends in several directions – and not only the policies of the outgoing government, or 'socialism', but also those of previous Conservative régimes, particularly those of her predecessor Edward Heath in the later stages of the 1970–4 government. In conformity with the 'New Right' philosophy that was also sweeping the United States, the decline of Britain was associated not only with policies of nationalisation and state control, but also with the whole twentieth-century British development of *welfarism* that had underpinned social provision from Asquith to Beveridge, Macmillan's 'middle way', and the 'consensus politics' of the *long boom*.

The first priorities of the new government in the economic field were therefore to 'roll back the state' by drastically cutting back on public expenditure, reducing taxes, and returning publicly owned industries and utilities to the private sector. Expenditure plans for 1980/1 were pruned by more than £1.5bn and a further £1bn of cuts obtained through cash-limiting programme budgets, with yet another £1bn to be found by sales of public-sector assets (Cmnd 7841). But public expenditure refused to come down. In March 1981 the White Paper (Cmnd 8175) blamed the recession. But by March 1982 (Cmnd 8494) the government was being forced to *increase* planned expenditure, mainly on social benefits to take care of growing unemployment, and on law and order; and although the 1983 plan for 1983/4 showed a reduction of £1bn from 1982's plan for that year, the outturn put most of it back on again. In the January 1985 White Paper (Cmnd 9428) much was made of the fact that the 'planning total' for 1985/6 had been held steady, at £132bn in cash terms, at what had been planned for that year in 1983 and 1984. But the budget statement in March 1986 estimated that outturn would be nearly £2bn higher. It seems that cutbacks in 1975–85 have not meant significant reductions in public expenditure, but at best, reductions in the rate of increase. The underlying dynamic of growth in public spending has simply been too strong for even a highly motivated axe-wielding Chancellor.

Table 1.2. *UK central government gross actual expenditure at constant prices, 1920/1 to 1930/1 and 1974/5 to 1984/5 (£m)*

Year	Amount	Year	Amount
1920/1	1,020.8	1974/5	70,758.8
1921/2	1,067.4	1975/6	74,313.4
1922/3	605.6	1976/7	72,257.0
1923/4	524.2	1977/8	66,946.7
1924/5	499.4	1978/9	68,792.7
1925/6	484.9	1979/80	70,486.7
1926/7	480.3	1980/1	73,602.5
1927/8	436.4	1981/2	72,558.9
1928/9	434.0	1982/3	73,178.5
1929/30	444.8	1983/4	75,325.2
1930/1	505.7	1984/5	77,924.7

Note: Constant prices: GDP deflator: 1920–31　1913 = 100
　　　　　　　　　　　　　　　　1975–85　1980 = 100
Source: Appropriation Accounts.

These events can be traced in the figures of Table 1.2, graphically represented in Fig. 1, which also present the contrast with the earlier decade of retrenchment in the twenties. The absolute falls in the twenties were, of course, much smaller (there is a marked difference in scale between the two halves of Fig. 1); but proportionately, they were considerably greater – between the peak and the trough of Gross Actual Expenditure (1921/2 and 1928/9), a drop of 59.3 percent; between 1975/6 and 1977/8 (trough), a fall of 9.9 percent only. Moreover, the cutback in the twenties was *sustained* for much longer: expenditure only began to rise again in 1929.

A picture of the relationship between planned expenditure and actual expenditure in the later decade can be gleaned from Table 1.3, which is compiled from the successive White Papers on Public Expenditure.[1] There is no easily discernible pattern. Leaving out the proposals of the Labour government in January 1979, the *plans* for expenditure for any particular year show an increase in successive White Papers, until

---

[1]　Or rather, from the versions of these figures given in later White Papers, since 1981, when the basis of forecasting was changed from the previous 'constant prices' assumptions to 'cash terms' (with assumptions about inflation built in). It is virtually impossible to recalculate earlier figures on the new assumptions, or project later figures on the old assumptions, so our comparisons are limited to those given in the table.

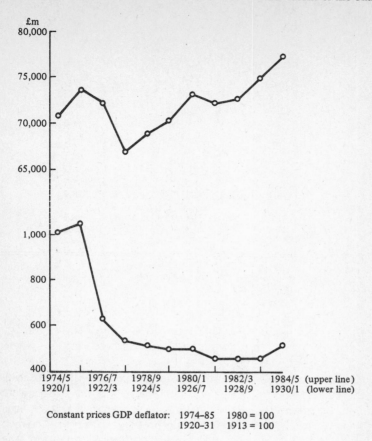

Constant prices GDP deflator: 1974–85   1980 = 100
                                 1920–31   1913 = 100

Source: *Appropriation Accounts*

Fig. 1. UK central government gross actual expenditure at constant
prices, 1920/1–1930/1 and 1974/5–1984/5.

1983/4, when the 1983 plan is lower than the 1982 plan, and this occurs
again in the successive plans for 1984/5, and the first two plans for
1985/6. The latest available outturn figure is *higher* than the latest plan
figure for 1981/2, and for 1983/4 and 1984/5, indicating overspend, but
lower for 1982/3, indicating shortfall on cash limits.

   Mrs Thatcher's government came to office pledged to reduce not only
public expenditure but also, as an end in itself, the size of the civil service.
Her open antipathy towards civil servants as such caused much trouble,
almost rebellion, from the civil service trade unions in the early years of

Table 1.3. *Public expenditure planning totals 1975/6 to 1988/9 (£m (cash))*

	1975/6	1976/7	1977/8	1978/9	1979/80	1980/1	1981/2	1982/3	1983/4	1984/5	1985/6	1986/7	1987/8	1988/9
Cmnd 7439 (January 79)					109,700	120,000								
Cmnd 7841 (March 80)						101,000	106,400	112,400						
Cmnd 8175 (March 81)							104,400	109,900	113,600					
Cmnd 8494 (March 82)	54,659	57,162	65,934	77,201	93,475	106,130	115,150	121,070	128,370					
Cmnd 8789 (February 83)		56,789	65,734	76,933	92,815	104,684	113,007	119,568	126,370	132,260				
Cmd 9143 (February 84)			65,752	76,922	92,672	104,676	113,377	120,238	126,353	132,080	136,680			
Cmnd 9428 (January 85)				76,971	92,683	104,676	113,430	120,298	128,111	132,092	136,750	141,480		
HC 273										129,600	133,900	139,100	143,900	148,700

Note: 12,345 = Outturn   12,345 = Estimate   12,345 = Plan

The 'Public expenditure planning total' comprises public expenditure programmes for central government, local authorities, certain public corporations, finance for nationalised industries and certain allowances. 'General Government expenditure' is an economic analysis category rather than a spending programme one but in effect includes the public expenditure planning total plus debt interest and non-trading capital consumption.

Sources: Cmnd 8494, *The Government's Expenditure Plans 1982–83 to 1984–85.* March 1982. col. 1, table 1.1 and chart 1.4 (for GDP ratios)
  Cmnd 8789, *The Government's Expenditure Plans 1983–84 to 1985–86.* February 1983. Vol.1, table 1.1 and chart 1.6 (for GDP ratios)
  Cmnd 9143, *The Government's Expenditure Plans 1984–85 to 1986–87.* February 1984. Vol.1, table 1.2 and chart 1.8 (for GDP ratios)
  Cmnd 9428, *The Government's Expenditure Plans 1985–86 to 1987–88.* January 1985. Vol.2, table 2.2; vol.1, chart 1.3 (GDP ratios)
  HC 273. *Financial Statement and Budget Report 1986–87.* 18 March 1986. Table 5.1
  National Accounts: *United Kingdom National Accounts,* 1985. Table 9.4. final line, 'Total expenditure', deflated, as percentage of line 'Gross Domestic Product at market prices' in Table 1.5 (1980=100)

Table 1.4. *UK civil service staff numbers, 1920–31 and 1974–85 (thousands, as at 1 April)*

Year	Non-industrials	Year	Non-industrials	Industrials	Total
1920	172.0	1974	511.8	180.2	692.0
1921	158.1	1975	524.1	177.3	701.4
1922	132.5	1976	568.5	179.1	747.6
1923	123.8	1977	571.1	174.4	745.5
1924	114.6	1978	567.3	168.4	735.7
1925	114.2	1979	565.8	166.5	732.3
1926	109.7	1980	547.5	157.4	704.9
1927	107.8	1981	539.9	149.7	689.6
1928	105.5	1982	528.0	138.4	666.4
1929	108.8	1983	518.5	130.4	648.9
1930	111.2	1984	504.3	119.7	624.0
1931	118.4	1985	498.0	101.0	599.0

Sources: 1920–31 *Treasury Staff Returns* (Cmd Nos. 690/1290/1658/1849/2119/2413/2653/2863/3106/3349/3619/3898
  1974–85 *Annual Abstract of Statistics.*

the régime. Within days of taking office the government announced a 3 percent cut in manpower, and by December 1979 the previous government's estimate of an (increased) total of civil servants by April 1980, at 748,000, had been turned into a forecast cut of some 20,000 posts, mainly by a ban on recruitment.

The 1976 Labour White Paper (Cmnd 6393) had promised a reduction in civil service staff (to save £140m in 1978/9), but no actual staff numbers were given. Table 1.4 shows, however, that staff figures continued to increase during 1976 (indeed, the numbers of industrial civil servants, mainly blue-collar workers in naval dockyards and ordnance factories, interrupted a long-term decline and actually increased in 1976); the total reached its peak in 1977. Staff totals were on the way down by 1979, then; but not fast enough for Mrs Thatcher.

On 6 December 1979 a further cut of some 39,000 posts by 1982/3 was announced, with a table setting out the financial and staff savings department by department, and giving their expected sources (e.g., 'savings from improved efficiency, computerisation, and some reduction in services'). On 14 March 1980 a further reduction of some 15,000 posts was made public; it was quite evident that a great deal of work was going on in Whitehall to find specific cuts in specific places, not just to massage

totals. Then, on 13 May 1980, just a year after taking office, the Prime
Minister made the definitive statement in the House of Commons:

In the past, Governments have progressively increased the number of tasks that
the Civil Service is asked to do without paying sufficient attention to the need for
economy and efficiency. Consequently, staff numbers have grown over the years.
The present Government are committed both to a reduction in tasks and to better
management. We believe that we should now concentrate on simplifying the
work and doing it more efficiently. The studies that Departments have already
carried out, including those in conjunction with Sir Derek Rayner, have
demonstrated clearly the scope for this.
   All Ministers in charge of Departments will now work out detailed plans for
concentrating on essential functions and making operations simpler and more
efficient in their Departments. The preparation of these plans will be coordinated
by my noble Friend the Lord President of the Council.
   When the Government took office the size of the Civil Service was 732,000. As a
result of the steps that we have already taken it is now 705,000. We intend now to
bring the number down to about 630,000 over the next four years. (HC Deb
13.5.80; quoted in Appendix 2 of the Fourth Report from the Treasury and Civil
Service Committee, Session 1979–80, HC 712–II.)

   Mrs Thatcher's announcement implied a reduction between 1 April
1979 and 1 April 1984 of 102,300, or 14 percent. Staff in post at 1 April
1984 actually numbered 623,972 (*Economic Progress Report*, No. 168,
June 1984). So that target was undeniably achieved, at least on paper.
   In the White Paper on Expenditure Plans of January 1985 (Cmnd
9428) the government published a fresh set of departmental targets for 1
April 1985 and each year until 1 April 1988, totalling respectively
(including a contingency margin) 606,565; 604,925; 600,439; and
590,447. The target for 1985 was subsequently revised downward to
603,765; but the actual staff in post as at 1 April 1985 totalled 599,026
(*Civil Service Statistics*, 1985, table 1), so that not only had the 1985 target
been met by then, but the original targets for 1986 and 1987 as well. In
contrast to experience on expenditure reductions, experience on staff
reductions appears to be a story of remarkable success.
   Table 1.4 and Fig. 2 present these staff figures in tabular and in graph
form, and also give a comparison with the twenties. For the earlier
decade, the staff story and the spending story are not very different: staff
numbers do not *plunge* as do the expenditure figures (see Fig. 1); but they
decline fairly steeply and then stay down. For the 1975–85 decade, the
staffing and the spending curves are quite dissimilar, almost reversed:
staff numbers go *up* rapidly at the beginning of the period, flatten out, and
then begin a long decline, whereas spending does almost the opposite.
We shall have to explore this curious phenomenon.

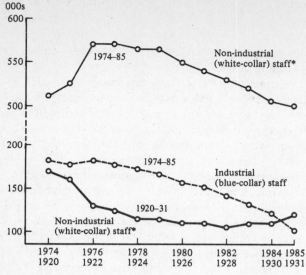

Fig. 2. UK civil service staff numbers, 1920–31 and 1975–85.

* Excluding Post Office staff

Sources: 1920 to 1931 Treasury Staff Returns (Cmd Nos. 690/1290/
1658/1849/2119/2413/2653/2863/3106/3349/
3619/3898)

1974 to 1985 Annual Abstract of Statistics
Figures are for 1 April in all cases

Comparing the 1920s staff cuts with the 1975–85 staff cuts, like the comparison of spending cuts, shows how much more severe the earlier cuts were. In the two eight-year periods between peaks and troughs on the graphs, numbers of white-collar civil servants (non-industrials) fell over 38 percent in the earlier period, as against approximately 13 percent in the later period (although we do not know whether or for how long the downward trend will continue in the eighties).

What we have seen, then, is that in terms of the totals of government spending on the one hand and civil service numbers on the other, the era of retrenchment in the 1920s meant severe and sustained reductions in both: but in the later retrenchment era from the mid seventies to the mid eighties, government spending was severely cut only temporarily and then resumed its long-term upward climb (in real terms), only starting to reduce in terms of share of GDP at the end of the period. Staffing cuts, however, though taking a long time to take effect, seem to have been set on a marked downward trend. As we saw, some degree of 'creative accounting' usually creeps into figures of staff cuts. But even allowing for a generous amount of 'massaging', it would be difficult to argue that a reduction in staffing of over 400 civil servants a week for over six years is wholly attributable to creative accounting.

Of course, a reduction of a certain percentage overall does not necessarily mean that each unit lost staff by that amount: some services could have lost many more, or lost in some years and gained in others, or even gained in every year over the period. Similarly with spending: an overall cut, or an overall rise in public expenditure, could well mask much more severe treatment for one programme and 'generous' treatment for another. We shall, obviously, not understand fully what retrenchment has meant in UK central government until we know what these patterns of differential cutback actually were, year by year – and until we can *explain why* some groups 'suffered' more than others, or did not suffer at all, and so on. This is what we shall go on to do in later chapters. But before we go on to look in more detail at what actually happened in British central government in these years, the next chapter surveys what, according to the various theories of bureaucratic behaviour (in cutbacks and otherwise), we might have *expected* to happen.[2] Without knowing what the actual patterns were, what patterns might we have predicted on the basis of what we think we know about government and about civil servants?

---

[2] The reader who would prefer to move on to the findings may go straight to Chapter 3, although it might then be necessary to refer back to Chapter 2 for the explanations of particular hypotheses.

2 Who is vulnerable?
The 64-hypothesis question

In the previous chapter, we spoke of cutback management only in terms of the central government as a whole: total spending, total staffing. Now we must begin to look inside these totals, at their component parts.

I Patterns and explanations

There are many ways in which total spending and staffing can be broken up. Parliament considers the estimates for next year's spending on the basis of *programmes* – for defence, for health and personal services, for housing, for education and science, and so on. But when the money is spent it is accounted for by *departments* – the Ministry of Defence, the Department of the Environment, etc. The boundaries of programmes and of departments by no means coincide: some programmes are carried out by a number of departments, some departments have a share in a number of programmes. And staffing is by department, not by programme; it is a department (or agency by another kind of title) which in law is the employer.

Civil servants, however, are not all of one sort; they can be grouped or classified in several ways. There are administrative occupational groups and specialist occupational groups; top ranks, middle ranks, and bottom ranks; white-collar people and blue-collar people (as we have already seen); men and women; temporary employees, part-timers, and other 'odd' groups. We might well expect that cutbacks could hit some of these groupings harder than others.

Although in common speech we talk of 'Whitehall' as if it were synonymous with 'the civil service', it is not, of course. It is the name of a street in London where indeed some of the older offices are located, linking the Palace of Westminster with Trafalgar Square; but most civil servants who work in London work in buildings which are not in Whitehall. More significant than that: most British civil servants do not work in London at all. They work in large 'central offices', like that of the Department of Health and Social Security in Newcastle upon Tyne, which draw their workload from the whole country but are far away from London; or in scientific laboratories and other such relatively separate units; or in the regional and local offices of ministries with public counters, such as Social Security or Employment or the Inland Revenue, to be found in every large city or town. So another way of dividing up the total civil service is by location – the region or part of the kingdom in which they work. Three important ministries are *territorial*: the Scottish Office and the other Scottish departments, the Welsh Office, and the Northern Ireland Office. But there are civil servants working in Scotland, in Wales, and in Northern Ireland who do not belong to these 'territorial' departments, but to a regional office of one of the UK ministries.

Spending as well as staffing can be categorised geographically; and it can be sorted by 'economic category' – first into current and capital spending, and then current spending into whether it is for the purchase of goods and services or for wages and salaries, or for 'transfer payments' to other people (cash benefits are transfers), or for debt interest, and so on. Cuts in spending in these various categories affect different groups of 'clients' or beneficiaries, so we shall want to know who suffers 'at second hand' in this way. Then again, spending can be categorised by 'spending authority': central government, local authorities, public corporations, etc.

These, then, are six distinct ways in which the totals we have been discussing up till now can be made up:

by programme
by department
by personnel group
by geographical location
by economic category
by spending authority;

and each may display a different pattern of treatment during an era of cutbacks. These six facets are not necessarily statistically independent (or 'orthogonal'), and we shall not try to present the complete picture for each (especially in the case of geographical location); but these six potential dimensions of the cutback management problem can bring out different aspects of the problem and provide the starting point for systematic analysis.

In principle, we can imagine a different pattern of spending and staffing representing the distribution of the total of public expenditure and the total numbers of civil servants for each of these facets; and each pattern can be different from one year to another. We assembled data from the published record to cover each of these six dimensions. But again: we shall not try to present all these data; we shall pick out the interesting bits.

Our aim, as mentioned in Chapter 1, is not merely to note these different patterns of spending and staffing, and to find out who got how much less, and when, and how, in the period of cutbacks we are looking at; but to *explain* these patterns – to make sense of them, if we can.

Good philosophical practice indicates that we should follow two maxims, or principles, in such an attempt. First, we should not use complicated explanations if simple ones will do just as well. Of two theories about what is going on, both of which fit the observed facts, choose the one with the fewer elements. Second, we should not invent special 'cutback management' explanations if we can adapt well-known theories of 'growth' – perhaps by turning the latter on their heads or back to front. Of two theories about how things fit together, both of which explain the observed facts, choose the one which embraces more of life, is the more general. Both of these principles are variants of the well-known 'Occam's Razor' – *entia non sunt multiplicanda praeter necessitatem.*

Broadly, we have come across four *kinds* of explanation of the patterns we are looking at. One: you don't have to look any further than the name of the political party in office at the time of any particular cutback. Tell me whether you have a Labour government or a Conservative government and I will tell you who wins and who loses. We shall call these *party-political* explanations, and we have already alluded to some of them in Chapter 1.

Two: patterns like these don't change overnight: they are the outcome of deep forces and pressures in society which shape the fortunes of the gainers and the losers, and your best bet about who will suffer next year is to see who suffered last year. We shall call these *trend* explanations; and unfortunately, some of them will fit two different sets of facts – 'first in, first out' is a 'trend' explanation, and so is 'last in, first out'.

Three: you won't ever explain patterns like these without getting inside the machine and really understanding how it works – the layout and structure, the work-flow and the technology. With the best will in the world, there are technical and organisational constraints on what can be cut and when. Some departments are more vulnerable to cuts than others, because of what they do and how they do it. We shall call these *bureaucratic process* explanations.

Four: really a variant of the last one, in that again it calls for insider knowledge; but this time of the internal rivalries and 'power game' in and between bureaucracies, the pecking order, the personalities. We shall call these *bureaucratic self-interest* explanations.

You may feel as we do that these four types of explanation run from the simpler to the more complex, and that whereas both *party-political* and *trend* types of explanation are 'general' ones, applying to changes during expansionary periods as well as periods of cutbacks, it may well be that there are *different* dynamics involved during growth and during cutbacks, for the *process* and the *self-interest* types of theory. From that point of view (bearing Occam's Razor in mind), we should always see whether one of the first two types of explanation will adequately account for the observed facts, before going for either of the latter two.

Within this framework, then, let us have a look at what theories are on offer. We can perhaps deal with *party-political* theories and with *trend* theories together, for there is not a great deal to be said; but for the other two types of explanation, we need a different approach. In the third section we shall examine theories about *bureaucrats* under each head of 'process' and 'self-interest'; and then in the last section of the chapter, go on to consider theories about *programmes* and *departments*, or 'bureaus'.

II   Party-political and trend explanations

The party-political explanation can rest on either of two theoretical bases, which in many cases generate mutually contradictory predictions. The first is the well-known Downs/Hotelling model (derived from commercial retail selling strategies) of competition between two major parties (Hotelling 1929; Downs 1957), where each competes for the votes of the marginal middle-ground voter. If we adopt this assumption we would expect the pattern of programme cutbacks to be exactly the same under governments of different parties, since those cuts would be made with the same marginal voter in mind. But we could derive our model from an alternative retail strategy of 'product differentiation', where the two parties strive to distinguish their position on every political issue from that of their rivals, and to create sharply discrete images that will give the voters (at least the illusion of) a clear choice, in the *adversarial politics* style (Finer 1975). If that is the model we have in mind, we might expect a sharp break in the pattern of which programmes suffer most, each time party control of government changes hands.

On popular perceptions, it could perhaps be said that the Downs/Hotelling model is closest to the usual stereotype of US party politics, while the Finer model is closest to the stereotype of contemporary British politics. As is well known, the two major British political parties derive their campaign finance and other support from sources that are both more stable and entrenched and more ideologically opposed than their US counterparts; they both have political mortgages to pay off when they achieve power, but to very different brokers and investors. Going from this popular version of UK party politics we might therefore expect a 'product-differentiation' model to give better predictions of cutback outcomes (cf. the discussion in Klein 1976). But Pommerehne and Schneider (1983) have ingeniously married the two approaches, suggesting that governments pursue their own goals (Finer model) when they can, only pursuing popularity (Downs model) when an election nears, or support in opinion polls slumps dangerously – a kind of *political business cycle* model (Nordhaus 1975): we shall investigate that also.

As to what policy programmes would be favoured by each major party (Conservatives and Labour), we could have conducted a detailed content analysis of the rival manifestos as applied, for example, by Laver (1984) to the 1983 general election. Instead, we have started with popular or 'saloon-bar' stereotypes (or 'what everyone knows') about the respective positions of the two parties. On these stereotypes, the Conservatives are committed to higher spending on defence and on 'law and order' than are Labour, and Labour to higher spending on social services (pensions, housing, education) than are the Conservatives. In the economic field, Labour are held to be more interventionist and committed to public ownership, and more sympathetic towards public expenditure generally, than are Conservatives. It is true, of course, that many of the key differences between parties refer to 'qualitative' matters rather than quantity of money devoted; for instance, nuclear arms as opposed to conventional weapon systems, retributive versus rehabilitative treatment of offenders, and so on. But it is party approaches to cutback management that interest us here, so we ignore such differences.

Conventional stereotypes about the two parties can also serve as a starting point for an analysis of bureaucratic staffing. Compared to the Conservative Party, the Labour Party has traditionally drawn its votes disproportionately from public- rather than from private-sector employees, from manual or blue-collar workers rather than from white-collar workers, and from occupational groups below the 'managerial and supervisory' grades (see Dunleavy 1980: Heath, Jowell, and Curtice 1985). Consequently, we might expect that a Labour government in a period of public-sector cutbacks would try to cut bureaucratic staff, and spending on bureaucrats' wages and salaries, by a smaller amount than would a Conservative government in the same position; would aim to cut blue-collar staff numbers by a smaller proportional amount than white-collar staff numbers; and would aim to cut lower-level staff grades by a smaller amount than top- and middle-level staff grades. The preferred Conservative strategy on staff cutbacks might be expected to be the opposite in each case.

Similarly on geographical distributions, it is well enough known that Labour votes are heavily concentrated in Scotland, Wales, and the North of England, while Conservative votes are thickest on the ground south of a line drawn between the Severn and the Wash. The naive expectation might therefore be that, in terms of the location of spending and staffing, the South-East would do better under the Conservatives, and the rest of the UK, under Labour. More subtly, perhaps, we might predict that regions with high concentrations of marginal seats will do better than other regions under either party.

On spending by economic category, conventional stereotypes or 'saloon-bar' expectations about the preferences of the two parties might well vary. Some might believe that a Labour government would be more inclined to cut capital spending than would a Conservative government, in order to protect current spending on public-sector employment (given the power of the public-sector unions in the Labour Party). Others might believe that a Labour government would cut capital spending by a smaller amount than a Conservative government, given that capital spending (especially on construction) tends to be a generator of employment. As between spending on 'goods and services' and 'transfer payments', we would on a conventional view of party platforms expect Labour to protect transfers, since so much of that total represents welfare benefits, while the Conservatives would target welfare for heavy cuts.

There is ambiguity also about what 'popular' expectations might be concerning the distribution of cutbacks among spending authorities. Labour have traditionally been the centralising party, with the defence of 'local self-government' in the hands of the Conservatives. But Labour are also conventionally in favour of municipalisation, and of intensive local services financed by high local taxes on property (the bulk of the proceeds coming from industrial and commercial business premises without votes as such), while the Conservatives are opposed to both – and in the 1970s and 1980s have been identified with marked increases in central control so as to limit public-sector borrowing and expenditure generally. So traditional roles have become reversed and it is under the Conservatives that we might reasonably expect local authority spending to decline relative to central government spending, while under Labour we might expect both to rise but the local to rise more, if anything.

But there is no confusion about what the conventional stereotype is concerning differences in the parties' attitudes to a third important class of spending authority, namely, nationalised industries and public corporations of one kind and another. Labour are expected to defend public ownership, and Conservatives are expected to be against it and to aim to 'privatise' as much as they can.

Theories about party-political rivalry can therefore generate a large number of hypotheses for testing against the observed behaviour, not necessarily in the following order:[1]

(1) on change of governing party, spending on no programme will increase or decrease markedly with respect to the previous year

(2) on change of governing party, spending on all programmes will increase or decrease markedly with respect to the previous year

(3) under Conservative government, spending on defence and on law-and-order programmes will increase, and spending on social services will decrease

(4) under Labour government, spending on social services programmes will increase, and spending on defence and law-and-order programmes will decrease

(5) under either party in government, spending on 'favoured' programmes will increase and spending on 'disfavoured' programmes will decrease in the year following an election; in the year preceding an election, spending on 'favoured' programmes will decrease and spending on 'disfavoured' programmes will increase

(6) public expenditure totals will increase under Labour and decrease under Conservative government

(7) under Labour government, spending on industry, trade, and employment programmes will increase, and will decrease under Conservative government

(8) under Labour government, numbers of civil servants and totals of spending on wages and salaries will increase, or will decrease by less than under Conservatives; under Conservative government, numbers of civil servants and spending on wages and salaries will decrease, or will increase by less than under Labour

(9) under Labour government, blue-collar staff numbers as a proportion of total civil service staff will not decrease; under Conservative government, white-collar staff numbers as a proportion of total civil service staff will not decrease

[1] In each case, change in spending implies *in real terms*, i.e., after allowing for inflation.

(10)   under Labour government, lower-level staff numbers as a proportion of total civil service staff will not decrease; under Conservative government, top-level staff numbers as a proportion of total civil service staff will not decrease

(11)   under Labour government, programme spending and staffing in the following Economic Planning Regions will increase or not decrease: West Midlands, North-West, Northern, Yorkshire & Humberside, Wales and Scotland; under Conservative government, programme spending and staffing in the following Economic Planning Regions will increase or not decrease: South-East, South-West, East Midlands, East Anglia *(for this purpose, Northern Ireland is left out of the analysis)*

(12)   programme spending and staffing will be higher than average in regions where the number of electorally marginal parliamentary seats is higher than average

(13)   under Labour government, revenue (current) expenditure will not decrease as a proportion of total government spending; under Conservative government, capital expenditure will not decrease as a proportion of total government spending

(14)   under Labour government, spending on transfer payments will not decrease as a proportion of total government spending; under Conservative government, it will

(15)   under Conservative government, spending by local authorities will not increase as a proportion of total public spending; under Labour government, it will

(16)   under Labour government, spending by other spending authorities than central government and local authorities will increase or not decrease; under Conservative government, it will decrease.

We turn now to theories about *trends* as an explanation of how cutback management works. As with party-political theories, we have to begin from two mutually exclusive sets of assumptions. A 'trend' explanation says that you can predict what will happen in the future from knowing what has happened in the past. But there are two alternative mechanisms: extrapolation and reversal. The first supposes that those elements that have been growing for a long time have been doing so as an outcome of social forces, or political pressures, that have historically been stronger than others and can be expected to continue being relatively stronger than rival forces (and *vice versa* for elements in historical decline). The second is predicated either on an appreciation that an era of cutbacks precisely and ineluctably is a reversal of growth, indicating that the previous engines of increase have lost their power and may therefore now be relatively *weaker* than other forces; or, more simply, that the fattest cats have more fat to lose and will therefore be prime targets for cuts. In either case, the prediction is that the past trend will go into reverse once the era of cutbacks begins. What was increasing fastest will decrease fastest, and some elements that were in relatively steep decline will find their fortunes improving.

As already noted, we seem to know a lot more about the growth of government than about the shrinking of government. A simple view of the past hundred years and more would yield the prediction that neither public expenditure nor public employment would suffer any more than temporary setback, however severe the environmental conditions. A less simple view, based on the *overload* thesis (Rose and Peters 1978), would nevertheless come to an equally simple prediction: public expenditure and public employment are *bound* to begin to decline in relative terms soon, if they have not already done so, since public expenditure must eventually reach a maximum sustainable level.

Perhaps more interesting than theories about total public expenditures, though, are theories which purport to explain which government *programmes* will increase and decrease because of underlying trends. The best known of these is probably Richard Rose's three-fold classification of programmes into defining, corporate (or resource-mobilising), and social (Rose 1976). The first includes those activities most basic to the state's territorial sovereignty: revenue-raising, defence and foreign policy, and internal security. The second includes activities undertaken by government because government alone commands the necessary scale of organisation, such as roads and railways legislation or health insurance or export credit guarantees; and the third uses the tax base to enhance the quality of individual lives, as in education, welfare benefits, and public parks. Rose's thesis, in a comparative survey of governmental development based upon an analysis of the *Almanac de Gotha*, is that state expansion began in the 'defining' field, moved into the 'corporate' field as first mercantilism and then the Industrial Revolution unfolded, and arrived in the 'social' field with the development of the liberal conscience. From such a theory, plus a 'reversal' assumption, we might predict that, in a period of severe cutbacks, 'social' programmes would be cut before 'resource-mobilising' programmes, and these before 'defining' programmes.

Other 'trend' theories rely on demographic history and projections to explain movements in public expenditure. Wilensky found in a cross-national study of trends in public expenditure that social security spending as a proportion of Gross National Product was correlated strongly with population structure, with the age of the social security organisational system itself, and with *per capita* GNP, but not with the policy views of the decision makers (Wilensky 1975; quoted in Klein 1976, 403). As Klein put it:

the discretion of the policy-makers may be limited to their ability to adjust to such forces . . . it would be misleading to concentrate exclusively on what the men in the life-boat are doing, without taking into account the sea current or the direction of the wind. (Klein, 1976, 402)

In cutbacks, then, on the basis of such a theory, we would predict that where there is (for example) a rising proportion of old people in the community, expenditures on retirement pensions and similar old-age-linked programmes will be hard to reduce and will go on growing, while school education and other youth-related programmes will gradually decline as a proportion of the total.

Some of the well-known Marxist explanations of the growth of public expenditure would perhaps count as 'trend' theories in our terms. A familiar instrumentalist account of the function of the state apparatus in advanced capitalist societies in Marxist theory is on the one hand to correct the mistakes of the market, regulating the economic cycle and saving private enterprises from their errors, and on the other hand to supplement market mechanisms by state action in the fields of foreign policy, defence and armaments, scientific research, technical and vocational training, and the infrastructure (roads and transport, housing, water supply, and the like) (see Dunleavy and O'Leary 1987, 203–70). The growth of welfare spending (unemployment pay, pensions, supplementary benefits, 'urban renewal', and environmental repair) is designed to keep the lid on the pot of social unrest brought about by the predations of capitalism (O'Connor 1973). From such an analysis, we could derive a prediction that, in public-sector cutbacks brought about by international economic recession or the like, social welfare spending will go *up* rather than down, as will spending on law and order, prisons, and 'inner-city' rescue.

Many other 'trend' theories could be canvassed. For instance, socio-economic trends in employment, coupled with anti-discriminatory legislation, would indicate that the proportion of blue-collar workers in the civil service will steadily go down (irrespective of overall staff expansion or decline), and that of women will steadily go up, in any period such as that we are studying. Industrial trends and the intensifying of international competition from countries where production is cheaper and more efficient confirm that British heavy industry is in long-term decline and that the expanding or 'sunrise' industries are in light engineering and in 'silicon-chip-based' manufacture, employing fewer people. That predicts the increase of public spending on welfare programmes, which in turn indicates higher amounts of transfer payments, and higher spending by central government authorities, so that socio-economic trends could have effects on the balance of economic categories and spending authorities.

From these 'trend' theories, then, we can as before generate a representative number of hypotheses for testing. For example (leaving out the simple 'inevitable growth' and 'inevitable decline' hypotheses, which if not essentially untestable are at least not testable on our data):

In the period 1975–85 in the United Kingdom:

(17) (based on historical development according to Rose 1976) social services programmes will be reduced more than industry, trade, and employment programmes, and those will be cut more than defence and law-and-order programmes

(18) (based on demographic trends) social security spending will increase or not decrease as a proportion of total government spending, and school education spending will decrease or not increase as a proportion of total government spending

(19) (based on Marxist analysis) spending on social security and unemployment relief programmes, on police, prisons, and 'inner-city' programmes will increase as a proportion of total government expenditure

(20) (based on employment trends) the proportion of blue-collar workers in the civil service will decrease, and the proportion of women will increase

(21) (based on industrial trends) expenditure under the head of transfer payments will increase

(22) expenditure by central government relative to spending by other spending authorities will increase.

These hypotheses are couched in terms of cutbacks, but they are derived from theories which are not specifically directed to cutback management. They must meet the second of the Occam's Razor requirements. The first requirement will be met if they account adequately for the observations made of what actually happened; for, complicated as they may seem, both 'party-political' and 'trend' theories are essentially simpler than 'bureaucratic process' and 'bureaucratic self-interest' theories. But if these theories fail to explain the outcomes of cutback management, we may need to look to others: so we must now survey what theories about bureaucrats, and theories about departments and programmes, have to offer.

III Theories about bureaucrats

What are bureaucrats like? You may think of them as did John Stuart Mill in the middle of the nineteenth century, as trained and skilled officials, 'governors by profession', paid and permanent, accumulating experience and practical knowledge, subject to a besetting flaw of 'routine', but – if properly selected, watched, and controlled by representative government – providing the essential advantage that work in the conduct of affairs which requires skill can be done by those who possess it (Mill 1861 (1910), 245–7). The *Report on the Organisation of the Permanent Civil Service* of 1853 by Sir Stafford Northcote and Sir Charles Trevelyan had made the same point on its first page:

It cannot be necessary to enter into any lengthened argument for the purpose of showing the high importance of the Permanent Civil Service of the country in the present day. The great and increasing accumulation of public business, and the consequent pressure upon the Government, need only be alluded to; and the inconveniences which are inseparable from the frequent changes which take place in the responsible administration are matter of sufficient notoriety. It may be safely asserted that, as matters now stand, the Government of the country could not be carried on without the aid of an efficient body of permanent officers, occupying a position duly subordinate to that of the Ministers who are directly responsible to the Crown and to Parliament, yet possessing sufficient independence, character, ability, and experience to be able to advise, assist, and to some extent, influence, those who are from time to time set over them. (C 1713, 1854, p. 3)

Alternatively, you may think that Adam Smith, writing in 1776 about the civil servants of the East India Company rather than those of the British Crown, but in terms which are perhaps generalisable, was being more realistic:

From the nature of their situation, too, the servants must be more disposed to support with rigorous severity their own interest against that of the country which they govern, than their masters can be to support theirs. The country belongs to their masters, who cannot avoid having some regard for the interest of what belongs to them. But it does not belong to the servants. The real interest of their masters, if they were capable of understanding it, is the same with that of the country, and it is from ignorance chiefly, and the meanness of mercantile prejudice, that they ever oppress it. But the real interest of the servants is by no means the same with that of the country, and the most perfect information would not necessarily put an end to their oppressions . . . I mean not to throw any odious imputation upon the general character of the servants of the East India Company, and much less upon that of any particular persons. It is the system of government, the situation in which they are placed, that I mean to censure; not the character of those who have acted in it. They acted as their situation naturally directed and they who have clamoured the loudest against them would, probably, not have acted better themselves. (Smith 1776, Bk IV, Chap. VII, Part III)

Walter Bagehot (possibly writing in reply to Mill) expresses the same point in nineteenth-century English terms:

Not only does a bureaucracy . . . tend to under-government, in point of quality; it tends to over-government in point of quantity. The trained official hates the rude, untrained public. He thinks that they are stupid, ignorant, reckless – that they cannot tell their own interest – that they should have the leave of the office before they do anything . . . A bureaucracy is sure to think that its duty is to augment official power, official business, or official members, rather than to leave free the energies of mankind . . . (Bagehot 1867 (1964), 197)

These quotations are representative of a vehement debate that took place all over Europe in the middle of the nineteenth century (Albrow 1970). The two positions are not necessarily incompatible with one another: the first could reflect aspiration, as it were – what *should* be the case – while the second could mirror reality, what human nature is like in such situations. Those who took the more positive view of the bureaucrat tended to take their evidence from what they knew of English political life and English officials, while those on the opposing side pointed to the fearful examples of the French and the Prussians, and even the Chinese of an earlier age.

The essence of each view was formalised in the twentieth century by, respectively, Max Weber (1921) in Germany, and a group of American economists of whom the leading names were Gordon Tullock (1965), Anthony Downs (1967), William Niskanen (1971), and Albert Breton (1974).

Weber's treatment was in a sociological tradition we now call 'Organisation Theory'; he believed that any *Verband* – association, firm, church, etc. – contained a leadership group determining directions, an administrative staff to sustain it, and the rest of the members to produce whatever was produced. *Bureaucracy* referred in Weber only to the administrative staff; and in his 'ideal-type' or model of a *legal-rational* administrative system he highlighted a hierarchical and functionally specialised structure, a routinised and rule-based procedure, and a disciplined, expert, qualified, and salaried staff who would deal with all decisions in an impersonal, disinterested way (Gerth and Mills 1946 (1961), 196–244; Albrow 1970, 44–5). This maps very well on to the J. S. Mill or Northcote–Trevelyan understanding of what bureaucrats should be like.

The economists take a rather different view. It is as it were an article of faith among them that bureaucrats are 'economic men', as are businessmen, maximising their personal advantage in whatever way they can in official operations; not in 'the market-place', to be sure, and not in terms of financial gain only, but with payoffs in intangibles such as power and prestige as well as salaries and perquisites. Just as businessmen compete for share of market, so bureaucrats compete for share of budget; part of any increase can be taken as 'private' benefits – an expansion in work means enlargement of staff, which in turn multiplies supervisory posts and enhances promotion prospects, and so on. It is not *corruption* which is being alleged; simply that bureaucrats live by the same lights as do the rest of us. This approach sees the world of bureaucracy, in fact, much as Adam Smith and Bagehot (editor of *The Economist*) did: bureaucrats will always be trying to give us more 'government' than we need, and will be more concerned with their own interests than in 'leaving free the energies of mankind' – or as the modern economists put it, allocating resources most efficiently.

What hypotheses will these theories generate about how bureaucrats will behave in a period of cutbacks? How, first, will a skilled, experienced, and independently minded official deal with the need for cutbacks, in an impersonal, disinterested way?

Much of the literature suggests that the first choice that presents itself to the manager faced with the need to reduce expenditure or staff numbers is between percentage cuts all round and selective cutbacks – between 'equity and efficiency', as Levine (1978, 320) puts it, or between incremental or quantum cuts (Glassberg 1978, 327), or between 'equal misery' and priorities (Hartley 1981, 143). There are many plausible reasons for expecting that the first reflex of central controllers suddenly given the task of making 'savings' of a certain amount will be to impose proportionate targets on each of the component units. (The same arguments, by and large, apply whether we are discussing the reactions of axe-wielders in a central ministry or of top people in each of the other ministries in respect of their internal allocating of cutbacks.) Proportionality may appeal to corporate sentiments of 'fairness', and preserve parity of esteem. Requiring each component unit to produce the same percentage sacrifices recognises a *status quo* that may very well have been brought about by decades of proportionate or incremental *growth* of budgets or staffing complements. Certainly, it avoids the recriminations, disruption, and delay that attend any attempt to upset such 'traditional' expectations. Another way of looking at this is that it transfers real decision costs lower down in the organisation (Levine 1978, 322).

Apart from those arguments for decrementalism as a rational response to declining resources, civil service bureaucracies are particularly subject to what in an earlier study (Hood and Dunsire 1981, 38, 114–15) we called the 'iron grid effect': that is, strong tendencies towards uniformity of structure, in the number of levels of hierarchy, span of control, and staff grading, which work to limit scope for adaptation to the environment. Less an argument than a fact of bureaucratic life, too, are the rigid rules of personnel management and historically strong labour unions with relatively easy access to management, creating powerful inertia forces working against rapid or radical redeployment of resources, whether in the civil service as a whole or within individual departments.

To those 'facts' we can add external pressures, from constituency Members of Parliament, lobbies, regional influentials, and others capable of mobilising resistance to selective 'attacks' on their preserves but who might be less vocal over smaller, well-spread reductions. Finally, perceptions of scale and timing may be important. If as many writers suggest (e.g., Glassberg 1978, 327) cutbacks initially tend to be seen as a temporary tightening of the belt, to meet a short-term, externally induced crisis which is expected to go away in due season, then the rational way to retain the capability for complete resumption of present levels of activity is to prune back everything a little, rather than immediately hacking off particular limbs of the bureaucratic tree.

Some theorists point out that decrementalism has its limits; you can do it once or twice, but if you go on meeting demands for overall savings by spreading the misery equally, complications ensue. Charles Levine (1979, 180) instances the 'paradox of irreducible wholes': organisations cannot be reduced piece by piece even if they were built that way. Public organisations are 'lumpy' in the way that critical masses of expertise, political support, facilities and equipment, and resources, have been assembled, and there may be unsuspected thresholds in any of these which when crossed cause unpredictable collapse of the whole. Other theorists note that many kinds of piecemeal 'saving' have their nemesis built in – a build-up of detrimental effects that will either cause eventual collapse or at best be more expensive to put right than the total of the savings. Sometimes it costs money to save money – for instance, investing in more efficient machinery or premises. But that is a 'long-haul' strategy.

Other theorists, therefore, postulate different *styles* of cutback management according to perception of the time-scale involved, and a 'cutback management dynamic' which progressively pushes the system from one style (or phase) to the next (Beck Jørgensen 1985, 1987). Chapter 7 will examine this idea.

We have had a plethora of arguments suggesting why percentage cuts all round are the 'natural' response of bureaucrats faced (at least for the first time) with demands for cutbacks; and a number of arguments indicating the drawbacks of such a course. If, then, a 'Weberian' bureaucrat chooses to cut *selectively*, what does theory suggest about how he or she might do it?

For example, which brings immediate benefits more easily: cutting budgets or cutting staff? Leaving aside all problems of opposition and recalcitrance, or self-interest, the logic of budget-making (annual allocations, upwards of 80 per cent of each year's budget inflexible, etc.) indicates that although one can cut budgetary *plans* for future years, it really is difficult – it takes a lot of time and effort – to find significant savings in sensible selective cutting of next year's budget, let alone this year's. Budgets have a long 'lead time'. The best one may be able to do is promise rigid *control* of expenditures, disapproving more items one by one as they come up (expenses, etc.), which is expensive in controller-time, or imposing cash limits – 'cuts by the back door', as Wright (1981, 25) called them. Selective cash limits, like percentage cuts, have the effect of passing down the line the choice of precisely *what* to cut and when; and although this may be seen as an avoiding of opprobrium, it can from another point of view be argued to be the most sensible way to make cuts, because it gives the decision to the programme managers, or even the 'street-level' bureaucrats, whose 'least harm' judgements can be expected to be at least better informed than those of their top-level superiors. But outcomes will take a year or so to become apparent.

Staff cutting, on the other hand, can in principle begin to have effect the day after the decision, because although staff complements and establishments are normally allocated annually, 'natural wastage' (through deaths, retirements, resignations, secondments, 'due cause' dismissals, etc.) occurs throughout the year with closely predictable incidence, and a ban on replacements, even if selective, will produce 'returns' within the year.

Here, then, is one area where a 'Weberian' model of bureaucratic

behaviour and an 'Adam Smith' one may perhaps generate contradictory predictions: the Weberian approach suggesting that staff will
be cut before spending, and most versions of the economistic approach
(as we shall see shortly) suggesting that almost *anything* will be cut
before staff.

When selecting *which* budget to cut, and which items of a budget to
cut, with a view to providing quick results, how will the stereotype
Weberian official react? This could take us into the subject of the next
section, theories about programmes and bureaus, rather than theories
about bureaucrats; but to keep it general and programme-non-specific,
there are (in principle) broad choices to be made about geographical
spread over the country; between current and capital spending; between
spending on goods and services, loans and grants or 'transfer payments',
and salaries; and between spending authorities.

Spending in the regions that is not programme-specific consists mainly
of the upkeep and staffing of regional and local offices by those
departments which maintain such networks. The workload of such
offices is, by and large, 'demand-driven'; the main hope of savings is
therefore either through greater economy and efficiency (mechanisation
and computerisation, amalgamation of offices into common premises
and even common staffs, and the like), or through planned deterioration
of the service (longer customer waiting times, more errors, poorer
working conditions). The first of these, however, takes time to produce
both the recommendations and the results. We can predict, therefore,
that for quick results the second will be employed; staffing will be
reduced, maintenance expenditures postponed.

The choice between cutting current or capital expenditure is of a
similar nature. Capital expenditure tends to be identifiable as specific
projects which can be reassessed individually, and it is often feasible to
postpone capital expenditure without immediately imperilling services.
We would expect the Weberian official faced with the need for quickly
apparent budget reductions to preserve current as against capital
spending.

The same reasoning does not apply, however, to selection among
other economic categories of expenditure. A hard-pressed official will
perhaps look to cut first the category over which the official already has
most control, and attempt to improve control over all categories in the
longer run. In general, transfer payments are either demand-led or
policy-led (which may amount to the same thing), and loans and grants
policy-determined (although conditions could quite promptly be tight-
ened up); so we might suppose that spending on goods and services

may tend to go down before spending on grants, etc. or on transfer payments does.

By and large, the same applies to cuts as between spending authorities. Control over local authority and public corporation is *long-linked*, or relatively remote, compared with control over central government authorities. We might expect, therefore, that although the machinery for controlling (and through these controls, reducing) local authority and other public authority spending might be rapidly overhauled and made more draconian, at first, spending by central government would go down more (or increase less) than spending by other types of authority.

What about the Weberian official's approach to cuts in staffing? Which groups of personnel are likely to be cut first, on an objective, impersonal analysis of the balance between speedy results and 'least harm'?

The main source of 'relatively painless' staff cutting (that is to say, avoiding compulsory redundancies and dismissals, with their attendant quasi-legal procedures and appeals, etc.) is, as already noted, the non-replacement of 'natural wastage'. Logic indicates, then, that the groups which have the largest incidence of natural wastage are the most vulnerable, all else being equal; and, although the *incidence*, or proportion, of it might be large in a category of civil servants which was nevertheless small in absolute numbers, significant total savings would only come from the larger groups. The larger groups are at the base of the pyramid. So we would predict that at the outset of cutbacks, at least, numbers of blue-collar workers and manual and clerical grades of white-collar workers would decrease more than other groups. In the slightly longer run, such groups are also the most vulnerable to 'savings' from computerisation and other measures to increase efficiency; and the jobs they do are also those most amenable to 'contracting out' – bringing in outside contractors to do what was previously done 'in house'. All in all, it seems a safe bet that the lower ranks will suffer more than the middle ranks. Numbers in the upper ranks, however, might be expected to have a relatively high 'wastage' rate through age retirements, and therefore if a truly Weberian logic of staff cutbacks is followed, we might expect quite high proportionate cutbacks in the upper ranks, even if the absolute numbers are small.

Where for any reason staff lost by natural wastage have to be replaced, it might seem a reasonable idea to appoint temporary staff, or part-time staff, who can keep the bureaucratic fabric in place for future restoration, if cuts are an ephemeral aberration in secular growth, but who can be 'let go' more easily if further cutbacks are required. We might expect, therefore, that at the outset of a period of cutbacks the numbers of temporary staff and of part-time staff, as a proportion of the total, would go up – and if the cutbacks continued, would then decline.

We could speculate further about where cuts could be expected, immediately, in the short term, and in the longer term, and as between the 'generalists' and the 'specialists', or as between different methods of achieving staff savings – lowering standards, greater efficiency, contracting out and privatisation, etc.; but perhaps such detail is better kept for a later chapter.

What we have discussed here produces a further batch of hypotheses for testing, concerning the responses to cutback pressures of the official whose motivations are solely of the 'Weberian' type – the informed, objective weighing-up of public pros and cons, resulting in judgements that produce the desired results while limiting damage:

(23)   at least at the outset of cutbacks, more or less equal percentage reductions will be applied to all spending units

(24)   in a period of cutbacks, total staff numbers will decrease before total spending does

(25)   at least at the outset of cutbacks, spending on and staffing of regional and local offices will be reduced

(26)   in a period of cutbacks, capital expenditures will be reduced before current expenditures

(27)   spending on goods and services will decrease before spending on subsidies and transfer payments does

(28)   spending by central government will decrease before spending by local authorities and other public authorities does

(29)   numbers (or proportions) of blue-collar workers will decrease before those of other civil service groups

(30)   numbers of clerical and other lower-grade white-collar civil servants will decrease before those of other civil service groups

(31)   at the outset of a period of cutbacks, numbers of temporary staff and of part-time staff will go up as a proportion of total staff, and as the cutbacks deepen, will decline again.

The *other* theory about bureaucrats with which we introduced this section of the chapter was what we are calling the 'Adam Smith' one: that is, as Adam Smith, Bagehot, and the later economists would have it, that bureaucrats are motivated just as the rest of us are, to look first after our own interests.

With some of the aspects of the economic approach to bureaucracy we are not going to be concerned in this book. Many economists (e.g.

Niskanen 1971; Ostrom 1974; Breton 1974; Williamson 1975; Posner 1977; Jackson 1982) have contrasted 'bureaus' and 'firms', according to whether ownership is transferable or not, whether they are financed by negotiated budget or by user charges, whether accountable by political clearance or by degree of profitability, and whether bankruptable or not; and reasoned that classic 'firms' will always be more *efficient* than classic 'bureaus', both in the allocative and in the value-for-money senses of the word. But these arguments have only marginal relevance to cutback management, and will not be investigated here.

It is only the root idea behind the economistic approach we are concerned with: the assertion that bureaucrats are *economic men* too, and evaluate any choice (at least partly) according to their own self-interest. The assumption is that increases in budget can be appropriated in some significant degree into 'private' benefits for the bureaucrats (using their discretionary powers), and that therefore bureaucrats will strive to push up budgets as far as they are allowed (ignoring the effect on costs). Cutbacks in budgets will, of course, diminish those benefits and so will be resisted strongly by bureaucrats. The 'private benefits' usually instanced depend on the 'hierarchical' nature of bureaucracies: a bigger budget means more staff to be hired to spend it, more staff (under traditionally fixed 'span of control' rules) means more managerial positions, and thus more promotion opportunities. More directly, bigger budgets can mean higher salaries and more 'perks' of one kind or another (even if not comparable in scale to managerial perks in firms).

Furthermore, the self-regarding bureaucrat is assumed to choose and recommend the most staff-intensive style of delivery of a service which is available in any given case (Breton 1974), since any other style (say, subsidising some other body to provide the service) will reduce the 'private' benefits which can be extracted. This kind of appreciation of bureaucratic motivation has perhaps by now 'passed into the language'. The enormous success of the British television comedy programme *Yes Minister* possibly arose from its articulating through humour 'truths' which are widely believed but not provable as objective description; as when the fictitious Permanent Secretary Sir Humphrey Appleby says:

The civil service does not make profits or losses. *Ergo*. we measure success by the size of our staff and budget. By definition, a big department is more successful than a small one . . . this simple proposition is the basis of our whole system. (Lynn and Jay 1981, 57)

Other observers of the British civil service have taken one of two lines of criticism of all this. The first points to some well-known differences between the bureaucratic milieux in Britain and in the United States: the latter much more decentralised and business oriented in any case, the former much more tightly knit and controlled, with the higher ranks socialised into an ethos that stresses service-wide standards, and places higher value on administrative operations that are 'lean' than on bureaucratic 'bloat' (Self 1972; Kogan 1973; Young 1974). In the British civil service, promotions at higher levels are centralised, and conditions of work (including accommodation and floor-space, furniture and fittings) are laid down by well-policed rules; staff complement and salary levels are not at the discretion of bureau heads. Some of the most prestigious and (to the ambitious) most desirable departments in British central government have relatively small budgets and staffs (Treasury, Cabinet Office). Not even the most acerbic 'mandarin' in real British life would be likely to agree with Sir Humphrey Appleby that the key to advancement in the higher reaches of the British civil service lies in simply raising your budget higher and higher. Some would say that the self-regarding British civil servant is more likely to *avoid* budgetary and other expansion if he can, as being irreconcilable with the 'on-the-job leisure' from which the bureaucrat may also derive utility (Leibenstein 1976, 95–117; Jackson 1982, 133; Peacock 1983, 128).

An important and more general extension of this line of argument is Dunleavy's (1985) critique of the Downs/Niskanen model, using the same analytic method but with different assumptions; showing that not all bureaucrats have identical utility functions, that strategies can be strung out on a spectrum of advantages from the highly personal to the collective-only, and that the definition of 'budget' (broadly, internal maintenance, external spending, or external funding) is very significant. Dunleavy's conclusion is that bureau chiefs, in contrast to lower-level bureaucrats, derive little benefit from many kinds of budgetary expansion; if they are self-interested, they may aim to 'shape' their bureaus in ways which might make these bureaus smaller, but containing more high-status staff and more highly discretionary budgets.

The other line of criticism of the economistic model of bureaucratic behaviour accepts that British civil servants resist cost-cutting and staff-savings exercises, but holds that this is accounted for less by the maximising of 'private' benefits by individuals than by collective preservation of the civil service's autonomy, a defence mechanism and closing of ranks against threats to their 'way of life' and accustomed modes of operation; cf. the fate of successive attempts to introduce 'business efficiency' methods into central government departments (Chapman 1978; Hennessey 1984; Fry 1985; Gray and Jenkins 1985).

Here is a clear case of our having plenty of ready-made theories to explain whatever behaviour we find, without anyone troubling to find what the facts actually are – the situation that set us on to what we call *bureaumetrics* in the first place.

Many of the theories about bureaucratic motivation are attempts to explain public-sector *growth* rather than cutbacks – and so should be used in preference to cutback-specific theories if they fit the observations equally well. But the cutback management literature, both American and British, is also replete with theories based on the image of the bureaucrat as fundamentally self-regarding and self-preserving.

Perhaps the basic supposition is that cutbacks bring out the worst in bureaucrats; if they seek to benefit themselves during a period of growth – when many can have a little more without any necessarily having less – how much more avidly will they guard their self-interest when it is a matter of who loses more, at whose expense? So we find authors using mean phrases like 'exploit the exploitable' (Levine 1978, 320), 'beggar thy neighbour' (Glennerster 1981, 191), 'hitting hardest at enemies and weaklings' (Hood and Wright 1981, 202), and the like. In cutbacks, the survival instinct is strong, and the weakest perforce go to the wall – or so it might seem. In this section, we shall concentrate on bureaucratic groups' sorties against other bureaucratic groups; in the next section, we shall discuss corporate survival tactics, or the agency-against-agency battle.

Hood and Wright (1981, 201) quote a former Prime Minister's policy adviser: 'it seems absolutely human and understandable that if cuts are imposed, those who decide where the cuts should be implemented decide "they should be on anybody else but us"' (Dr Bernard Donoughue, in *The Times*, 2 April 1980). If the watchword is 'Axeman, save thyself!', who gets axed? The Treasury and Civil Service Committee of the House of Commons evidently had some suspicions of that kind in 1980, when they called for detailed quarterly progress reports of how actual staff cuts were made. (We shall describe the results in Chapter 6.)

They may have expected that the 'mandarins' (the highest-ranking civil servants, who on the whole make these decisions) would ensure that the burden of cutbacks would fall on the middle and lower ranks, but certainly not on 'top brass'; this, after all, is often bitterly alleged whenever cuts occur, whether in government or in other fields – and not only in class-conscious Britain. The long-standing rivalry between the 'generalists' and the 'specialists' for succession to top jobs is well known: would it not be a safe bet that the administrative occupational group would protect itself at the expense of the specialist and technical occupational groups? Similarly, that the white-collar workers would see that it was the blue-collar workers who suffered; that the people at headquarters would chop the people in the regions before they cut London staff; and so on. In extension of the idea, we might guess that in cutbacks, well-entrenched male civil servants would prune female staff before other males; that temporary staff would be the first to go; that part-time employees would be next.

These are all eminently testable propositions – or at least, actual outcomes can be matched against putative outcomes if these were the intentions operating. So we have a further series of hypotheses to investigate:

(32)   when central government expenditure is rising, total numbers of civil servants will rise with it

(33)   when central government expenditure is rising, expenditure on salaries and associated costs for civil servants will rise at a greater rate than the total expenditure – i.e., it will absorb an increasing proportion of the total

(34)   when central government expenditure is rising, programmes where spending on wages and salaries is a dominant proportion of the total (e.g., over half) will increase at a rate greater than that of total expenditure; when central government expenditure is falling, such programmes will increase, or decline at a rate smaller than that of the total

(35)   in cutbacks, numbers of top civil servants will not decrease, or will decrease less than those of middle- and lower-level ranks

(36)   in cutbacks, numbers of staff in administration groups will not decrease, or will decrease less than those in other occupational groups

(37)   in cutbacks, numbers in the non-industrial civil service will not decrease, or will decrease less than those in the industrial civil service

(38)   in cutbacks, numbers of civil servants employed in the London region will not decrease, or will decrease less than those employed in the other regions

(39)   in cutbacks, numbers of male civil servants will not decrease, or will decrease less than those of female civil servants

(40)   in cutbacks, numbers of established (permanent) staff will not decrease, or will decrease less than those of temporary staff

(41)   in cutbacks, numbers of full-time staff will not decrease, or will decrease less than those of part-time staff.

Now let us look at theories about bureaucracies, about the differences between departments, and how to tell which are more vulnerable than others in an era of cutbacks. Once more, we shall begin with a *bureaucratic process* approach, and then go on to a *bureaucratic self-interest* analysis.

IV   Theories about programmes and bureaus

The mood in the last section was *active* – what do we know about bureaucrats that would explain how they are likely to *behave* in an era of cutbacks? The mood here, by contrast, must be *passive*: what do we know about programmes, or about bureaus and departments, which will tell us how they are likely to *be treated* during a time of cutbacks?

That requires a characterisation of the different ministries and their spending, some form of descriptive classification, a way of indicating for each its degree of *vulnerability* to cutbacks, less or greater than its fellows. Comparisons of this kind, one ministry with another, are surprisingly few, and surprisingly recent. The literature of the nineteenth century has many discussions of *bureaucracy* in the abstract, or as a type of government – a disease the Continentals suffered from, but from which England was blessedly free; and discussions also of the *roles* of Ministers and their civil service advisers. But not even such acute observers as Sir Henry Taylor (1836) or Walter Bagehot (1867) give us their adversions on the nature of the Colonial Office as compared with the Home Office or the War Office, or the like.

In general, even in most of the Public Administration textbooks which began to appear after the Second World War, the *bureaucratic process* is described as a generic one; at best, as in Mackenzie and Grove's *Central Administration in Britain* (1957), the structure (in terms of numbers of different classes and grades of civil servants) and functions (tasks, or programmes) of half a dozen ministries were given, as illustrations of the diversity and complexity of the subject. Yet Mackenzie and Grove give hints of something more: as in their brief *characterisation* of the Home Office as at once 'an aristocrat and a maid of all work' (228), or the following:

The Commonwealth Relations Office is concerned largely with high policy, but manages directly only the affairs of its own small staff at home and overseas. The Home Office also makes policy; it manages a larger office directly, and controls other services indirectly through minor Departments and local authorities. When we come to the Air Ministry a further dimension is added: not so much because this is a service Department concerned with defence policy, as because the Ministry is directly responsible for the administration of a very large body of Crown servants, the Royal Air Force (about 240,000 strong in 1956), and for the provision of their extremely expensive equipment. (Mackenzie and Grove 1957. 232)

Later, the Ministry of Pensions and National Insurance is given as an example of 'a great Executive and Clerical Class Department' (239). If we had such thumbnail sketches for *all* departments, we would perhaps have the basis for a multidimensional categorisation of the sort we need, that might give us something to go on in estimating vulnerability to cutbacks – are 'high policy' departments more, or less, likely to be cut than 'great Executive and Clerical' departments?

The idea to be explored is that there is some factor or factors in their bureaucratic processes which may determine which departments are cut more than others, when selective cutbacks are made (there is no problem if all cuts are on the 'equal misery' basis). Now it is possible that it is the *programmes* with which a department is associated, and nothing about its processes as such, which determines its fate; and if this were so, an obvious strategy for a departmental chief seeking to preserve his or her departmental position would be to guard against programme instability (the pattern of distribution of resources among programmes being at the mercy of party-political swings) by assembling a 'portfolio' of programme holdings, spread across the preferences of rival parties. For instance, a predominantly 'law and order' department might aim to acquire stocks in inner-city aid programmes, or programmes to combat racial or sexual discrimination, as well as in the more traditional punitive approaches; a defence department might target its contracts towards marginal constituencies and highlight its employment-generating capacities.

The most sophisticated analysis of differences between spending programmes is that of Klein (1976). He notes that one budgetary pound is not necessarily equal to another budgetary pound: they can vary in three main ways. First, in *economic significance*: programmes that employ people or buy goods pre-empt resources directly, while programmes that merely shuffle resources from the taxpayer to the beneficiary have a much less certain economic effect – the Treasury will, for example, recoup some of the resources in taxation. Second: in *administrative feasibility and time-horizon*: transferring money can be implemented more quickly than creating staff or putting up buildings; capital spending plans can be dropped more easily than can existing services. (It is also, Klein says, less politically invidious to export unemployment into the construction industry than to dismiss public employees – but he is writing in 1976.) Third: different programmes are distinguished by the extent to which they *commit* governments to expenditure *outside their control*. Spending on pensions to retired persons is a precise commitment, and subject to demographic changes the government cannot alter – but the rates of benefit are within the government's control; subsidies to agriculture are both imprecise and subject to vagaries of weather (and nowadays to European Community decisions).

The implication is that governments using public expenditure to manage the economy will switch resources from programme to programme according to the requisite mix of economic effect, immediate or longer-term effect, and predictability of effect that the circumstances demand (subject, as he says elsewhere in the article, to political/ideological acceptability to the party in power, and to the degree of organised pressure they are under from groups whose votes or co-operation they need). We might interpret the model for an era of cutbacks thus: governments will be less worried about transfer-payments programmes than about programmes which are heavy on purchases of goods and services; they will cut capital spending before current spending; they will try to abandon altogether programmes where commitments are open-ended, to put cash or other limits on commitments wherever feasible, and to reduce the rates of payment where they can.

Klein notes also an inverse relationship between the size of a programme and the part played by party-political decisions; where expenditures are very large, it takes considerable shifts of resources to make more than a marginal adjustment. Again, there is a relationship between the volatility of spending totals (whether or not annual change is incremental) and a programme's characteristics in terms of (a) manpower-intensiveness and (b) cash-intensiveness. Where a programme's budget is largely wages and salaries of employees, change is slow; where its essence is to move money around, totals can change quite markedly from year to year. In cutbacks, therefore, we might expect that small programmes will suffer earlier, and proportionately more, than large programmes; and that money-moving programmes will suffer earlier, and more, than employment-heavy programmes. (To some extent this prediction is inconsistent with that above, about government being less worried about transfer-payments programmes.)

Using Downs' theory (Downs 1960) that political support for a government will be maximised when the visible benefits from public expenditures outweigh the visible burdens of taxation, Klein notes that there is no pressure group which mobilises the vague aspiration towards lower taxes by a single-minded demand for tax cuts, while there are many groups which translate wants for increased spending into clearly articulated demands backed by threat of one kind and another. The visibility of programme benefits, he suggests, is at maximum when the programme scores high on specificity of beneficiary group and on clarity (he says 'certainty') of benefit. 'Public goods' programmes like defence and law and order score low on specificity of beneficiary: they are too general in their impact. Attendance allowances, and school education, score high: who benefits is obvious. School education, again, scores high on clarity – the accessibility and tight causality of the relationship between demands and provision: more children (demand) means more teachers and books (provision), and everyone can see that. Health services, however, or university education, do not have such a simple formula: it is not obvious whether more old people, or even more sick people, means more doctors, or more medicine, or more hospital beds, or what; or how the demand for graduates translates into facilities for higher education. Klein postulates that expenditure will be highest on services that offer clear benefits to specific groups: you do better to aim to please parents than to please the sick – and the former are in any case more politically active than the latter, and more likely to exert pressure. Moreover, if you spend your resources highly visibly, in this way, you may achieve equal political impact for less cash; for example, if aiding industry, put all your effort into one industry, or one region, rather than offering general subsidies.

Perhaps this translates, in hard times, into expectations that programmes providing public goods (in the welfare economist's sense) will suffer more than programmes providing cash benefits to individuals; that programmes whose clients are organised into groups will suffer less than programmes whose clients are less well organised; and that less complex programmes (with comparatively few subheads, indicating clearer ties between demand and provision) will suffer less than more complex ones. In such a rich panoply of theory, it is not always easy to operationalise the concepts. But we have been given enough, perhaps, to encourage us to feel that we now 'know' something about how programmes may differ, in cutback-relevant ways. We have at least the following hypotheses to examine:

(42) programmes which are proportionately high in purchases of goods and services will be cut before and more than programmes which are proportionately high in transfer-payments to individuals

(43)   programmes which are proportionately high in capital spending will be cut before and more than programmes high in current expenditure

(44)   programmes with open-ended commitments will be abolished or cash-limited or cut before others: specifically, spending on agriculture will be cut early and deeply

(45)   programmes small in absolute size (total spending) will suffer earlier and proportionately more than large programmes

(46)   programmes proportionately heavy in grants, loans and subsidies will suffer earlier and more than programmes proportionately heavy in wages and salaries of employees

(47)   programmes providing public goods (e.g., defence, law and order) will suffer earlier and more than programmes providing cash benefits to individuals (e.g., social security, pensions)

(48)   programmes with many subheads (complex programmes) will suffer earlier and more than programmes with few subheads (simple ones).

Much of the cutback management literature concentrates on bureaus rather than programmes (although the distinction is not always sustainable), and suggests that cutbacks can be predicted on characteristics of individual bureaucracies. Levine (1978) describes four types of *cause* for the decline of public organisations: *problem depletion* (their *raison d'être* disappears); *environmental entropy* (general or specific regional economic decline, technological changes, and so on, lead to a fall in support from the public purse, whatever the 'need'); *political vulnerability* (fragility arising from small size, internal conflicts, changes in leadership, lack of a 'corner' in expertise, absence of a history of achievement or excellence, organisational 'youth' in general); and *organisational atrophy* (e.g., perverse incentives, role confusion, inappropriate rules, weak oversight, lack of self-evaluation, high turnover of staff, constant reorganisation, technological obsolescence, etc.).

The problem there seems to be the length of this list; if any of these attributes can make you vulnerable, who shall be saved? If it needs a combination, what combination? Such a catch-all list would produce a large number of hypotheses for testing, it is true; but the testing would need such a variety of data as to be prohibitively expensive, in practical terms. For our purposes we really want to identify a few key factors which will predict outcomes with reasonable comprehensibility.

Besides, much of this closely mirrors more general discussions of the sources of bureaucratic power, so that it appears to say that if you lose power you lose resources – not a very new thought. Rourke (1976), for instance, said that bureaucratic power is based on (a) possession of expertise vital to reaching decisions in important areas of policy; (b) ability to mobilise an influential constituency; (c) corporate strength and effective leadership.

Some British commentators have elaborated on the *political vulnerability* theme. Cutting road-maintenance is politically less 'immediate' than sacking staff or closing schools (Midwinter and Page 1981, 72); programmes attractive to vote-sensitive governments in terms of alleged social benefits – jobs, aid to the balance of payments, technological spin-off, etc. – are less vulnerable (Hartley 1981, 125); the most vulnerable units often are the bureaucrats whom bureaucrats do not like – planners and research staff (Glennerster 1981, 186). But we need further exploration of how 'political weakness' is to be defined and measured.

Probably the most sophisticated, systematic and fine-grained attempt to produce a bureaucratic-process account of vulnerability to cutbacks is that offered by Beck Jørgensen (1985, 1987). As part of a wider discussion of cutback management processes, he identifies three dimensions of vulnerability, and implies that a bureau's fate over a period of cutbacks is predictable from its overall profile on these three dimensions. The three dimensions are as follows (the labelling is ours, not Beck Jørgensen's):

A *invisibility* – the probability of being identified as a potential target for cutbacks
B *output effects vulnerability* – the extent to which cutbacks if imposed will cause immediate and publicly visible damage to the public services produced by the bureau in question
C *political 'clout'* – the ability to mount effective resistance to cutbacks if proposed.

Invisibility (or identificational vulnerability, as Beck Jørgensen calls it) refers to the ease with which central allocators of manpower and spending budgets can 'see' a department, when looking for targets for the axe. One factor that clearly plays a part here is the extent to which a department finances its budget from fees and charges rather than drawing on general tax funds. It is suggested that budgets which do not require large lump-sum grants from an overstrained exchequer will be relatively 'invisible' to budgetary allocators, even though a 'rational-comprehensive' approach to cutback management might imply equally rigid scrutiny of all types of public expenditure, however financed.

Beck Jørgensen suggests that another factor in visibility may be the *complexity* of a department's budget (complex budgets are harder for

budget allocators to 'take in', and so more opaque than simple ones –
complexity confers protection, *pace* Klein). This relates to his general
argument that the more 'transparent' a department's structure and
production functions are, the more difficult it will be to conceal
organisational slack or reserves.

Obviously there are many possible dimensions of 'visibility'. It has a
social-psychological aspect which might be tapped by in-depth inter-
viewing. Moreover, visibility may be linked to party-political differences
to some degree, since governments of differing colour may not 'see'
certain programmes that are dearest to their political hearts, when
looking for candidates for cutback; it is more likely to be activities
peripheral to their central political values which are most carefully
scrutinised. Similarly, as Beck Jørgensen suggests, bureaucracies performing politically controversial tasks – say, matters of artistic and
dramatic taste – may be more visible than bureaucracies with a more
'consensus-based' area of operations. Unfortunately, there is as yet no
reliable scale of 'controversiality' in bureaucratic activities, although it
would be in principle possible to construct such a scale from attitude
surveys or from content analysis of parliamentary reports and/or party
manifestos.

Output effects vulnerability (or operational vulnerability, as Beck
Jørgensen terms it) refers to the extent to which cuts in a department's
staff or budget will have a large and instant impact on its activities in the
world outside. Beck Jørgensen instances situations where the technology
imposes an on/off threshold (outputs are useless if inputs drop below a
certain level, e.g., population censuses); where there can be no buffer
stocks between production capacity and demand (product is highly
perishable, e.g., news, or the work cycle is very short, with turnaround
within the day or even the hour, e.g. the first-class post); where fixed
recurrent expenditures are high in relation to total budget (discretionary
expenditure is small, e.g., pensions administration). All of the items
discussed by Beck Jørgensen in this category refer to structures or
technologies which do not permit the accumulation of organisational
'slack', implicit reserves of energy, or 'cushions' against shock; such a
bureau is operationally brittle, and cuts that another department might
absorb, at least for a time, can spell quick disintegration. Highlighting
and playing on this 'fragility' can paradoxically offer such a department
some protection against *any* cuts. It is an interesting speculation, but it
does not readily lend itself to systematic testing because of lack of
consistent data describing public bureaucracies in this dimension.

Another kind of output effect, almost the opposite, may make a department vulnerable in the short term. 'Seed-corn' activities – tasks such as research, planning, policy development, staff training, plant maintenance, and the like – are tempting to the axe-wielders because cuts, rather than having instant effect, have consequences that only build up gradually over time; and nemesis always seems a long way off. We would expect, therefore, that departments with a relatively high proportion of their total budget going on research and development would fare worse than other departments during cutback.

A third possible dimension of output effects vulnerability is the extent to which the activities of a department are suitable for the contracting out or hiving off of work to a legally independent body – a strategy which can play a notable part in cutbacks. Given that hiving off and contracting out tend to concentrate on routine functions, and on blue-collar work, it might be supposed that the proportion of a department's total staff consisting of blue-collar staff or staff in lower clerical grades might be a good predictor of its degree of suffering, at least in staff reductions.

As with *visibility*, Beck Jørgensen's ideas about output effects vulnerability are rich and subtle, but do not always lend themselves to ready measurement – even for fairly down-to-earth matters like maintenance expenditures, which are often said to be more vulnerable to cutbacks than other kinds of bureaucratic activity (e.g. Midwinter and Page 1981, 72).

Political clout (or allocational vulnerability in Beck Jørgensen's terms) is closely related to invisibility – a mugger casting round for a victim does not 'see' a passer-by built like a prize-fighter. Even if a department is highly visible in the categories discussed earlier, it may yet be saved from staff or spending cutbacks if it has 'clout' – the ability to muster political support when attacked. Empires can hit back.

Echoing some of Klein's analysis, Beck Jørgensen suggests that bureaucracies low on 'clout' will be those which are not closely in touch with their clients; which are not buttressed by professions (well known for their ability to resist change successfully); whose client groups do not have easy access to budget allocators in order to 'scream' about cutbacks; and the benefits of whose outputs are enjoyed in small amounts by many people, whereas the costs are paid in large amounts by few people – large and scattered beneficiary groups have low incentive to mobilise, and more difficulties in doing so, than does the smaller 'benefactor' group, especially when the latter is well used to collective action. Such are the characteristics that go to make the bureaucratic 'political weakling', feeble in inspiring or organising political 'voice'. The problems arise in operationalising the arguments for testing by readily available documentary data. However, the archetypal bureau meeting the specifications for 'low clout' is the social security department, while the health bureau (buttressed by well-entrenched professions) ought to have 'high clout'; so it ought to be instructive to compare the fortunes of the two main parts or bureaus in the (then) single UK Department of Health and Social Security (since 1988, split into two distinct departments).

Many other scholars of the cutback management process have focussed on political vulnerability. For instance, Levine (1978) associates frequent changes in leadership with political vulnerability. As noted in Chapter 1, conventional wisdom about the British Cabinet (e.g., Heclo and Wildavsky 1974) holds that since spending Ministers 'fight their corner' in Cabinet to defend their departments' interests and to resist Treasury pressures for cutbacks, departments without a Cabinet Minister at their head are politically vulnerable to budgetary cuts (at least). Again, the nature of the political decision process over spending cuts might be expected to benefit departments whose interests were closely related to those of other departments: that is, since 'voting' in Cabinet and other committees is open, there should be ample scope for log-rolling. If this were the key to the Cabinet decision process over expenditure, we would expect departments with the highest degree of 'interconnectedness' with other departments, through shared programmes, to benefit most from log-rolling in protecting their budgets.

The complementary risk-spreading 'portfolio effect' has already been mentioned. The argument is that the larger the number of separate programmes a department has, the more different pressure groups it has available to support its operations, and the more it is protected from the vagaries of party-political preference – among a range of programmes there is always likely to be one or two 'glamour stocks' whatever the party in power, whereas a single-programme endowment has a much higher political downside risk.

Finally, it seems possible that political clout will be augmented by a strategy of devoting the largest feasible proportion of a bureau's budget to payments to outside groups, as opposed to the payment of bureaucrats' salaries. Political screams coming from outside groups are more likely to be heard by Treasury and Cabinet and by party whips than are screams from disgruntled bureaucrats. Bureaucracies behaving according to the classic economistic model, in other words, devoting as much as they can of available funds to bureaucratic salaries and perks, will find few allies in the outside world to rally to their cause when their budget is under attack.

These arguments give us another range of hypotheses to be tested against the data, as follows:

(49) bureaus that are highly self-financing (through fees, charges, etc.) will be cut less or later than bureaus which depend heavily on central allocations

(50) bureaus with complex budgets will be cut less or later than bureaus with simple financial structures (cf. 48 above)

(51) bureaus with a relatively high proportion of total spending going on research and development will be cut earlier and more than other bureaus

(52) bureaus with a high proportion of staff in lower clerical grades or in industrial grades will be cut in staff earlier and more than other bureaus

(53) the social security bureau (part of the then Department of Health and Social Security in the UK) will be cut earlier and more than the health bureau (another part of the same department).

In discussing *political clout* the analytical distinction we have made between a Weberian bureaucratic-process approach and an economistic bureaucratic self-interest one has become very blurred; the line between a bureau's being vulnerable to cuts by the central axe-wielders because of its lack of strong pressure-group support and another bureau's deploying its high political clout in self-preservation at the expense of its fellows is too fine to draw clearly. But let us not worry about that, but go on to consider now not vulnerability, but straight power play. *Programmes* have no power as such, but they can attract external support which can then be manipulated by their host bureaus; how will the self-interested bureau, bent on corporate survival in a harsh environment, react to the threat of cuts?

Its main strategy, according to some writers, is to 'lighten ship' by sacrificing first what is less essential, while preserving the 'principal resource' (Hartley and Lynk 1983), 'defending the base' or 'protecting the core':

For example, in the 1970s, the non-core elements of education – school meals, adult education and nursery schools – bore the brunt of spending cuts. The core – the teaching of 5–16 year olds and the provision of courses in working skills for 16–18 year olds – suffered only marginally. (Wright 1981, 16)

On this basis, then, we could expect the following: bureaus with a preponderance of staff in general administration grades will protect that generalist corps by selectively sacrificing the main alternative, their 'specialists'; on the other hand, bureaus with a preponderance of specialists will protect specialist operations. Departments whose main functions are of a 'money-moving' kind – broadly, paying other people to do things – will protect their contract and grant funds; departments whose main functions are of a 'labour-intensive' kind – broadly, performing tasks through direct employment of staff – will protect their staffing complements, and/or the salaries/wages component of their budgets. Departments with many branch offices as their main characteristic will protect this resource; departments with few outlying locations will sacrifice these (and so become more concentrated in one or two regions).

Departments differ in many other ways: for example, a 'functional' breakdown of staff by their types of work, as the Treasury has done in some years, into *public-service delivery, trading and support services,* and *policy/parliamentary* work, would show departments varying in their proportions of each type of work. We would therefore expect that departments conspicuously oriented towards any one of these types of work would protect that one at the expense of the other two.

As we saw in the last section, an even blunter argument simply says that those who have the power to wield axes use them on anyone but themselves. The self-interested bureau will 'look after Number One'. If this were the case it ought to manifest itself in at least the following ways. The central controlling departments (in the UK, mainly the Treasury and the Cabinet Office) would be the last to suffer; cuts would fall earlier and more heavily on the 'spending departments'. The bigger departments would use their weight in Cabinet and elsewhere to divert cutbacks on to the smaller departments. Central government as a whole would protect itself by squeezing the rest of the public sector first. The public sector would see that cuts were exported into the independent and private sectors: by trying to do more 'in house' and purchasing services less; grants, loans, and contracts would decrease before and more than bureaucratic salaries.

The 'economistic' approach to the reactions of bureaus in hard times thus yields a final set of theoretical propositions to be tested against the data for the period 1975–85 in the United Kingdom:

(54)　during cutbacks, bureaus with a preponderance of staff in general administrative grades will cut numbers of specialists disproportionately more than the numbers of generalists

(55)　during cutbacks, bureaus with a preponderance of staff in specialist grades will cut numbers of generalists disproportionately more than the numbers of specialists

(56)   in bureaus where salary costs are a small proportion of total budget, the proportion will fall or not rise during cutbacks

(57)   in bureaus where salary costs are a large proportion of total budget, the proportion will rise or not fall during cutbacks

(58)   highly dispersed departments with significant proportions of staff in several regions will not become more concentrated during cutbacks

(59)   highly concentrated departments with significant proportions of staff in only one region will not become more dispersed during cutbacks

(60)   in bureaus where a high proportion of staff are found in one type of work (service-delivery, common services, policy/parliamentary work), the proportion will rise or not fall during cutbacks

(61)   during cutbacks, the relative ranking of Treasury and Cabinet Office in 'league tables' of central government staffing and spending will improve

(62)   during cutbacks, the proportion of total central government spending and staffing allotted to the largest departments will rise

(63)   during cutbacks, the proportion of total public expenditure allotted to central government will rise

(64)   during cutbacks, central government funding of outside research, etc., and expenditure on contracted goods and services generally, will fall in comparison with spending on bureaucrats' wages and salaries.

As we have tried to show, there is no lack of theory which can be applied to produce testable hypotheses about how cutback management processes will operate. Some of this 'theory' is rooted in popular stereotypes and expectations, some of it in scholarly attempts to analyse the cutback process. What we now need to do is to see which of these expectations is consistent with the observed behaviour of cutback managers in Britain from the middle 1970s to the middle 1980s, as revealed by staffing and spending data for central departments over that period.

3 Winners and losers 1: party and trend explanations

In this chapter we shall begin to look at what actually happened in British central government during the period 1975–85 (with occasional glances at earlier periods), against these hypotheses about what, by one theory or another, you might have expected to happen. We shall deal with *party-political* and *trend* types of hypothesis now (the first 22 hypotheses out of the 64 presented in the previous chapter), and in the next chapters go on to examine hypotheses based on theories about *bureaucratic politics* and *bureaucratic process*.

I Party-political explanations

Conveniently for our research, the period of public-sector cutbacks in which we are principally interested, the decade from the middle of the seventies until the middle of the eighties, is divided by the 1979 General Election into a period of Labour government and a period of Conservative government. Consequently we are able to test some of the propositions which hang on party-political explanations of cutback patterns, even if with rather short runs of data. If it matters which party is in power, it should show up somewhere – in differential treatment of different *programmes*, or of different *departments*, or of different groups of *personnel*, or of different *regions*, or of different *economic categories*, or different *spending authorities*. The first sixteen hypotheses set out in Chapter 2 on pp. 27–8 are concerned with the supposed effects of party on cutbacks.

But, as we saw in the previous chapter, at least one influential theory about the strategies of political party competition suggests that it will *not* matter which party is in power, because the two major parties with the potential of forming a government will always gravitate towards the middle ground of politics, in the attempt to attract voters away from the other party. That is the 'Downs/Hotelling model', or 'D/H' for short. So the first proposition we should test is whether or not, on these data in this decade, it seems to matter which party is in power. An alternative theory of party competition we called the 'Finer model', and, as we saw, it predicts that the parties will sharply differentiate their political products because of the way that they draw support from different interests and incur political debts to different paymasters. As discussed in the previous chapter, we fill out the 'Finer' model with popular or 'saloon-bar' stereotypes of the parties and of how the party platforms differ – thus 'F/SBS' for short.

If the first model is the better one, we should find 1979 an insignificant date in spending patterns (Hypothesis 1); if the second model is the better one, 1979 should show a marked change in patterns (Hypothesis 2). If neither prediction is borne out, then we should look at *any* significant dates of apparent pattern changes, and see whether these are predicted by the third or *political business cycle* model referred to in the previous chapter. Authors such as Pommerehne and Schneider assert that a government in our kind of political system will have an incentive to behave in one way at the beginning of its period of office, and in another way towards its end. Because their model is similar to an account of the 'political business cycle' by Nordhaus (1975), we will designate as the 'NPS' model the possibility that a government might start its period in a 'Finer' frame of mind, rewarding its supporters and paying off its debts, and then gravitate towards a 'Downs/Hotelling' attitude as the next General Election approaches, so as to attract some of the waverers (Hypothesis 4). These models are presented diagrammatically in Table 3.1.

As a first test let us look at Table 3.2, which presents the figures for total public expenditure for each year from 1966 to 1983, giving us two periods of government by each party and three changes of party. The D/H model would lead us to expect no marked differences in the trends of total public expenditure on these changes of party. But the figures do not bear this out; on the first change, a distinct downward trend is replaced by an upward trend, and on the second change there is another reversal; only on the third change is the trend difficult to discern. Hypothesis 1 is not supported. But before we conclude that the Finer model is the better predictor of what happened in these periods, we had better see whether the changes in total spending are those we would have expected, according to the 'saloon-bar' stereotypes to which we referred in the previous chapter. And they are not: the figures contradict the supposition that public expenditure totals increase under Labour government and decrease under Conservative government (Hypothesis 3). Of the eighteen numbers in the right-hand column in Table 3.2, fifteen are positive (increases over the previous year), and three are negative; and none of the negative ones are under Conservative governments. If the

Table 3.1. *Party-political explanations: popular expectations and expectations drawn from academic theories*

Name	Description	Hypothesis
Saloon-bar stereotypes	Conservatives favour law and order, reduced public spending; Labour favour social services, economic intervention, and higher public spending	Spending on favoured programmes will be higher under each party in office and lower under their opponents
Downs/Hotelling	Product competition – parties compete for middle voter	No marked differences in spending patterns before and after General Elections
Finer	Product differentiation – adversarial politics: reward friends and punish enemies	Marked changes in spending patterns after General Elections
Nordhaus/ Pommerehne/ Schneider	Political business cycle – pursue ideological goals at first, popularity only when support slumps or General Election nears	Marked changes in spending patterns immediately after General Election, reversed just before succeeding General Election

parties are engaged in adversarial politics or product differentiation in this regard (as the Finer model asserts), they would appear to be fighting under the other side's colours. Hypothesis 2 is not supported either.

What of the 'NPS' hypothesis? Under this, Labour should be favouring public expenditure at the beginning of each period of office, while gravitating towards a centrist position (decreases, or less high increases) towards the end of it; while the Conservatives play the opposite game. Now it might possibly be unfair to saddle an incoming government with the figures for its first year of office, since in many cases these will be conditioned by 'inertia' commitments from the previous government. So let us compare spending in the second year of each period with spending in the final year, just before (but not including) the General Election. If this is done, support for the 'political business cycle' hypothesis does indeed appear.

Comparing 1967 with 1969, we see Labour cutting back markedly on public expenditure; while the Conservatives increased public spending just as markedly in the 1973 pre-election year (compared with 1971), as also (though less markedly) in the 1982 pre-election year (compared with 1980). Labour's 1974–9 period of office, however, does not conform – as might be predicted, since the government party did not command a

Table 3.2. *Percent change (constant prices) in total public expenditure: annually 1966–83*

Year	Total public expenditure (£m)	Total public expenditure cp	% change*
Labour			
government			
1966	15,317	68,686	+ 3.5
1967	17,520	76,507	+11.4
1968	19,106	79,941	+ 4.5
1969	19,778	78,484	− 1.8
Conservative			
government			
1970	21,866	80,985	+ 3.2
1971	24,327	82,186	+ 1.5
1972	27,375	85,547	+ 4.1
1973	32,316	94,491	+10.4
Labour			
government			
1974	39,229	99,819	+11.6
1975	51,553	103,106	+ 3.3
1976	58,643	101,987	− 1.1
1977	61,962	94,598	− 7.2
1978	72,199	99,039	+ 4.7
Conservative			
government			
1979	85,483	102,505	+ 3.5
1980	104,110	104,110	+ 1.6
1981	116,966	104,527	+ 0.4
1982	128,489	106,896	+ 2.3
1983	138,306	109,506	+ 2.4

Note: *Change from previous year (at constant prices)
Sources: 1966–73 *National Income and Expenditure*, 1965–75, table 10.2
   1973–83 *United Kingdom National Accounts*, 1984, table 9.4
   GDP deflator: 1980=100

stable voting majority in the House of Commons over most of that period and therefore could not control the election date. 'Finer'-type spending in the first two years apparently gives way to 'Downs/Hotelling'-type behaviour in the succeeding two years; but the centrism, it may seem, was overdone, and needed a swing back to higher spending in the final year if party supporters were not to be outraged. If Mr Callaghan (Labour Prime Minister, 1976–9) had called a General Election in Autumn 1978, however, as he was widely expected to do, the pattern would have fitted nicely.

Table 3.3. *Percent change (constant prices) in General Government expenditure by programme, in four four-year periods (two Labour majority, two Conservative majority)*

		Pre-cutbacks era		Cutbacks era		
Programme (in order of 1983 size)		Labour 1966/7–1969/70	Conservative 1970/1–1973/4	Labour 1975/6–1978/9	Conservative 1980/1–1983/4	Comment
		1	2	3	4	5
Social Security		+22.6	+11.3*	+21.7*	+20.3*	— ***
National Health Service	†	+11.6	+16.7	+ 2.6	+ 9.2	***
Defence		− 8.0	− 9.4*	+ 0.6*	+10.3*	—
Education	†	+17.4	+22.1	−10.2	+ 1.8	*
Housing		+ 6.6	+48.5	−18.8	−27.6*	*
Roads, Public Lighting		+29.0	+ 5.4*	−24.0	+ 6.0	
Industry/Trade		+33.8	+ 6.4	−51.2	−41.4	
Police	‡†	+18.7	+15.6	+ 3.9*	+17.2*	— **
Personal Social Services	‡†	+63.6	+59.9*	+ 0.6	+ 6.4	— *
Employment Services		+44.6	+30.1*	+63.2*	+38.5*	***
External Relations		− 5.6	+50.1*	+103.7	− 5.9	*
Agriculture, Fisheries, Food		+12.3	+ 3.0	−59.5*	+22.4*	**
Transport/Communications	†	+ 4.2	+18.9	−46.5	+32.4	
Miscellaneous Local Government		+ 4.2	+49.1	−26.0	+ 9.8	
Water/Sewerage/Refuse Collection	‡†	+26.7	+23.9	−25.5	− 5.9	—
Parliament/Law Courts	‡†	+38.8	+56.9*	+ 2.2*	+28.5*	— ***
Parks/Pleasure Grounds		+18.7	+35.6	−10.2	+ 5.8	
Research		+ 7.7	+ 0.4*	− 3.5	+ 6.1	— *

	†					
Libraries/Museums/Art Galleries	†	+19.9	+40.6	+ 0.1	+ 5.8	
Fire Service	†	+20.5	+15.7	− 2.8*	+11.5*	— **
Prisons	†	+45.7	+29.9	+11.9*	+ 9.8	— *
School Meals/Milk	†	+ 2.1	− 9.3*	−13.3	−10.9	—
Public Health	†	+ 3.6	+ 5.7	+ 3.9	+ 5.6	— *
Land Drainage/Coast		+ 9.7	+22.8	+26.3	−23.8	— —
Records/Surveys	†	+25.8	+ 3.0*	−10.3	+ 0.8	— *
Civil Defence		−86.7	+44.7*	− 0.2*	+46.0*	***

Note: † = wages/salaries 50 % or more of total expenditure

Underlining = Labour changes and Conservative changes within 5 % of each other

* = expected difference, on party stereotypes

The programmes are listed in order of budget size in 1983

Sources: 1975–1983 *United Kingdom National Accounts, 1984,* table 9.4.

1966–1973 *National Income and Expenditure 1965–75,* table 10.2

GDP deflator: 1980 = 100

On this first test of the party-politics explanatory models, then, only the 'political business cycle' approach (Hypothesis 4) seems to offer a reasonable prediction. Of course, it may be objected, this was an unusual period, and the parties were 'blown off course' by external demands for public-sector cutbacks and so on; to judge solely by the crude totals of public expenditure in these years is hardly an exhaustive test of the rival propositions. Conscious of this, we ran tests on a similar four-period basis using figures for changes in expenditure programme by programme.

Table 3.3 takes two four-year periods of Labour government, and two four-year periods of Conservative government, allowing us to compare 'before and after' for three changes of ruling party; and compares the percentage change in central government expenditure over each period, programme by programme for the 26 programmes listed in the official Blue Book[1] for these years. (The programmes are listed according to their relative size in 1983, large to small.) The D/H model would lead us to expect no great difference in expenditure on any programme across these General Election events – say, that a percentage increase or decrease in spending over a Labour four-year period would be within five percentage points of the increase or decrease over a Conservative four-year period.

This expectation is not borne out. In Table 3.3, where a change in one column is within 5.0 points of change in the previous column, underlining links the two changes. In only one programme (Public Health – mainly environmental health) is the percentage increase within this range over all three changes of party. Of the 78 possible underlinings, only 13 appear. There is very little sign of a 'Downs/Hotelling effect' (Hypothesis 1).

It would seem, therefore, that 'party does matter' – a change of governing party means a greater-than-minimal change in spending measured in four-year periods. But once again, we had better be cautious about a conclusion that the Finer model gives the best fit, until we investigate whether the changes in spending patterns are those we would have expected, according to our popular stereotypes of party preferences among programmes. These, as pointed out earlier, are not 'scientifically' generated, but based on our interpretation of popular expectations. For those, we postulate an expected Conservative commitment to higher spending on defence and law-and-order activities and lower spending on social services (Hypothesis 5); and an expected Labour commitment to employment services, housing (public housing tenants traditionally constitute part of Labour's 'payroll vote'), and social

---

[1] *National Income and Expenditure*, later *United Kingdom National Accounts*.

services generally (Hypothesis 6). But we have left out three programmes where popular stereotypes about party positions are less clear or constant (the three local government programmes, including Water and Public Health).

In Table 3.3, an asterisk attaches to a change in columns 2, 3, and 4 if in our opinion that change conforms to these party stereotypes. For example, in the top line (the Social Security programme), each change on change of party is what the 'saloon-bar expert' would expect, so this row accumulates three asterisks. Only four other programmes rate three asterisks in this way. Of a possible 69 asterisks, only 29 appear; and the patterns of spending change in six programmes go clean counter to stereotype. In these four four-year periods the product-differentiation model of party competition appears to fare no better overall than did the product-competition model in accounting for changes in spending on individual programmes. But we cannot test the 'political business cycle' model with this table, since the data are not annual.

We devised another, more detailed, test of the simplified party stereotypes to let us do so. Hypotheses 5 and 6 state that spending on defence and law and order programmes will increase under a Conservative government and decrease under Labour, and that the contrary will occur in respect of spending on social services programmes. To test these hypotheses we have taken the 'Social Services' grouping that is used in the Blue Books, and constructed a 'Law and Order' grouping that embraces the Military Defence programme, and the Civil Defence, Police, Prisons, Parliament/Law Courts, and Fire Service programmes; Table 3.4 shows percentage changes in spending for these groupings not by four-year periods, but annually as in Table 3.2, with the change of governing party marked.[2]

Hypotheses 5 and 6 are sustained for the first two periods, if rather weakly. Under the 1966–9 Labour government, all but two of the changes for Social Services programmes are positive, while there are six decreases in the period in Law and Order programmes, including two in the total column. Under the Conservative government of 1970–4, all the changes in Law and Order programmes are positive, while there are three decreases in Social Services programmes (all in the School Meals and Welfare Foods programme). Nevertheless, percentage increases in Social Services programmes were larger in total under that Conservative government than were Law and Order programmes in three years out of four.

[2] To avoid too large a table some smaller programmes do not have a column to themselves but are included in the totals.

Table 3.4. *Percent change (constant prices) in General Government expenditure by selected programme: annually 1966–83*

Year	'Social services' programmes					'Law and order' programmes				
	Education	National Health Service	School Meals	Social Security	Total*	Military Defence	Civil Defence	Police	Prison Service	Total†
	1	2	3	4	5	6	7	8	9	10
Labour government										
1966	+ 6.5	+ 4.9	+ 7.5	+ 2.2	+ 4.3	+ 0.1	− 12.6	+ 9.6	+ 4.8	+ 1.2
1967	+ 8.5	+ 7.9	+ 11.1	+ 9.6	+ 9.0	+ 6.4	+ 2.2	+ 9.8	+ 9.2	+ 7.0
1968	+ 6.1	+ 4.2	− 9.5	+ 10.4	+ 7.2	− 2.9	− 64.1	+ 4.3	+ 21.1	− 2.0
1969	+ 2.0	− 0.7	+ 1.7	+ 1.4	+ 1.7	− 10.9	− 63.6	+ 3.5	+ 10.4	− 8.4
Conservative government										
1970	+ 5.0	+ 6.6	− 1.7	+ 2.5	+ 4.5	+ 0.3	+ 83.3	+ 9.0	+ 8.6	+ 2.0
1971	+ 4.4	+ 3.5	− 14.4	+ 0.2	+ 2.2	+ 2.4	+ 9.1	+ 6.4	+ 6.6	+ 3.3
1972	+ 8.9	+ 6.8	− 3.6	+ 9.9	+ 8.8	+ 3.5	+ 16.7	+ 1.0	+ 8.2	+ 3.8
1973	+ 7.3	+ 5.7	+ 10.2	+ 1.1	+ 5.0	+ 3.2	+ 14.3	+ 7.5	+ 12.6	+ 4.5
Labour government										
1974	+ 1.3	+ 13.8	+ 18.9	+ 7.5	+ 7.6	+ 2.4	+ 3.1	− 28.0	+ 20.4	− 0.2
1975	+ 12.0	+ 5.5	+ 8.4	+ 2.4	+ 6.5	− 0.5	− 33.3	+ 55.2	+ 2.4	+ 5.1
1976	− 4.0	+ 3.1	+ 5.1	+ 9.7	+ 3.7	+ 4.5	+ 122.7	+ 9.3	+ 5.4	+ 5.2
1977	− 4.8	− 3.2	− 14.6	+ 3.1	− 1.4	− 3.1	− 59.2	− 8.1	+ 3.2	− 4.0
1978	− 1.7	+ 2.9	− 3.4	+ 7.5	+ 3.8	− 0.6	+ 10.0	+ 3.4	+ 2.8	+ 0.3

Conservative
government

1979	− 1.3	+ 1.6	− 8.5	+ 2.3	+ 1.2	+ 3.5	+118.2	+ 6.1	− 5.1	+ 3.9
1980	+ 3.2	+ 7.4	−15.8	+ 0.2	+ 2.6	+ 6.2	−33.3	+ 2.6	+14.6	+ 6.1
1981	+ 0.3	+ 3.2	− 9.0	+10.6	+ 5.7	− 2.4	−28.1	+ 9.5	+ 3.6	− 0.0
1982	− 0.1	− 2.0	− 2.0	+ 8.5	+ 3.6	+ 8.5	+ 8.7	+ 5.1	− 5.5	+ 7.4
1983	+ 1.5	+ 7.9	− 0.2	+ 0.2	+ 2.3	+ 4.2	+88.0	+ 1.8	+12.2	+ 4.5

Note: *Total for 'Social Services' includes also Personal Social Services
†Total for 'Law and Order' includes also Parliament and Law Courts and Fire Service programmes
Sources: 1966–73 *National Income and Expenditure, 1965–75*, table 10.2
1973–83 *United Kingdom National Accounts, 1984*, table 9.4
GDP deflator: 1980 = 100

The picture is less clear for the later two periods, because spending cutbacks began in 1976. The first two years of the 1974–9 Labour government can, however, be seen to conform to the hypotheses. Social Services programmes changes are all positive, while there are some negative ones among the Law and Order programmes; and in four out of the five years, the totals show Labour favouring Social Services programmes over Law and Order programmes. The Conservative period 1979–83 is more mixed, in individual programmes: only two (one on either side – Social Security and Police) show no cuts at all. But again, in four years out of the five, the totals columns show the Conservatives favouring Law and Order programmes over Social Services programmes.

By and large, then, the 'saloon-bar' stereotypes about what governments of each of the two main parties will do when in office achieve weak support, on these groups of programmes; 'F/SBS' is at least preferred to 'D/H'. How will the 'NPS' approach fare? We can test Hypothesis 4 also with Table 3.4.

If that hypothesis is to hold, a Labour government should be favouring 'Social Services' programmes at the beginning of its period of office, while cutting back 'Law and Order' programmes; towards the end of the period, the imbalance should be reduced or reversed; and similarly for a Conservative government, in the opposite sense. As before, we will compare spending in the second year of each period with spending in the last year before the General Election.

As can be seen from Table 3.4, the differences between columns 5 and 10 in the second year of each government bear out the first part of the hypothesis (both parties favour 'their own' programmes), but the second part (both parties favour the 'other side's' programmes) is sustained in only one out of the four pre-election years – 1973, when the Conservative government increased its spending on Law and Order by less than on Social Services. So the 'political business cycle' model does not do well on these figures in the run-up to an election.

Another saloon-bar expectation of the same general sort is embodied in Hypothesis 7, concerning spending on industry, trade, and employment programmes. We can test this, and also test our three main models again, with the figures in Table 3.5, where four individual programmes are aggregated into a 'Total industry and employment' figure. If Hypothesis 7 is to hold, there should be more pluses than minuses in columns 1 to 4 under Labour governments, and more minuses than pluses under Conservative governments. In fact, it is an exceedingly close-run thing: there are 21 Labour pluses out of 36, and 20 Conservative pluses out of 36. Governments of both parties increased

Table 3.5. *Percent change (constant prices) in General Government expenditure, by selected programme (Industry, Trade and Employment): annually 1966–83*

Year	'Industry and employment' programmes				
	Roads/ Public Lighting	Transport and Communications	Employment Services	Other Industry & Trade	Total
Labour government	1	2	3	4	5
1966	+ 3.4	+ 1.9	+50.7	+15.5	+ 9.8
1967	+15.9	+12.8	+30.5	+38.6	+27.0
1968	+174.7	+13.6	+15.9	+ 3.3	+36.8
1969	−59.5	−18.7	− 4.4	− 6.6	−27.9
Conservative government					
1970	+10.3	+12.2	+ 3.0	− 2.6	+ 3.4
1971	− 5.1	+20.3	+26.2	+ 6.8	+ 3.8
1972	+ 2.3	− 6.5	+ 8.7	−10.3	− 6.1
1973	+ 8.4	+24.6	− 5.1	+11.1	+12.9
Labour government					
1974	− 5.4	+74.3	+ 8.9	−14.7	+ 5.5
1975	− 1.5	−13.5	+41.7	+58.9	+20.3
1976	− 7.1	−37.9	+27.3	−31.7	−23.8
1977	−16.5	−20.2	+21.8	−71.4	−37.6
1978	− 1.9	+ 7.9	+ 5.3	+150.0	+33.2
Conservative government					
1979	+ 3.0	+ 7.0	− 5.1	+24.4	+10.6
1980	+ 0.2	−29.9	+13.2	− 2.6	− 4.4
1981	− 2.0	+44.4	+24.6	−23.0	− 0.6
1982	+12.4	− 6.1	− 8.6	− 7.9	− 2.7
1983	− 3.7	− 2.4	+21.6	−17.3	− 2.6

Sources: 1966–73 *National Income and Expenditure*, 1965–75, table 10.2
1973–83 *United Kingdom National Accounts*, 1984, table 9.4
GDP deflator: 1980 = 100

spending on industry and employment programmes. The hypothesis is clearly rejected.

What of the more general models? Once again, the governments of 1966–70 and 1970–4 conform better to the F/SBS expectations than to the D/H expectations, and better than do the later governments. Labour increased spending on every programme in this sector until the cuts of late 1968 and 1969, while the Conservatives cut some programmes in every year, and increased others by smaller amounts. Then cutbacks bite more harshly, and even Labour cuts the road programme and some others, while there is no easily discernible pattern in the Conservative cuts and increases during 1979–83.

On the NPS model, Labour should show a relative decrease on these programmes when the pre-election year is compared with the second year; and the Conservatives a relative increase. Using the total column 5, the model does predict the outcome in three of the four periods, with (once again) the Labour government of 1974–9 failing to conform – though, as once before, if the General Election had come in 1978 instead of 1979 the predictions would have been good in all four periods. On this particular set of spending programmes, therefore, the 'political business cycle' predicts better than the 'Finer' model.

Putting precise numbers on judgements such as these is perhaps a spurious exercise; but for what it is worth, the proportion of observations conforming to each of the three models in these four tests (based on the numbers of pluses and minuses shown in Tables 3.2, 3.4, and 3.5, and on the underlinings and asterisks in Table 3.3) is as follows:

	D/H	F/SBS	NPS
Total public spending, 1966–83	<.33	.33	>.75
26 public spending programmes, 1966–83	.17	.42	n/t
Social services/law and order	.00	.57	.25
Industry/employment	.00	.51	.75

So all in all, in trying to account for different spending patterns among programmes of various kinds – total public spending, defence and law and order, social services, industry and employment – the 'Finer' model, as expanded by man-in-the-street or 'saloon-bar' party stereotypes, did about as well as spinning a coin, but rather better than the Downs/Hotelling model; the 'political business cycle' type of explanation, on the other hand, although it failed on one of the tests, predicted better than 'Finer' on total public spending and industry/employment, and seems worthy of closer investigation.

Departments

Before we go on to explore the hypotheses about what will happen to different groups of civil service staff under each party, it may be useful to consider whether particular *departments* are more vulnerable to cutbacks under one party than under the other. Departmental vulnerability is somewhat more complicated than programme or staff grouping vulnerability. Programmes lend themselves to measurement in terms of spending, and groups in terms of numbers of staff. But both dimensions are relevant for departments and can feasibly be measured; conceivably a department could fare well on one and poorly on the other. Table 3.6 summarises the fate of 36 UK central government departments (or sometimes, because of changes in departmental boundaries, groups of departments – see Appendix I), in the two five-year periods 1975/6 to 1979/80 and 1980/1 to 1984/5, in terms of both staff and spending.

What Table 3.6 shows is that a third of all the departmental groups listed there had a consistent fate under the two different party régimes, in that they continuously prospered or suffered, in both staff and spending. This would be consistent with a Downs/Hotelling model – though it is not easy to see just what set of voters each party was trying to attract in dealing similarly with, for example, the Land Registry, the Charity Commission, and the Ordnance Survey.

For the other two-thirds, some mixture of fortunes is observable, consistent with a product-differentiation or 'Finer' model. To take staffing first: in all but five cases out of the 36, the Conservatives cut staff more heavily, or increased staff less, than had Labour – just as party-political stereotypes would predict; and four of the five exceptions are amongst the smaller departments, so that a small absolute change might register as a large percent change.

However, there is no similar pattern observable on the spending side. The picture is broadly similar to that for programme outcomes shown in Table 3.3, but it is not exactly the same. Where Labour had increased spending, the Conservatives increased it by more in about half the cases; where Labour had cut spending, the Conservatives cut it by more in about half the cases (all of the last among the 'all-round loser' departments). No 'product differentiation' visible there.

The Conservatives increased spending in 20 departments to Labour's 25, and made cuts in 16; but the *average* increase by the Conservatives was of 46.48 percent as against Labour's average increase of 20.67 percent, while the average Conservative cut was of 33.21 percent, compared with Labour's 27.79 percent. Thus although the Conservatives increased spending in fewer departments, the overall increase was much greater than under Labour (as we know from Chapter 1), offset by larger cuts in more departments. Conservative action seems to have been more selective, even draconian (in both directions) – not, perhaps, to be expected on ideological grounds, but possibly consistent with the personalities involved.

Table 3.6. *Percent change in departmental staff and real-terms spending, 36 departments, in two five-year periods (one Labour majority, one Conservative majority)*

Department		1975/6–1979/80		1980/1–1984/5	
		Staff	Spending	Staff	Spending
(a) All-round winners					
Registrar of Friendly Societies	33	+ 1.75	+ 0.72	0	+71.32
Employment*	4	+45.15	+39.26	+11.16	+56.92
Land Registry	14	+19.92	+23.30	+14.46	+51.99
Charities Commission	28	+ 1.51	+ 8.10	+ 0.91	+42.75
Office of Fair Trading	29	+74.42	+ 5.53	+ 4.05	+42.49
Home Office	6	+10.71	+14.34	+ 4.88	+10.71
Treasury Solicitor	26	+ 7.95	+13.34	+ 2.52	+ 5.77
(b) Mainly winners					
Intervention Board for Agricultural Produce	25	+10.74	− 36.74	+11.64	+202.95
Public Record Office	27	+ 5.29	+14.72	− 6.27	+142.08
Lord Chancellor's Department†	11	+ 4.39	+18.15	− 1.22	+67.26
Welsh Office	18	+104.72	+42.10	−14.14	+52.33
Inland Revenue	3	+15.72	+ 1.37	−10.69	+26.21
Customs and Excise	7	+ 6.52	+ 5.04	− 7.26	+15.12
Dept of Health and Social Security	2	+12.61	+33.95	− 5.38	+ 9.81
Registers of Scotland	24	+11.89	+36.00	+49.47	−99.98
(c) Mixed fortunes					
Scottish Record Office	32	− 3.60	+ 3.37	− 9.56	+26.58
Foreign and Commonwealth Office	12	− 5.27	+29.57	− 4.78	+21.61
Department of Energy	22	+ 7.71	−52.57	−14.05	+21.04
Ministry of Defence	1	− 6.73	+ 1.70	−16.06	+ 6.44
Government Actuary	35	− 6.45	− 0.57	+ 6.90	+ 4.22
Overseas Development Administration	21	+ 2.16	+17.58	−10.00	− 9.16
Scottish Office	10	+10.59	+14.25	− 6.02	−11.35
(d) Mainly losers					
Privy Council Office	36	−20.00	−12.61	−20.51	+53.10
Northern Ireland Office	31	− 0.89	+56.55	−14.61	− 5.62
Central Office of Information	23	− 9.50	+20.48	−18.44	− 5.95
Department of Education and Science‡	17	− 6.17	+16.16	− 7.71	−17.17
Export Credits Guarantee Department	20	+11.89	−77.92	− 7.78	−37.15
Crown Estates Office	34	− 7.81	+ 1.63	− 4.39	−37.24
Department of Trade and Industry§	8	− 4.19	+87.59	−22.07	−46.59
Treasury/Cabinet Office (TCC)‖	15	− 1.70	+11.91	−18.65	−78.37
(e) All-round losers					
National Savings Department	13	−20.74	−13.00	−22.14	−13.43

Table 3.6 (*cont.*)

Department		1975/6–1979/80		1980/1–1984/5	
		Staff	Spending	Staff	Spending
Department of the Environment¶	5	− 4.54	− 8.10	−21.21	−24.32
Ministry of Agriculture, Fisheries and Food	9	− 7.57	−56.15	−13.48	−24.54
Office of Population Census and Surveys	19	− 7.93	−16.14	−17.73	−25.54
General Register Office (Scotland)	30	−13.16	−12.16	−28.49	−35.41
Ordnance Survey	16	−20.86	−19.75	−18.45	−59.60

Note: Spending figures are from annual Supply Estimates
Staffing figures are from annual *Civil Service Statistics*
*Employment Group includes MSC, ACAS, HSC/E
†Lord Chancellor's Department includes Public Trustee
‡Department of Education and Science includes Arts and Libraries but excludes Museums
§Trade and Industry includes DI, DTI, DTr and Prices
‖TCC Group includes Treasury, Cabinet Office, Civil Service Department/MPO
¶Department of Environment includes Property Services Agency and Department of Transport
Figures after department name indicate rank order by staff size at 1 January 1984

Why some departments are consistent winners and some consistent losers under either party may have more to do with the department than with the party – we discuss that aspect in Chapter 5. Party-political explanations do not leap to mind, and hold water even less than they did in discussing the distributions of programme success and failure. It was suggested in Chapter 2 that shrewd departmental chiefs, seeking to preserve their departmental positions against the possibility that *programmes* would be vulnerable to change of party, would make sure to amass a 'portfolio' of programme holdings spread across the preferences of rival parties.

Departments do differ in the number of programmes in which they participate. Such bureaucratic risk-spreading would lead to a logic of large conglomerate departments, and a prediction that none would either gain or suffer unduly over a representative period. But if we focus in Table 3.6, particularly on the largest departments – those numbered 1 to 10, say – it does not appear that they operated such a strategy, or if they did, that it worked. Two of the 'giants' appear among the all-round winners, two among the all-round losers, and there is at least one of them in each of the other three categories.

Staff groupings

In the remainder of the section we shall test only the 'popular stereotypes' predictions embodied in Hypotheses 8 to 16. There are 'saloon-bar' expectations about what will happen to different groups of staff under each party. Labour, in this view, will want to keep up total numbers of civil servants, to preserve blue-collar staff rather than white-collar staff, and lower-grade staff rather than top- and middle-grade staff; while Conservatives will have the opposite priorities. Table 3.7 gives the comparisons, for two four-year periods under each party. It is indeed true that Conservative cuts in staffing were proportionately much heavier than any Labour cuts (Hypothesis 8). The prediction that Labour would protect lower grades staff as against top and middle grades (Hypothesis 10) is partly met; top grades alone, amongst white-collar staff, were cut. But it is perhaps not expected from the common stereotype that the Conservatives' cuts, too, would fall much more heavily on top staff than on lower-level staff, in proportionate terms. So Hypothesis 10 is only half supported.

Both parties cut the numbers of blue-collar workers, in the pre-retrenchment period as well as the retrenchment period. In the earlier period Labour, in comparison with how they treated white-collar staff, in fact dealt more harshly with their blue-collar staff than did the Conservatives (although the Conservative cut is in itself larger); and in the later period, although the Conservatives again cut blue-collar staff more heavily, they also cut white-collar staff, while Labour did not. So the expectation that Labour would aim to cut blue-collar numbers proportionately less than white-collar numbers (Hypothesis 9) is not borne out, in either era.

It was predicted by Hypothesis 8 that spending on wages and salaries will be safeguarded under Labour more than under the Conservatives. In fact (as will be seen shortly in Table 3.9), central government spending on wages and salaries in the pre-cutbacks period went up more than twice as fast under the Conservatives as under Labour; and in the cutbacks era, spending was *cut* under Labour while being increased under the Conservatives. So that prediction, too, is not fulfilled.

Putting the staffing figures and these spending figures together, we can see that Labour in their cutbacks period increased civil service staff overall, but cut wages and salaries costs; the Conservatives cut staff numbers, but *increased* salaries costs overall – clearly to the benefit of those who kept their jobs. This does not quite fit with the simple popular stereotypes of the parties that we discussed in the previous chapter, but it

Table 3.7. *Percent change in numbers of selected civil service groups, in four four-year periods (two Labour majority, two Conservative majority)*

	Pre-cutbacks era		Cutbacks era	
Group	Labour 1966–9	Conservative 1970–3	Labour 1975–8	Conservative 1980–3
Total civil service staff*	+ 3.8	− 0.7	+ 4.9	− 8.0
Blue-collar civil servants*	−7.5	− 9.0	− 5.0	−17.2
White-collar civil servants*	+9.9	+ 2.8	+ 8.2	− 5.3
Part-time white-collar†	n.a.	−14.1	+30.5	− 9.9
Female white-collar†	n.a.	− 4.1	+ 7.0	− 2.7
Top staff white-collar‡	n.a.	n.a.	− 0.4	−13.5
Middle staff white-collar‡	n.a.	n.a.	+ 3.8	− 7.1
Bottom staff white-collar‡	n.a.	n.a.	+ 5.4	− 4.2
Administrative grades§	n.a.	n.a.	− 6.0	− 3.5

Sources:*Annual Abstract of Statistics. Blue-collar = industrial staff. White-collar = non-industrial staff
†*Civil Service Statistics* (from 1970 only)
‡ 'MANDATE' (Treasury) (from 1975). Top Staff = Under Secretary and above. Middle Staff = Assistant Secretary to Higher Executive Officer. Bottom Staff = below Higher Executive Officer
§ Staff in Post returns (from 1972 only). Administrative Grades = staff in Administration Group, Clerical Assistant to Senior Executive Officer

can be seen to fit with 'rational strategy' for each of the two parties, given that a great proportion of Labour's support traditionally comes from lower-income workers and from public-sector workers than is the case with the Conservatives, so that it would be in Labour's electoral interest to make a given salary budget buy the largest possible number of public bureaucrats.

Some other differences in cutback patterns revealed by Table 3.7 are not immediately ascribable to the party stereotypes; for instance, that the Conservatives cut both women and part-time staff more heavily than did Labour, and that Labour cut the Administration grades (no longer a synonym for top staff, but covering ranks from the bottom to upper-middle) more heavily than did the Conservatives. We may need to look at other kinds of explanation.

Regional discrimination

Geographically, as is now well known, Labour Party support resides predominantly to the north and west of a line joining the Severn and the

Table 3.8. Marginal seats (5 % majority or less) at General Elections 1979 and 1983, by Economic Planning Region; and average percentage change in numbers of non-industrial staff in periods 1979–82 and 1983–6 by Economic Planning Region

Region	Marginal seats 1979					Average change in non-industrial staff 1979–82	Marginal seats 1983					Average change in non-industrial staff 1983–6
	Con.	Lab.	Other	Total	%		Con.	Lab.	Other	Total	%	
South-East	9	3	1	13	14.0	− 2.5*	4	1	1	6	5.5	−4.1
South-West	1	2	—	3	6.5	− 5.2	3	—	—	3	6.2	−2.1
Greater London	4	5	—	9	9.8	− 6.3*	7	4	—	11	13.1	−6.7
East Anglia	1	1	—	2	11.8	− 7.5	—	1	—	1	5.0	+8.3
East Midlands	2	4	—	6	15.0	− 2.4	5	4	—	9	21.4	−3.0
West Midlands	4	5	—	9	16.1	− 1.7	4	5	—	9	15.5	−0.3
Yorkshire and Humberside	5	3	1	9	16.7	+ 0.3	5	5	1	11	20.4	−2.0
North-West	5	9	—	14	18.4	− 6.1	3	1	1	5	6.8	−8.2
Northern	—	1	—	1	2.7	− 5.5	1	3	—	4	11.1	−8.7
Scotland	7	5	1	13	18.3	− 3.6	5	1	3	9	12.5	−1.6
Wales	—	2	—	2	5.5	− 5.7	5	4	1	10	26.3	−6.8
Northern Ireland	—	—	2	2	16.7	−10.8	—	—	4	4	23.5	−3.1
All regions	37	40	4	83	13.1	− 6.0	42	29	10	82	12.6	−4.5

Sources: Marginal seats: *The Times Guide to the House of Commons*, May 1979, pp.257–61; June 1983, pp.259–78, 282
NB: The Regional Analyses in these sources were not used; the figures were reassembled where necessary to fit Economic Planning Regions boundaries
Non-industrial staff changes: *Civil Service Statistics* (annually)
Note: * Average non-industrial staff change 1980–2, not 1979–82: separate figures for Greater London only available from 1980

Humber; the number of Labour-held parliamentary seats to the south-east of that line is quite small. A naive hypothesis of what party politics is all about would, therefore, predict that in a period of Labour government civil service jobs and spending on programmes would increase disproportionately in the North and West, while under the Conservatives the South-East would be favoured (Hypothesis 11). Unfortunately, we do not have good data for this item. Staffing totals for non-industrial civil servants by Economic Planning Region are available only from 1977 (see Table A3 in Appendix II); and spending totals by Economic Planning Region are not available at all, from official sources – the only figures we could find are for 1974–7 (Short 1981). We do not therefore provide tables for this item. For what it is worth, however, neither source bears out the hypothesis.

Staffing in the regions north and west of the dividing line, aggregated and expressed as a percentage of total staffing for Great Britain, increased steadily throughout the period 1977–86, whatever the party in power, from 41.8 percent to 43.9 percent. Taking it region by region confirms the picture. If anything, the prediction about staffing is reversed; but it is probably safer to say that party-political explanations of this naive kind do not work for regional discrimination in staffing.

A more sophisticated version of a hypothesis about regional discrimination, however, might suggest that parties in power will tend to favour regions where there is a concentration of marginal parliamentary seats (Hypothesis 12). Table 3.8 presents the data about the number of seats at the General Elections of 1979 and 1983 in each Economic Planning Region which the elected member held with a majority of 5 percent or less (according to *The Times Guide to the House of Commons*, 1979, 257; 1983, 282); along with, first, that number expressed as a percentage of the total number of seats in the region, and second, the average change in percentage terms in civil service 'white-collar' staffing over the three years following each election, for each region (drawn from Table A3 in Appendix II).

If the hypothesis is to hold, the regions with an above-average share of marginal seats should (on average) show smaller cuts in staffing than those with fewer marginal seats. There were seven regions in 1979 with an above-the-average percentage of marginal seats, and five below: the average cut in staffing for the former group was 3.83 percent, and for the latter, 6.04 percent. This conforms to the hypothesis. In 1983, there were six regions with above-average percentage of marginals (but only four overlapping with the 1979 group), and six below: the average cut in staffing for the former group was 3.65 percent, and for the latter, 2.73

percent – contrary to the hypothesis, unless we leave out East Anglia, which had the lowest percentage of marginals (5.0) but a massive *increase* in staff (+8.3 percent) over these three years, probably due to the progressive transfer of HMSO to Norwich. If we exclude that region, the average cut for the five remaining regions with below-average number of marginals becomes 4.94 percent. On this rather simple analysis, there does seem to be something in the hypothesis: regions with higher numbers of marginals attract smaller cuts in staffing.

A more formal analysis indicates, however, that there is no significant correlation between either numbers of marginal seats or percentage of seats that are marginal and average non-industrial staff change, in either the 1979–82 period or the 1983–6 period, with or without East Anglia in either period ($r < 0.22$, or negative). But if we take marginal seats held by Conservative MPs only, after the 1979 election, the correlation becomes quite strong ($r = 0.66$, or 0.71 excluding East Anglia). The effect is quite absent after the 1983 election, however ($r < 0.11$, or negative). So it would indeed appear that, on these figures, at least after the 1979 election, there is some evidence that the party in power may well have tended to favour regions with a concentration of marginal seats, as Hypothesis 12 predicted.

Others

The remaining hypotheses about party-political explanations covered spending by economic categories, and by different kinds of authority. Labour will favour current expenditure, Conservatives capital (Hypothesis 13): Labour will favour transfer payments, Conservatives will not (Hypothesis 14); Labour will favour other types of spending authority over central government, Conservatives the opposite (Hypothesis 15). Table 3.9 shows the picture, taking as before two periods of equal length under both Labour and Conservative governments, before and after the onset of cutbacks.

In this table, current spending as a percentage of total spending is not listed, but it is the reciprocal of capital spending: the expectation that current expenditure will go up under Labour and down under Conservatives can be tested by the sections on capital spending (lines 9–18), from which it can be seen that in the pre-retrenchment period the proportion of expenditure going on capital went up under Labour and down under Conservatives (contrary to prediction), except for local authority spending; but in the cutbacks periods, there is some support for

Hypothesis 13. Line 12 shows that in central government Labour capital spending went down and Conservative up (predicted).

Transfer payments consist of subsidies and other grants, but are dominated by social welfare benefits. Hypothesis 14, that such spending is favoured by Labour more than by Conservatives, is not really supported in either era: the increase under Labour in the cutbacks era was a third of that under the Conservatives (line 27), and in each era, the budget share of such payments reached its highest point under the Conservatives (line 28).

The stereotype view that Labour will favour other types of spending authority before central government (Hypotheses 15 and 16) receives little support from the table. Lines 5 and 8 are reciprocals: although the respective shares of central and local government are pretty stable in the pre-cutbacks era, they indicate in the cutbacks era an increasing predominance of central government, under either party. The effect is most marked in capital spending (lines 13 and 17). Indeed, local government's heaviest losses occur under Labour (lines 7 and 16). Not in Table 3.9, but extractable from the same sources, is evidence about 'other spending authorities' than merely central government and local authorities, which perhaps better accords with the stereotype (Hypothesis 16): spending by public corporations increased by 23.9 percent and 25.8 percent in the two Labour periods, as against 6.4 percent and 3.4 percent respectively in the two Conservative periods (table 6.1 in each of the Blue Books cited as sources in Table 3.8).

In general, then, party-political explanations of how cutback management works give mixed results. Sometimes, particularly in respect of some spending programmes, a sophisticated 'political business cycle' model yields good results where the common saloon-bar stereotypes of what you would expect from the two major parties in government are but weakly supported if at all. There is a hint that the proportion of government-held marginal seats in a region may play a part in mitigating cuts in staffing. But more often, and particularly when we are speaking of different groups of personnel, or wages and salaries, or regions, or economic categories, or transfer payments, or types of spending authority and the like, party-political explanations simply fail to explain, and we need to look for other types of explanation. We turn now to what we have labelled *trend* explanations.

Table 3.9. *Changes in selected items of central and local government expenditure in four four-year periods (two Labour majority, two Conservative majority) (constant prices (£m); 1980=100)*

	Pre-retrenchment				Retrenchment era			
	Labour		Conservative		Labour		Conservative	
	1966/7	1969/70	1970/1	1973/4	1975/6	1978/9	1980/1	1983/4
1 Total spending*	68,318	81,825	84,185	98,997	112,950	112,535	115,795	125,377
2 % change in period		+19.7		+17.6		− 0.4		+ 8.3
3 Total central government spending†	47,650	57,214	58,574	67,535	79,628	83,588	86,393	95,573
4 % change in period		+20.1		+15.3		+5.0		+10.6
5 as % of total spending	69.7	69.9	69.6	68.2	70.5	74.3	74.6	76.2
6 Total local government spending†	20,668	24,611	25,611	31,462	33,322	28,947	29,402	29,804
7 % change in period		+19.1		+22.8		−13.1		+1.4
8 as % of total spending	30.2	30.1	30.4	31.8	29.5	25.7	25.4	23.8
9 Total capital spending‡	8,857	12,985	12,693	14,260	12,742	9,548	8,208	7,722
10 as % of total spending	13.0	15.9	15.1	14.4	11.3	8.5	7.1	6.2
11 Central government capital spending	2,740	5,925	5,719	5,444	4,994	4,647	4,113	4,594
12 % change in period		+116.2		− 4.8		− 6.9		+11.7
13 as % of total capital spending	19.9	21.7	23.8	21.3	25.2	27.7	31.4	45.7
14 as % of total central spending	5.7	10.3	9.8	8.1	6.3	5.6	4.8	4.8
15 Local government capital spending	6,117	7,060	6,974	8,816	7,748	4,901	4,095	3,128
16 % change in period		+15.4		+26.4		−36.7		−23.6
17 as % of total capital spending	80.0	78.3	76.2	78.7	74.8	72.3	68.6	54.3
18 as % of total local spending	29.6	28.7	27.2	28.0	23.2	16.9	13.9	10.5
19 Wages and salaries§	18,632	20,437	21,651	26,327	31,266	29,142	30,837	32,783
20 Central government wages and salaries as % of total	50.8	49.0	49.6	46.5	48.0	49.6	50.3	49.7

21 Wages and salaries as % total central government spending	19.9	17.5	18.3	18.1	18.9	17.3	17.9	17.1
22 % change in period		+ 5.8		+14.0		− 3.6		+ 5.1
23 Local government wages and salaries as % of total	49.2	51.0	50.4	53.5	52.0	50.4	49.7	50.3
24 Wages and salaries as % total local government spending	44.3	42.3	42.6	44.7	48.8	50.7	52.1	55.3
25 % change in period		+13.7		+29.0		− 9.7		+ 7.5
26 Transfer payments‖	16,013	19,467	19,970	24,135	27,914	29,540	30,785	45,584
27 % change in period		+22.7		+20.9		+ 5.8		+17.2
28 as % of expenditure	24.6	26.0	25.9	27.0	27.1	29.8	29.6	33.0

Note: *The sum of lines 3 and 6. Total spending = central government current spending plus central government capital spending plus local government current spending plus local government capital spending

†Includes: *current expenditure*: expenditure on goods and services, subsidies, grants to personal sector, debt interest, central grants to local authorities, grants overseas, national insurance and war benefits paid to non-residents: *capital expenditure*: gross domestic fixed capital formation, increase in stock value, capital transfers (excludes net lending and debt interest)

Source: central government 1966–73: *National Income and Expenditure, 1965–75*, tables 7.1, 7.2

central government 1975–83: *UK National Accounts, 1984*, tables 7.2, 7.3

local government 1966–73: *National Income and Expenditure, 1965–75*, tables 8.1, 8.2

local government 1975–83: *UK National Accounts, 1984*, tables 8.2, 8.3

‡The sum of lines 11 and 15

§Includes: employers' contributions to national insurance, superannuation etc.; amounts included in trading services, financed by grants, and charged to capital account

Sources: 1966–9: *National Income and Expenditure, 1972*, table 44

1970–3: *National Income and Expenditure, 1965–75*, table 9.2

1975–83: *UK National Accounts, 1984*, table 9.4

‖Includes subsidies and current grants, for (1966–73) 'Combined Public Authorities'; (1975–83) 'General Government'

Sources: 1966–73: *National Income and Expenditure, 1965–75*, table 9.1

1975–83: *UK National Accounts, 1984*, table 9.4

NB: in line 28, percentage is of 'General Government' total expenditure, not of line 1 in this table

II   Trend explanations

In the previous chapter we outlined seven hypotheses drawn from 'trend' expectations about retrenchment. As we saw, this kind of explanation predicts the future (or explains the present) from the past; either by revealing the underlying and continuing force of some process of *development*, or by laying bare the dynamics of *homoeostasis* in the system, whereby things that have gone too far will be brought back. We might assume, for example, that departments most rapidly or most recently growing just prior to the onset of cutbacks would be the least vulnerable to reductions, on the ground that whatever secular movements or sectional lobbies supported their growth in the fat years would carry over to the lean years. Against that, the alternative principle would predict the opposite: growth rates might go into reverse, on the 'last in, first out' argument, hitting the 'Johnny-come-lately' departments hardest. This would chime to some extent with Downs' (1967) idea about the vulnerability of new bureaus against longer-established ones (but see Kaufman 1985).

Table 3.10 shows pre-cutback-era staff growth over a long-run period (1961–75) and a short-run period (1970–5), as against cutback-era staffing changes (1975–85), for 12 departments where the data are available. It shows that extrapolation of pre-cutback trends predicts cutback-era outcomes for about half the cases, in direction though not very well in amount. But for the rest, pre-cutback growth turned into subsequent slump (or stagnation, in the case of the Scottish Office).

Thus discovering a trend does not by itself tell you whether to extrapolate it or reverse it. In the previous chapter we discussed Rose's (1976) theory about the development in Europe of the functions of the state: first 'defining', then 'corporate', and then 'social' functions. If an era of growth comes to an end, and cutbacks set in, which functions suffer first? 'Social' functions (Hypothesis 17), obviously – if one assumes that the later functions are the least vital to the state, and that decision makers will go along with destiny in this way; but the 'social' functions are (in a country which is 'developed' enough to have them) those that are most modern, most manifest, possibly most 'political'. It might be too risky, in an electoral sense, to cut 'social' functions first. Thus 'political' trends would indicate an *extrapolation* hypothesis. Only if one rather believed in one of the 'overload' theories, suggesting a *reversal* mechanism, would it be logical to assume that history would simply turn itself back.

Let us see how these different theories square with observed behaviour

Table 3.10. *Percent change in department staff before 1975 compared with changes 1975–85: selected departmental groupings*

Department	1961–75	1970–5	1975–85
(a) 'Prosper rain or shine'			
Home Office with Lord Chancellor*	+ 81.59	+22.60	+16.30
Department of Health and Social Security	+ 94.00	+24.23	+ 4.99
Employment†	+197.04	+66.85	+ 3.31
(b) 'From prosperity to slump or stagnation'			
Scottish Office	+ 45.65	+10.11	− 0.42
Chancellor of the Exchequer's Departments‡	+ 51.20	n.a.	−11.96
Department of Education and Science, including Arts and Libraries	+ 3.42	+27.96	−16.41
Trade, Industry and Export Credits Guarantee Department	+ 26.13	−40.36	−25.60
Department of Environment§	+593.92	+59.41	−75.88
(c) 'From bad to worse (or no better)'			
Ministry of Defence‖	− 10.02	− 4.56	−27.63
Ministry of Agriculture, Fisheries and Food	− 14.34	− 3.61	−26.32
Foreign and Commonwealth Office and Overseas Development Administration	− 5.06	− 3.78	−22.63
Department of Energy	− 42.92	n.a.	−14.66

Notes: NB: departmental titles and boundaries have changed considerably over the period dealt with here, especially 1961–75; figures have been constructed by taking the 1961 equivalents of the 1975–85 departments (e.g., Ministry of Pensions and National Insurance and National Assistance Board and Ministry of Health in the case of the contemporary Department of Health and Social Security). For that reason, figures should be taken as approximate only.

* Staff figures for LCD include Public Trustee Office

† Base year for staff changes is 1976, not 1975, because of 1976 accounting changes

‡ Treasury, Civil Service Catering Organisation, Customs and Excise, Inland Revenue, Central Office of Information, Registry of Friendly Societies, Royal Mint, HM Stationery Office. Figures exclude Government Actuary, National Investment and Loans Office, and National Savings Department

§ Base year for staff changes is 1977, not 1975, because of boundary changes in 1976; figures exclude Property Services Agency

‖ Figures in third column (only) exclude Royal Ordnance Factories, because of change in accounting base: decline in third column would be greater if Royal Ordnance Factories were included

Sources: Memorandum by the Chief Secretary to the Treasury on the Supply Estimates 1975/6 to 1985/6 (annual tables of staffing of central government departments)

Table 3.11. *Percent annual change (constant prices) in General Government expenditure by selected programme groups and by total: 1977–85*

Year	Community and Social Affairs				General Government Services			'Economic Services'	All programmes
	Education	Health	Social security	Total*	Defence	Public order and safety	Total†	Economic affairs‡	Total public expenditure§
	1	2	3	4	5	6	7	8	9
1978	−1.4	+3.1	+7.3	+3.1	−0.6	+2.6	+3.0	+22.3	+4.8
1979	−1.5	+1.1	+2.0	+1.7	+3.7	+3.9	+3.3	+11.8	+3.5
1980	+3.1	+7.0	+1.4	+2.2	+6.4	+6.5	+1.6	− 3.3	+1.7
1981	+0.3	+2.7	+9.1	+0.8	−1.3	+4.6	−2.4	− 2.1	+0.3
1982	−0.7	−2.0	+8.4	+2.1	+6.4	+4.4	+5.8	− 1.2	+2.4
1983	+2.4	+7.6	+3.4	+4.6	+4.3	+3.9	+3.0	− 1.2	+2.7
1984	−0.6	+0.8	+3.4	+1.8	+3.9	+6.5	+3.6	− 7.8	+1.4
1985	−2.0	+1.6	+2.9	+0.1	−1.4	−0.1	+5.5	+ 5.1	+2.5

Note: * Total for 'Community and Social Affairs' includes Education, Health, Social Security, Housing and Community Amenities (embracing Water and Sewerage), Recreation and Cultural Affairs
† Total for 'General Government Services' includes General Public Services (embracing Parliament, Tax Collection, and External Services), Defence, and Public Order and Safety (which itself embraces Police, Fire, Law Courts and Prisons)
‡ Total for 'Economic Services' includes Fuel and Energy, Agriculture/Forestry/Fishing, Mining/Mineral Resources/Manufacturing/Construction/Consumer Protection, Transport/Communication, and Other Economic Affairs and Services. All of these, as well as several of their component elements, are *net* totals: that is, after offsetting income from public corporations, disposal of shares, etc. Thus this column is not comparable with the other columns in this table
§ Total for All programmes includes also Other Expenditure (mainly debt interest)
Source: 1977–85 *United Kingdom National Accounts,* 1986, table 9.4. GDP deflator: 1980=100

over the 1975–85 period. Because of the way the official statistics come, we have a choice between taking the period 1974–83, as before (Table 3.4), or the period 1977–85, as in Table 3.11.[3] However, the figures for the overlap years 1977–83 agree tolerably well in the two versions, if we stick to the totals columns. For simplicity, we shall use the later version, and sacrifice 1975 and 1976 from the reckoning. It is clear enough that although the *increases* in social spending go up and down a bit year by year, there have been no swingeing cuts since 1975 – and the same is true for Law and Order programmes.

The only fairly clear evidence of attempts at real cuts comes in the 'Economic' programmes – and the more so, since the figures here are *net* ones, the balance of expenditures after receipts are deducted. The newer categorisation is complex, with large swings from year to year (and Employment Services lost altogether into the depths of 'Other'); still, taking Economic Affairs programmes as a whole, and the period as a whole, 1977–85 shows an *increase* of 23.7 percent, and an increase in share of budget from 9.2 percent to 9.4 percent. Between 1979 and 1984, however, the figures are quite different: a *decline* of 13.9 percent, and share of budget down from 11.6 percent to 9.2 percent. Whatever the explanation of this set of priorities (preserve social functions and defining functions and sacrifice corporate functions), it does not seem to be a 'developmental' one; neither the extrapolation nor the reversal approach to Hypothesis 17 predicts the actual outcome from the Rose model.

Demographic trends are often seen as the real ineluctable driving forces of social functions – the sea currents or winds, in Klein's metaphor quoted above (p. 30), to which the ship of state and its policy makers can only adjust. In the United Kingdom during these years, the two most policy-relevant demographic trends are probably the continuing increase in the proportions of old people in the population, and the decline

[3] The groupings used in the *United Kingdom National Accounts* changed (to conform to international practice) after 1984: programmes were henceforth arranged under three main categories:
   (a) *General Government Services*
       (including legislature, taxation, and external services; defence; and public order and safety)
   (b) *Community and Social Affairs*
       (including education, health, social security, housing and community amenity, recreational and cultural); and
   (c) *Economic Services*
       (including fuel and energy; agriculture, forestry and fishing; mining and mineral resources, manufacturing and construction; consumer protection; transport and communications; other, including distribution and 'general labour services').
This categorisation conforms remarkably well to Rose's conception of, respectively, 'defining', 'social', and 'corporate' functions.

in the proportions of school-age children (Griffin 1987, chap. 1). Predictions based on these trends would be that social security payments, disproportionately taken up by the older age-groups, would be resistant to cuts, while education would not (Hypothesis 18). For what it is worth, the evidence in Tables 3.4 and 3.11 supports both suggestions, in the columns of *plus* figures in the former case, and the predominantly *minus* figures in the latter. The hypothesis itself gives no explanation of the variations in the *plus* figures – for example, in column 3 of Table 3.11, between +9.1 in 1981 and +2.9 in 1985. Nor can it suggest *how much* of the increases or decreases are due to trend factors alone, and how much to implementation of other policy aims. Demographic factors (an ageing population will make more use of the health services) could also be behind the column of *plus* figures under Health. But there are equally consistent columns of *pluses* under Defence and under Public Order and Safety; it is not clear that demographic trends would explain those.

The working out of historical trends according to a *Marxist* analysis of the driving forces of social change is also sometimes seen as irresistible, explaining the policy-shifts that may ostensibly have other justifications. If the cutback era itself is seen as a crisis of capitalism, then the ascribed role of the state in such a situation yields predictions of what will happen to spending on unemployment pay and social security, on police, on prisons, and on palliatives for urban unrest (Hypothesis 19). We cannot isolate unemployment pay in the data used above, but if the older-style *National Accounts* are used it is true that Employment Services spending between 1975 and 1983 went up by 142.6 percent, from under 1 to over 2 percent of budget.

We have already dealt with the Social Security figures. Police and Prisons spending is obtainable: Police, between 1975 and 1983, up by 32.5 percent (budget share, 1.8 percent to 2.2 percent); Prisons, up by 32.9 percent (budget share, 0.37 percent to 0.47 percent). Between 1977 and 1985, with the new classification, the figures are very similar: Police up by 39.6 percent and Prisons by 24.7 percent. From the *Appropriation Accounts* we can get figures (between 1979 and 1984 only) for Urban Programme Grants in England (Class VIII: Other Environmental Services), which went up by 35.3 percent over these years, from 0.13 percent of budget to 0.16 percent. As predicted, spending on all these services increased as a proportion of total government expenditure. Again, the analysis does not tell us what other factors might be in play, or explain annual variations; but so far as it goes, the figures certainly support Hypothesis 19, and a Marxist analysis of what is happening.

Economic and socio-economic trends, movements on a larger scale than that of the individual nation, are often felt to be fundamental in policy change; like demographic factors, governments can adjust to them, but are not in control of them. Technological change could be said to 'dictate' that blue-collar employment will decrease in the last quarter of the century in all advanced countries, and all that boom or slump conditions will do is vary the incidence slightly. It is partly technological change, and partly a massive movement of ideas, that might similarly 'dictate' a disproportionate increase in the numbers of women in the workforce (Hypothesis 20).

Such trends ought to be visible in civil service figures. Some indications have already been given, in Table 3.7, showing indeed a steady decline in blue-collar ('industrial') employment in the civil service, which in fact has been continuous ever since 1956: the industrial civil service then represented 46.8 percent of the total civil service, was 35.0 percent in 1966, down to 24.2 percent in 1976, and 21.7 percent in 1981 – a decline of 251 in every thousand over twenty-five years, or about 100 a year – out of a total that had declined in that time only from 745,700 to 695,000. According to the *Annual Abstract of Statistics*, industrial civil servants were 25.3 percent of the civil service of 701,400 in 1975, and 16.9 percent of the civil service of 599,000 in 1985: a decline of 84 per thousand each year. The reduction of blue-collar numbers during the retrenchment period is clearly mainly explicable as a *trend* phenomenon.

Women in the civil service made up about 35 percent of it in 1971, and of that number, nine out of ten were in the non-industrial (white-collar) service – predominantly in the lower grades (*Civil Service Statistics*, 1975, p. 12). The proportions of women in the white-collar civil service began to climb steadily: 39.9 percent in 1972, 42.2 percent in 1975, 45.3 percent in 1978, 46.4 percent in 1981, 47.0 percent in 1984, and 47.2 percent in 1985 (*Civil Service Statistics*, annually). A definite trend seems to be established, and Hypothesis 20 is supported. (We shall return to these figures in a later section.)

The general proposition, based on industrial trends, that transfer payments expenditure will increase (Hypothesis 21), is of course borne out well, as we have already seen. Between 1975 and 1985, 'General Government' (which brings together central government and local authority spending) subsidies and current grants to the personal sector increased in real terms from £28 billion to £39 billion, and in budget share from 27.1 percent to 34.1 percent.

But the prediction that central government spending on subsidies and grants to the personal sector would increase in relation to spending by local authorities (Hypothesis 22) is not supported: whereas in 1975, for every local pound spent in subsidies and current grants to the personal sector central government spent over £15, this figure by 1985 had become only £9. For current spending on goods and services, however, the share of central govenment did go up, but the ratio stayed remarkably steady; in 1975, central government spent £1.45 for each local pound; in 1985, it was only £1.68.

Trend explanations, in the items where we have examined them, seem to have done quite well. Though neither in staffing changes nor in the very broad categorisation of functions of government did historical trends predict what happened between 1975 and 1985, demographic trends can predict changes in spending on education and social security, and perhaps on health. And in so far as 'capitalism in crisis' theories are 'trend' explanations, they find support in the patterns of government spending in that decade. Large-scale socio-technical change predicts the decline in blue-collar public employment that certainly took place; and other employment trends predict the increase in public employment of women.

Much is left unexplained. Trend predictions are seldom precise about the amount of change to be expected; essentially, they are predictions of direction of change. But if the philosophical mentor, Occam's Razor, needed any empirical help, it receives it here: to the extent that observations are explicable by secular trends, such explanations should be preferred, since they embrace more of the world. As Klein (in the piece already quoted) warned us, we should not concentrate exclusively on what the policy makers say or *think* they are doing. Now we shall take a look at these policy makers, and what is expected of them.

4   Winners and losers II: the bureaucrat factor

If you are looking for explanations of patterns of cutbacks, the next approach says, you have to take into account the kind of people bureaucrats are, and the pressures they work under. We have two broad theories about the kind of people they are, or possibly, two pictures of them – one as they should be, and one as they really are: the first, bureaucrats as rational civil servants, following the logic of each situation on the best information they have, and under the pressures of, broadly, the demand for quick results, the noise from the wounded, and the ever-present competition for resources; the second, bureaucrats looking after themselves, using their position to protect their interests. In Chapter 2, these two types were designated the 'Weberian' and the 'Adam Smith' bureaucrats, for reasons explained there: the strategies in retrenchment that we would expect from each are summarised in Table 4.1.

I   The 'Weberian' bureaucrat

Much writing about cutbacks and bureaucratic behaviour, as we saw in Chapter 2, suggests that both in the character of the bureaucrat and in the pressures of the situation there are several reasons for expecting that the response to a demand for reduced expenditure or staffing is (at least at first) to prune *everything* back by the same necessary amount, or proportion (Hypothesis 23). What does the evidence show on this point?

Table 4.2 shows in its two halves, and crudely, the incidence of cuts in spending and in staffing among 36 departments in the decade under review (without indicating amounts or proportions of individual cuts). It is clear, first of all, that 'misery', if not 'equal', was more widely shared in staffing than in spending – the average number of departments showing a decrease was 16.44 in spending but 24.22 in staffing; second, that 'widespread cuts' seldom means cuts for more than around two departments in three – even in staffing, in all but two years the departments *not* suffering are in double figures. Third, within those

87

Table 4.1. *'Weberian' and 'Adam Smith' bureaucrats: strategies in cutbacks*

The Weberian bureaucrat	The Adam Smith bureaucrat
Aim: to 'subordinate himself to the chief without any will of his own'* – in this case, to bring about effective cutbacks quickly	Aim: 'to support with rigorous severity [his] own interest against that of the country which [he] govern[s]'† – in this case, to minimise his own injury in cutbacks
Expected strategy	Expected strategy
Prune everything back equally at first	Resist cutbacks by offering 'fairy gold'
Cut staff before budget	Cut budget before staff
Cut capital rather than current spending	Cut anything before salaries share of expenditure
Cut goods and services spending before grants and transfers	Cut money-moving rather than salaries-heavy programmes
Cut central spending before local	Cut central spending last
Cut big battalions	Cut any but top echelons
At outset, increase temporaries and part-time staff	Cut temporaries and part-time staff

Note: * Weber, in Gerth and Mills 1948, 208
† Adam Smith 1776, bk IV, chap. VII, part III

limits, there is some support for the idea that the first response is to cut widely by a little. The first two years are the Callaghan years; cuts were required by the IMF, and are found both in spending and in staffing, but could well have been seen as necessary only to weather the storm – there is a relaxation in the third year; the later years are Thatcher years, and events are policy-driven rather than crisis-driven, with the emphasis on a manifesto promise to reduce the public bureaucracy. But the Conservatives, on the common stereotype, are the party expected to cut public expenditure; are these figures also evidence that whereas they have been able to cut staff, they have been unable to cut spending – that it is *easier* to cut staff than to cut spending?

The graph in Figure 3 presents another picture. The assertion was that the 'Weberian' bureaucrat finds it easier and speedier to cut staff *before* cutting spending (Hypothesis 24). It is certainly not true that in this period of cutbacks staff were cut before spending: spending went down immediately and quickly in 1976, staffing much more slowly – but then steadily, *as if* people had learned how to do it. Spending, however, began to climb again in 1977, more or less steadily – *as if* people, having managed by some kind of brute force to get it down, had not learned how to *keep* it down. Perhaps, therefore, it is (contrary to the 'Weberian' assumption) easier to cut spending before cutting staffing, but easier to

Table 4.2. *Incidence of cutbacks in spending and staffing 1975–85: 36 departments*

(a) Spending. Number of departments showing decrease and increase in gross expenditure between one year and the next; and change in total government gross expenditure (£m at constant prices: 1980 = 100)

	1975/6–1976/7	1976/7–1977/8	1977/8–1978/9	1978/9–1979/80	1979/80–1980/1	1980/1–1981/2	1981/2–1982/3	1982/3–1983/4	1983/4–1984/5
Decrease	24	25	23	10	9	19	18	9	11
Increase	12	11	13	26	27	17	18	27	25
Increase/ decrease in total spending	−2,056	−5,310	+1,846	+1,694	+3,116	−1,044	+620	+2,147	+2,599

(b) Staffing. Number of departments showing decrease and increase in total staff from one year to the next: and increase/decrease in total civil service

	1 January 1976 to 1 January 1977	1 January 1977 to 1 January 1978	1 January 1978 to 1 January 1979	1 January 1979 to 1 January 1980	1 January 1980 to 1 January 1981	1 January 1981 to 1 January 1982	1 January 1982 to 1 January 1983	1 January 1983 to 1 January 1984	1 January 1984 to 1 January 1985
Decrease	23	23	18	26	20	31	29	24	24
Increase	13	13	18	10	16	5	7	12	12
Increase/ decrease in total civil service	+1,041	−8,177	−4,808	−25,556	−12,550	−19,646	−22,890	−19,943	−13,021

Sources: (a) *Appropriation Accounts* (annually)
(b) *Civil Service Statistics* (annually)
'Total civil service' = industrial + non-industrial

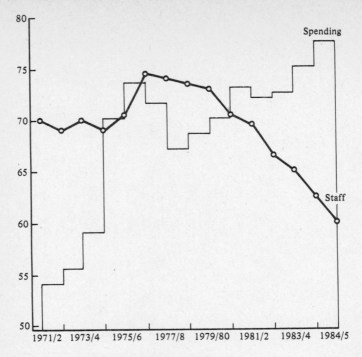

*Vertical scale: spending, £000m; staffing, 000s

Sources: Spending, *Appropriation Accounts* (annually)
GDP deflator: 1980 = 100
Staffing, *Annual Abstarct of Statistics*. Totals include
industrial plus non-industrial staff

Fig. 3. UK central government gross actual expenditure at constant
prices, 1971/2–1984/5 (bar chart) and total civil service staff as
at 1 April 1971–85 (points).

maintain staffing cuts than to maintain spending cuts. (Alternatively,
that 'Adam Smith' bureaucrats can prevent cuts in staffing for a while,
but not for long.)

   On the other hand, the suggestion (Hypothesis 26) that a 'Weberian'
official faced with the need for quick-acting reductions in public
expenditure will cut capital spending before current spending is amply
supported, as shown in Table 4.3. Whether one takes the inflation-
adjusted figures for central government current and capital expenditure,
or those for local authorities, or the combination of both of them (called
'General Government' in the Blue Book, *UK National Accounts*), current

Table 4.3. *Central, local, and General Government current and capital expenditure 1975–85 (£m) (constant prices: GDP deflator, 1980 = 100)*

Year	Central government current expenditure	Local government current expenditure	General Government current expenditure	Central government capital expenditure	Local government capital expenditure	General Government capital expenditure	Column 4 as % of column 6
	1	2	3	4	5	6	7
1975	75,432	25,576	83,088	4,980	7,738	12,380	40.23
1976	78,294	25,442	85,732	4,922	7,263	11,917	41.13
1977	76,064	24,050	84,166	4,339	5,658	9,773	44.39
1978	78,853	24,069	87,385	4,630	4,911	9,235	50.13
1979	80,587	24,599	89,929	4,127	4,550	8,357	49.38
1980	82,365	25,323	92,824	4,070	4,000	7,775	52.35
1981	85,878	25,175	95,839	3,795	2,703	6,214	61.07
1982	88,342	25,249	98,634	4,114	2,191	6,027	68.26
1983	91,059	26,721	101,375	4,508	3,447	7,703	58.52
1984	94,946	27,108	104,888	4,258	3,879	7,875	54.07
1985	97,314	27,324	107,702	5,058	3,046	7,470	67.71

Source: UK National Accounts, 1986, tables 7.1, 8.1, 9.1

Table 4.4. Central, local, and General Government expenditure on goods and services and on transfer payments, 1975–85 (£m) (constant prices: GDP deflator, 1980 = 100)

Year	Central government goods and services	Local government goods and services	General Government goods and services	Central government transfer payments	Local government transfer payments	General Government transfer payments	General Government total expenditure
	1	2	3	4	5	6	7
1975	26,468	18,238	44,624	26,182	1,716	27,914	103,106
1976	27,530	17,918	43,628	26,374	1,746	28,193	101,987
1977	26,608	16,814	43,421	26,139	1,748	27,887	94,336
1978	26,996	17,209	44,204	27,656	1,889	29,545	98,909
1979	27,384	17,455	44,893	28,861	1,969	30,627	102,328
1980	29,298	17,892	47,190	29,087	2,147	31,234	104,060
1981	29,680	18,224	47,733	31,619	2,053	33,551	104,381
1982	30,230	18,450	48,639	32,987	2,229	35,186	106,982
1983	31,628	18,975	50,563	32,742	3,683*	36,397	109,788
1984	32,299	19,237	51,380	34,479	3,941	38,303	111,308
1985	32,347	19,193	51,912	34,909	3,794	38,984	114,071

Note: * New housing benefit scheme introduced
Source: UK National Accounts, 1984 and 1986, tables 7.2, 8.2, 9.4

expenditure between 1975 and 1985 goes up initially while capital expenditure goes down. Although current spending goes down between 1976 and 1977 for all three spending authorities, it then begins a steady climb (a slow and weak one in the case of local authorities), while the capital spending figures only begin to recover (weakly) after 1981. Thanks to a large rise between 1984 and 1985, central government capital spending (deflated) ends up higher than it began – though not, of course, as a proportion of total spending.

The expectation about the choices of hard-pressed but 'objective' officials is that they will use whatever quick-acting levers of control they possess, before attempting to deploy controls they know are slower to take effect. Cutting capital before current spending is one example; another, within current spending, involves the distinction between purchases (of goods and services, including wages and salaries) and transfers (pensions, grants, benefit payments, etc.). The suggestion is that it is easier and quicker to make cuts in the first than in the second, so purchases should decrease before transfers do, or increase by less (Hypothesis 27). The figures give some support to this hypothesis also, if equivocally. Table 4.4 shows that in local authorities and general government purchases (at constant prices) go down initially, while transfers (a much smaller element in local authority spending than in central government spending) go up.

For central government, however, purchases increase from 1975 to 1976 by much more than transfers, and from 1976 to 1977 both purchases and transfers decrease.[1] From 1977 purchases begin to climb again in central, local, and general government spending, but in no case do they climb as much or as fast as do transfers. These figures do, therefore, support a conclusion that controls on purchases are not only quicker acting but also more effective than are controls on transfers. Assuming that bureaucrats expend equal ingenuity, energy, etc. on attempting to control both purchases and transfers, they seem (as we would expect) to be more successful in keeping rein on purchasing goods and services than they are on limiting transfer payments.

The same theorising about reaction speed of controls on spending would suggest that, since central government has central departments on a shorter rein than it has local authorities or public corporations,

---

[1] This is true for General Government also if we remove the wages and salaries element from purchases. Wages/salaries form a steadily decreasing proportion of purchases (from 66.4 percent in 1975 to 61.0 percent in 1985), but there is a blip in 1977, when the proportional spending on salaries goes up slightly (because spending on non-salary purchases goes down a little).

spending by central government itself will decrease before that of the other spending authorities (Hypothesis 28). This is only half true, as can be seen in Table 4.5. First, between 1975 and 1976 central government total expenditure (current plus capital) goes *up*, and only decreases in the following year; whereas local authority total spending goes down immediately, and faster in the following year. After that, central spending begins its steady climb, while local spending continues a fitful decline, increasing only after 1982.

If we are ascribing these outcomes to the variation in the effectiveness of central controlling mechanisms (the objective of keeping down all spending being assumed to be constant), then control over local authority spending was more effective, not only initially but in the longer term, than was central control over central spending. (Local authority capital spending was under particularly close control, as can be judged from column 7 in Table 4.3: central government capital expenditure in the decade took an increasing share of a declining total.) However, if we apply the same assumptions to public corporation spending (remembering that 'public corporations' here cover such bodies as New Town Corporations but exclude the 'nationalised industries'), then the original expectation gets more support. Total expenditure of public corporations does not decline at all until very late in the period, between 1984 and 1985:

In all of these comparisons, we are making heroic assumptions: that if expenditure (at constant prices) goes up in a period of cutbacks, that is evidence of a 'failure of control', and if it goes down, that is evidence of success. We are not comparing what we perhaps should compare (the counter-factual): the actual rate of increase of spending with what we might call its 'natural' or uncontrolled rate – that is, the rate by which it would have increased if some quite efficacious controls had not been in operation to limit it. We do not have the data for that.

Nevertheless, some of the expectations we formed on theoretical grounds about how a 'Weberian' bureaucrat will behave in trying to meet a political demand for instant spending cuts are borne out by the actual patterns of spending found between 1975 and 1985 in the United Kingdom, and some are not: there is little evidence of initial 'equal misery', but it is not true that staff are cut before budget; capital spending is quite clearly cut before current spending, and perhaps we can say that spending on goods and services does not rise as much as does spending on grants and transfers; but it is certainly not true that central spending is cut before local spending. What do the figures on *staffing* cuts show?

Staffing cuts, it was suggested, can be the more easily made the greater

Table 4.5. *Central government current and capital expenditure as percent of General Government expenditure, 1975–85 (constant prices: GDP deflator, 1980 = 100)*

Year	Central government current and capital expenditure	Local authorities current and capital expenditure	Public corporations total expenditure	General Government current and capital expenditure	Column 1 as % of column 4
	1	2	3	4	5
1975	82,512	33,314	37,516	95,468	86.43
1976	83,216	32,705	40,090	97,649	85.22
1977	80,403	29,708	41,234	93,939	85.59
1978	83,483	28,980	43,059	96,620	86.40
1979	84,714	29,149	46,211	98,286	86.19
1980	86,435	29,323	45,935	100,599	85.93
1981	89,673	27,878	46,928	102,053	87.87
1982	92,456	27,440	47,078	104,661	88.34
1983	95,567	30,168	48,064	109,078	87.61
1984	99,204	30,987	47,085	112,763	87.98
1985	102,372	30,370	40,290	115,172	88.89

Source: UK National Accounts, 1986

the rate of 'natural wastage'; not only because non-replacement is less painful than making staff 'redundant', and under existing legislation cheaper, but because it is also procedurally quicker. Accordingly, we can expect the earliest and also the most sustained cuts among those groups of staff with highest 'natural' turnover. 'Weberian' officials looking for significant numbers of 'staff savings' will also look first at the larger groups. The most vulnerable groups are therefore those which are both large and high in natural wastage. These are found among the lower grades. As mentioned earlier too, it is these ranks which are most susceptible to mechanisation and computerisation, and to contracting out. By and large, it will be surprising if it is not the manual grades of the civil service, and the lower clerical grades, who suffer earliest and most when retrenchment sets in (Hypotheses 29, 30).

However, since there is a correlation between length of service (i.e., age) and rank, we might also expect that 'natural wastage' through age retirement might be quite high at 'the top'. This logic would lead us to predict proportionately more severe cuts at the 'top' and 'bottom' than in the 'middle'. Let us see what happened.

We have already adverted to the fact that the decline in numbers and proportion of blue-collar staff is a long-term trend in the United Kingdom.

Table 4.6. *Numbers and proportions of white-collar (non-industrial) civil servants in top, middle, and bottom grades, and blue-collar (industrial) civil servants, 1975–85*

Year	Top		Middle	Bottom	Blue-collar
1975	828	(0.17)	91,649 (18.54)	401,915 (81.29)	177,300 (25.3)
1976	870	(0.16)	96,768 (17.95)	441,542 (81.89)	179,100 (24.0)
1977	848	(0.16)	97,284 (17.92)	444,641 (81.92)	174,400 (23.4)
1978	833	(0.15)	98,074 (18.12)	442,324 (81.73)	168,400 (22.9)
1979	819	(0.15)	98,770 (18.23)	442,106 (81.62)	166,500 (22.7)
1980	813	(0.15)	98,905 (18.51)	434,626 (81.34)	157,400 (22.3)
1981	778	(0.15)	97,340 (18.38)	431,418 (81.47)	149,700 (21.7)
1982	738	(0.14)	94,561 (18.27)	422,355 (81.59)	138,400 (20.8)
1983	702	(0.14)	92,224 (18.14)	415,416 (81.72)	130,400 (20.1)
1984	717	(0.14)	91,220 (18.40)	403,917 (81.46)	119,700 (19.2)
1985	687	(0.14)	90,252 (18.44)	398,436 (81.42)	101,000 (16.9)

Definitions:
'Top' = Grades 1–3 of the Open Structure, formerly Permanent Secretary, Deputy Secretary, and Under Secretary
'Middle' = Grades 4–7 of the Open Structure, formerly (Grade 4). Director and equivalents; (Grade 5) Assistant Secretary and equivalents; (Grade 6) Senior Principal and equivalents; (Grade 7) Principal and equivalents; together with Senior Executive Officer, Higher Executive Officer (D), Higher Executive Officer, Administration Trainee, and equivalents
'Bottom' = Executive Officer, Clerical Officer, Clerical Assistant, 'Clerical Officer' and 'Clerical Assistant' grades are now designated 'Administration Officers' and 'Administration Assistants'

(Figures in parentheses in 'white-collar' columns represent absolute figures as percentage of a total derived by removing unattributed grades from the gross total. These unattributed grades decline in significance from being 4.06 percent of the gross total in 1975 to 0.02 percent in 1985)
Sources: Non-industrial staff: HM Treasury ('MANDATE') all departments
Industrial staff: *Annual Abstract of Statistics*
NB: figures for total civil service staff differ in the two sources, so percentages are not of the same figure

Nevertheless it is true that, as can be seen in Table 4.6, in the decade we are focussing on (1975–85), the numbers of blue-collar staff do not decline at all in the first two years of the period, but increase (though the proportion goes down). Thereafter the proportion of blue-collar civil servants declines steeply in what is a steadily declining total, so that indeed the manual grades are hit harder than the 'white-collar' grades over the decade.

For the lower administrative and clerical grades, it is a more complicated story. The data is drawn from the Treasury 'MANDATE' computer record, and we have defined 'top' as comprising the ranks of

Under Secretary and above (Grades 1 to 3), 'middle' as comprising the band from Assistant Secretary (Grade 5) to Higher Executive Officer inclusive (or equivalent grades), and 'bottom' the remainder (see definitions in Table 4.6). 'Bottom' grades in the non-industrial service are heavily dominated by Executive Officers and 'clerical' staff in the administrative and Social Security Groups.

Throughout the period, the 'bottom' of the white-collar pyramid, so defined, represent 81 percent of the whole; the decimal points accommodate the variation from year to year. Table 4.6 gives the figures. From this it can be seen that the hypothesis that 'bottom' grades will be cut first is not borne out. As we know from Table 1.4 and Fig. 1, the cuts in the civil service as a whole did not begin until 1977, and the 'bottom' grades declined, both in numbers and as a proportion of the whole, between then and 1978. But the number of 'top' civil servants declined from 1976.[2] As a proportion of the total, 'bottom' grades *rose* at first, then varied a little but ended up higher than they began in 1975. Of course, in absolute terms the numbers of lower-grade white-collar civil servants went down between 1977 and 1985; but by 10.4 percent, compared with 19.0 percent for 'top' grades, and 7.2 percent for 'middle' grades. The logic of the 'wastage rate', and cutback by non-replacement, was a good predictor of what happened.

The final prediction we arrived at in considering the Weberian bureaucrat's reactions to demands for staff cuts was that savings would be made, at least initially, by replacing permanent staff by temporary staff – for as long as that ploy 'worked'; but as the climate worsened, and the possibility of keeping the main staff fabric in being (against the return of better times) was seen to be a chimera, proportions of temporary staff would decline again (Hypothesis 31). As between 1975 and 1985, part-time white-collar staff formed 2.5 percent of the total in 1975 (just under 13,000 people), and rose steadily year by year – but rather too many years for the theory, for they did not begin to decline until 1982; and even thereafter, again reached their highest point in 1985, at 3.3 percent of the total, or about 16,500. So recourse *was* being had to employing more part-time staff, but not apparently on the reasoning supposed.

In the next section we substitute for the Weberian assumption about the motivations of bureaucrats the Adam Smith one – in the present context, that any axe-wielding official is going to 'look after Number One'.

---

[2] What is equally notable is that the 'middle' does not begin to decline until 1980. This is an aspect of what we call the 'Law of Bureaucratic Slimming', which we shall go into in the next section.

II   The 'Adam Smith' bureaucrat

The egregious Sir Humphrey Appleby surely sums up popular ideas in assuming that a bureau chief's standing is measured by the size of his department's staff and budget – and the bigger the budget, the bigger the staff: the bigger the staff, the higher the pyramid, or at least, the more supervisory jobs to be allocated. Dunleavy's more sophisticated (1985) analysis, however, describes 'expanding career prospects', 'increased demand for skills and labour', and 'triggering upward regrading' as welfare gains which primarily benefit 'bottom' and 'middle' ranks rather than top people; and middle and bottom ranks do not have a great deal of influence to deploy, so that the costs of advocating the expansion fall most heavily not on them but on the top people, who have more influence but gain least. So Dunleavy would *not* predict that top civil servants will strongly wield such influence as they have in the direction of increasing the complement. Nevertheless, it remains a popular expectation that if central government expenditure is rising, numbers of civil servants will rise with it (Hypothesis 32).

A glance at Figure 3 will have shown that, in the decade 1975–85 at least, this expectation is not realised. It is true that from 1975 to 1976, both spending and staffing go up, and that then they both fall in the next two years; but whereas spending then 'recovers', and begins its fairly steady climb to a very high level (all after taking inflation into account), the decline of total staffing continues just as steadily. It is apparently not the case that when you spend more public money you need more civil servants to do it.

Perhaps, then, the 'private benefits' which bureaucrats are expected to cream off from budgetary expansion were taken in higher salaries, or in rises in pay-related items such as pensions? Again, Dunleavy (1985) notes that salaries are a matter of 'core' budget (mainly internal maintenance), so that not all increases in overall spending need provide increases in salary (for example, a rise in state pension rates will increase a bureau's external spending but will entail no effect on civil service salaries). Further, a utility maximising strategy of general pay increases is a *collective* strategy rather than an *individual* one (examples of the latter are personal promotion and job regrading); in bottom ranks the opportunities for improving individual welfare are few, so that general pay increases often represent their best hope, while top ranks have more scope for individual betterment and so their propensity to go for all-round pay increases is less. So it is not nearly as clear as might be supposed that the top bureaucrats (who have the power) will aim for general salary increases. Nevertheless, it is again a staple of popular lore on self-regarding bureaucrats that when public expenditure is rising, expenditure on public servants' salaries will rise by at least as much, if not more (Hypothesis 33).

As in a previous analysis (Hood and Dunsire 1984) but using a different source and period, we shall explore four sub-hypotheses to see which best fits the facts. The source is the Blue Book (*UK National Accounts*) for 1986, which in one series gives a figure for expenditure on 'Wages and salaries etc.' from 1977 to 1985 – quite convenient for our purposes, since there is an almost-unbroken expansion; but the figures are for 'General Government', a consolidation of central and local spending, which gives us a broader classification of 'bureaucrat'. The four sub-hypotheses are these:

1 The *whole* or a large proportion of any real increase in general government spending is appropriated in the form of pay and/or pay-related perks for the public servants. If all real budgetary increases were spent in this way, we would find over time an increase in the proportion of the total government budget devoted to wages and salaries, etc.

2 As government spending changes, a constant proportion of it is devoted to pay and perks, as if following the old 'poundage' principle once used for remunerating tax collectors. By this, self-interested bureaucrats would still be strongly motivated to seek increases in government spending, since they would share in them *pari passu*. If that were the case, we would find that wages/salaries, etc. of the public servants constituted a more or less constant percentage of total General Government spending as the latter increased.

3 As the real level of government spending rises, there is *no* rise in the real level of pay and pay-related perks of the public service. If that were the case, we would find the level of wages/salaries, etc. spending remaining no more than constant in real terms, although total spending went up in real terms.

4 As the real level of government spending rises, the real level of pay and pay-related perks of public servants *falls*. In these circumstances, a real increase in general government spending does not serve even to maintain the real level of bureaucratic wages/salaries, etc.

Findings consistent with sub-hypotheses 1 and 2 might be said to be consistent with the conventional budget/utility theory of bureaucracy; findings consistent with sub-hypotheses 3 and 4 would leave the exponents of that theory with the need to explain what precisely is the utility to bureaucrats of budgetary increases, or perhaps confirm Dunleavy's (1985) critique of its crudeness. Figure 4 gives the results. There are three lines: the upper one shows what spending on public servants' wages and salaries would have been over the period 1977–85 if it had remained at the 1977 ratio to total General Government spending (i.e., 29.59 percent). That line therefore represents sub-hypothesis 2; and a level of actual spending on wages and salaries anywhere above that line would be consistent with sub-hypothesis 1. The lowest of the three lines shows what spending on public servants' wages and salaries would have been over the period if that spending had been maintained at a constant real level (rising only in line with inflation as measured by the GDP index). That line therefore represents sub-hypothesis 3, and a level of actual spending on wages and salaries below that line would be consistent with sub-hypothesis 4.

The middle line shows what the total amount spent on public service wages and salaries etc. actually was (as reported in *UK National Accounts*, 1986, table 9.4). Clearly sub-hypothesis 1 is rejected by this observation, and the same goes for sub-hypothesis 4. What actually happened falls somewhere between sub-hypothesis 2 and sub-hypothesis 3. The lower two curves are very close together in the earlier years of the period, but after 1979 it is the upper two curves which are closer. Sub-hypothesis 2 would appear to be a better predictor than sub-hypothesis 3 over the period as a whole.

Public servants' pay did, therefore, go up more or less in line with public spending, even if it did not proportionally beat that rise. This is a very similar result to that which we found in the earlier exercise, over the period 1971–83, and covering only central government spending and the pay of civil servants rather than, as here, central and local government together. These results are not clear cut. Pay goes up by more than would be required simply to match inflation, but not by quite enough to match total budget increase. Dunleavy's explanation would possibly be that this result is consistent with top management's interest in 'reducing conflict in bureau management' – the only type of welfare gain from an increase in 'core budget' in which top ranks are more interested than middle or bottom ranks (Dunleavy 1985, 309).

But perhaps by taking only aggregate figures for government as a whole we are, as Dunleavy would note, missing significant differences between bureaus or programmes in this regard? Some programmes are 'staff-heavy' (much of their spending is on wages and salaries; 'core budget' is a high proportion of the total), while others are comparatively 'staff-light' – they move money around, rather than spend it on

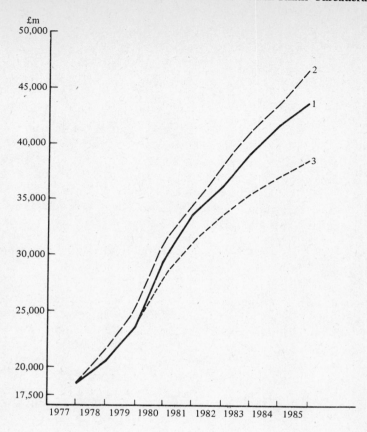

Notes: Curve 1   Actual wages and salaries, etc. (£m, current prices)

Curve 2   What wages and salaries, etc. would have been if they had remained as a constant proportion of total General Government spending

Curve 3   What wages and salaries, etc. would have been if they had increased only in line with inflation (GDP deflator: 1980 = 100)

Source: *UK National Accounts*, 1986, table 9.4

Fig. 4. General Government: wages and salaries, etc. as constant proportion of total expenditure, as reported, and as increased only by inflation, 1977–85 (£m).

themselves (external spending and/or external funding is a high proportion of total budget). If there is anything in the suggestion that the 'Adam Smith' bureaucrat will for preference choose the staff-intensive mode of delivery rather than any other (Breton 1974), then we might expect that when real total spending is growing, the spending in staff-heavy programmes will grow faster (Hypothesis 34).

We have looked into this also, using 'General Government' again, and for the years 1977–8 to 1984–5. In that period, four out of the thirteen spending programmes listed in the Blue Book consistently devoted more than half of their expenditure to wages and salaries, etc. These were General Public Services (including Parliament, Tax Collection, and External Affairs), Public Order and Safety (including Police, Fire, Law Courts, Prisons), Education, and Health. In 1985 the proportion of total budget going on wages and salaries in these four averaged 60 percent, while the average for the other nine was only 16 percent, Recreation and Cultural Affairs (a small programme) being the most staff-heavy of the nine at 43 percent.

Taking one year with the previous year, these four staff-heavy programmes *did* beat the percentage increase in total General Government spending in some years, but none of them in all years, and in no year did all four increase proportionately more than the total. Public Order and Safety came closest, with better-than-total increases in five years out of the eight; the others achieved it in only two (Education) or three. Moreover, Defence (not staff-heavy in these terms) achieved it in five, and Social Security (even less so – consistently under 8 percent spent on wages and salaries) in six years out of the eight. It does not look as though the bureaucrats, profiting from their position of 'information-impactedness' (Williamson 1975) and other power-resources, have managed to steer increases in total government spending into staff-intensive channels.

Up till now in this section, we have been concerned with expenditure and so have not, in this period, been able to investigate *cutback* strategies to any great extent: public expenditure was rising for most of the period, even in real terms. When we turn to consider staffing, however, cuts do appear. And here, many fears and allegations about the behaviour of self-regarding bureaucrats are less based on those of the economistic academic writers, and arise more from a jaundiced view of human nature in general, rather than of *homo bureauensis* in particular. If bureaucrats are obliged to wield axes on other bureaucrats, this view holds, they will make sure the axe falls on someone else, not on themselves. Does not that stand to reason?

Table 4.7. *Percentage decreases in numbers of selected civil service groupings, 1975–85 and 1977–85*

Grouping	1975–85	1977–85
Top	17.09	19.04
Middle	1.52	7.23
Bottom	0.86	10.39
Blue-collar	34.24	34.02
Base	11.07	17.10

'Top'
'Middle' } see note to Table 4.6
'Bottom'
'Blue-collar' = industrial civil service
'Base' = 'Bottom' + 'blue-collar'
Source: HM Treasury ('MANDATE'): all departments

Let us examine first the common assumption that whoever suffers, it will not be the 'top brass', the bosses, those at the peak of the pyramid (Hypothesis 35). We have already seen the figures: Table 4.7 shows both the absolute decrease in numbers in the three highest grades of the civil service (the 'top'), and how these ranks diminished even as a proportion of a shrinking total, between 1975 and 1985. The total, however, did not begin to shrink until 1977, and as we saw in an earlier table (Table 1.4), the total of white-collar civil servants did not become less than it had been in 1975 until 1983. Recognising this, if we nevertheless measure the shrinkage in each group over the decade 1975–85, the differential effect on the 'top' shows up very clearly (see the first column in Table 4.7). Whereas no other group of white-collar civil servants lost more than 2 percent of its numbers from the beginning to the end of this decade, the highest ranks lost 17 percent of their numbers.

The total began to decline in 1977. The second column measures the relative decreases in 'top', 'middle', and 'bottom' over the period 1977–85. It can be seen again that the highest ranks, far from imposing cuts more severely on anyone other than themselves, imposed the greatest cuts on themselves – among white-collar civil servants, that is; the blue-collar civil service declined by more than one-third in that time.

What is interesting about this table, however, is not so much the fortunes of the top civil servants as those of the *middle* grades. Since middle grades supervise blue-collar workers as well as 'bottom' white-collar grades, a truer picture of their relative 'suffering' over the decade as a whole is obtained by replacing 'bottom' by 'base' – a combination of the lower white-collar grades and blue-collar grades. 'Middle' can then be seen to have declined by 1.52 percent over the decade, or 7.23 percent in the 'cuts' period, compared with 17 percent and 19 percent for the 'top' and 11.1 percent and 17.2 percent for the 'base'. This cannot be merely a 'size effect', or else it would surely have been even more marked in the 'top' grades. It is partly a reflection of the point we have already noted, that the 'middle' ranks did not begin to decline until much later than the other groups – they continued to grow, *in absolute numbers* as well as in share of the total, until 1980. If we measure decline from 1980 onwards, the 'middle' still suffered less than the 'base' in that period – 8.75 percent as against 13.32 percent – and less than the 'top' (15.5 percent). As a proportion of the total civil service, the top grades decline over the cuts period very slightly (from 0.12 percent to 0.11 percent), the 'base' also (86.35 percent to 84.99 percent); but the middle grades climb steadily year by year (from 13.53 percent in 1977 to 14.90 percent in 1985).

This appears to conform to a general 'Law of Bureaucratic Slimming' which states that during retrenchment, in proportion to overall cuts, the middle tends to expand at the expense of the top and the base. A drift to 'middle-heaviness' has been observed as characterising bureaucracies in decline in the USA: Martin (1983, 51–4) noted this for police agencies, city administrators, and the federal government service. Official federal figures showed that the lowest grades (GS 1–3) and the top grades (GS 16–18) all indicated a decline, while there were big increases in grades GS 10–15 inclusive, particularly GS 14.

One type of explanation would accord with the 'axeman, save thyself' hypothesis we are investigating: this points out that the civil servants most closely associated with detailed 'establishment' work (promotions, postings, hirings and firings) do not inhabit the highest reaches of the bureaucracy at all, but the middle. It is much more likely to be Assistant Secretaries and Senior Executive Officers (or GS 14s), rather than their exalted superiors at the Under Secretary and above level, who are charged with finding and delivering staff savings. If there are any 'axemen' they will be in the middle ranks; *of course* the middle ranks suffer later and less than other groupings.

Another mode of explanation, however, lies in a more mechanical effect altogether. In a civil service like the British one where promotion to a higher grade is still at least partly according to length of service, there is a linkage between turnover rates (flows between the grade and the outside world), promotion rates (flows between grades), and average age and length of service in a grade. If promotion criteria remain unchanged, a grade (or group of grades) with low turnover rates will tend to swell and to age in comparison with a grade (or group of grades) with higher turnover; and this effect will increase if normal promotion out of that grade (or group of grades) is checked. Martin attributed the US findings to hiring freezes on entry-level grades, automatic career-ladder promotions, high attrition in lower grades, contracting out of less complex and lower-graded work, and automation which replaces lower-graded clerical and administrative personnel by electronics, which in turn requires higher-graded technical and professional personnel to operate and maintain the systems. We shall go into this in a later chapter.

The figures for shares of the total taken by different grade levels may, of course, mask significant changes in the *kind* of bureaucrats being employed. In particular, we might expect that, under the pressures of retrenchment, the civil service will 'revert to type'. 'Specialists' will be shed rather than 'generalists' (Hypothesis 36); blue-collar workers will suffer disproportionately in relation to white-collar workers (Hypothesis 37); part-time staff will be the first to go (Hypothesis 41); and the proportion of women staff (as relative latecomers to the bureaucratic world) will gradually decline (Hypothesis 39). If all these things happened in the period since 1975, then the traditional stereotype of the 'civil servant' as a male clerk with life tenure and pension would more and more represent the reality.

If we translate 'generalists' into the Administration Group together with the Secretarial Group (we could add the Open Structure posts, but they are numerically insignificant in this context), and regard the rest (or possibly the rest of the white-collar civil service) as being 'specialists' to some degree or other, we can test Hypothesis 36 readily. Table 4.8 gives the various numbers and proportions. In the first year of the period the growth in the civil service takes place disproportionately *outside* the 'generalist' groups: whether measured against the whole civil service or against the white-collar civil service only, their proportions in 1976 are much smaller than in 1975. (In fact, if we extended the table backwards, we would find the proportion of generalists in the total climbing to its *peak* in 1975, and not again dropping back to what it was in 1972 (35.3 percent of the all-in total).)

When the cuts begin, they are seen in the secretarial grades first (column 2), in 1976, and then in the other groups in 1977. Thereafter the proportion of secretaries in the total remains remarkably constant (columns 5 and 9). The proportion of Administration Group people in the total falls a bit, until 1980, but then begins to rise steadily (column 4), or somewhat more erratically if you measure against white-collar grades

Table 4.8. *Proportions of Administration Group and Secretarial Group civil servants in total civil service as at 1 January 1975–85*

Year	Administration Group	Secretarial Group	Total civil service	% 1/3	% 2/3	% 1+2/3	Total non-industrial civil service	% 1/7	% 2/7	% 1+2/7
	1	2	3	4	5	6	7	8	9	10
1975	267,822	27,391	693,921	38.5	3.9	42.4	517,030	51.8	5.3	57.1
1976	251,851	29,369	745,120	33.8	3.9	37.7	564,800	44.6	5.2	49.8
1977	252,747	28,916	746,161	33.9	3.9	37.8	569,900	44.3	5.1	49.4
1978	251,758	28,535	737,984	34.1	3.9	38.0	567,000	44.4	5.0	49.4
1979	250,908	28,540	733,176	34.2	3.9	38.1	566,000	44.3	5.0	49.4
1980	240,137	27,595	707,620	33.9	3.9	37.8	548,553	43.8	5.0	48.8
1981	238,297	27,327	695,070	34.3	3.9	38.4	542,790	43.9	5.0	48.9
1982	236,274	26,599	675,424	35.0	3.9	38.9	532,805	44.3	5.0	49.3
1983	231,662	25,919	652,534	35.5	4.0	39.5	520,339	44.5	5.0	49.5
1984	224,944	25,083	632,591	35.6	4.0	39.5	508,867	44.2	4.9	49.1
1985	223,275	24,646	619,570	36.0	4.0	40.0	503,253	44.4	4.9	49.3

Sources: columns 1 and 2, *Staff in Post*
columns 3 and 7, *Civil Service Statistics*

only (column 8). The generalists taken together (columns 6 and 10) follow the fortunes of the Administration Group, more or less. The proportion of the generalists increases from 1977 to 1985 (the years of cutback), if you consider the whole civil service, but that could be explained by a more than proportionate fall in the numbers of blue-collar civil servants (which we know took place). If you consider only the white-collar workers, the proportion between 1977 and 1985 is pretty constant – not much sign there of the generalists taking the cuts out of the specialists rather than themselves. On the other hand, not much sign either of the Fulton Committee's (1968) bold assertion that the cult of the generalist administrator was obsolete.

The same table can yield figures about the relationship between cuts among white-collar and cuts among blue-collar civil servants, since the difference between columns 3 and 7 gives the size of the industrial civil service each year. This is 176,261 in 1977 and 116,317 in 1985, a decline of 34.0 percent; over the same period the non-industrial civil service declines by 11.7 percent. However, as we have noted before, the blue-collar civil service has been in long-term decline; using a different series (from the *Annual Abstract of Statistics*, presented in *Civil Service Statistics* 1985, p. 11), we can show that since its post-war peak in 1946 of 366,000 the industrial civil service has declined by over 60 percent – 10 percent in the first decade, 30 percent in the next, 23 percent in the third decade (1966–76), and 44 percent since then, according to this series (which is as at 1 April rather than 1 January, and has certain other differences of counting). There is no question, then, that the blue-collar workers have suffered more than white-collar workers during the recent retrenchment, and even more drastically than their own historical trend.

The figures for the numbers and proportions of part-time civil servants and women civil servants (white-collar only in each case) are given in Table 4.9. Because of changes in the presentation of statistics we have strictly comparable figures (i.e., from the same table in each annual issue of *Civil Service Statistics*) only from 1978. But it can clearly be seen that, in these cases, the supposition that (in the tendentious phrase used above) the civil service will 'revert to type' by discriminating against part-timers and women is not borne out. The proportion of part-timers *rises*, then falls a bit, but leaps remarkably (by more than a quarter) in the final two years of the period. The proportion of women civil servants shows a fairly steady climb over the period. Indeed, if the trend continues for another decade the traditional stereotype of the civil service (along with terms like 'manpower' and 'manning') may have to change, since women will

Table 4.9. *Numbers and proportions of part-time civil servants and women civil servants among white-collar (non-industrial) civil servants, 1978–86*

Year	Total non-industrial civil service	Part-timers	% 2/1	Women	% 4/1
	1	2	3	4	5
1978	559,898	16,584	3.0	253,765	45.3
1979	559,025	17,025	3.0	255,186	45.6
1980	541,645	17,932	3.3	248,613	45.9
1981	536,218	17,675	3.3	249,908	46.6
1982	526,416	16,715	3.2	247,250	47.0
1983	514,061	16,151	3.1	241,928	47.1
1984	502,426	15,760	3.1	235,937	47.0
1985	496,783	16,537	3.3	234,460	47.2
1986	491,531	20,344	4.1	234,617	47.7

Source: *Civil Service Statistics*, annually, table 4

be in the majority. Women staff already predominate in the lower ranks of the Administration Group (70 percent in 1986), in the Secretarial Category (over 99 percent women), and in the Social Security Category (68 percent in 1986). (Women also form a large proportion of part-time staff: 94 percent in 1986.) The numbers of women in the top grades of the civil service (grades 1–3) reached a peak of 32 in 1982 (4.3 percent of total 1–3 staff), and have dropped to 25 in 1986 (3.8 percent). Proportions in the rest of the Open Structure (grades 4–6 from 1984, 4–7 from 1986) are, however, climbing: 4.5 percent in 1984, 5.0 percent in 1985, 5.7 percent in 1986 if one excludes grade 7, 7.3 percent if one includes it. All these figures back up a national stereotype of the 'role' of women, in the civil service and elsewhere, which is changing but slowly.

Another variant of the 'axeman, save thyself' hypothesis is that in a period of retrenchment cuts are decided at headquarters, and that therefore you could expect that headquarters staff would impose reductions on field offices and the like, before they imposed cuts on themselves (Hypothesis 38). There is an obvious parallel with multinational corporations closing down peripheral plants during hard times. Indeed, there might be some 'managerialist' logic in differential cuts in HQ staff compared with regional staff, since by and large it takes just as big a unit in a bureaucracy's head office to control a network of, say, 900 field staff as a network of 1,000: it may need a much greater magnitude of field cuts than this before obvious redundancies appear at HQ.

We can test this proposition in only a limited way, since we do not have staff figures for 'headquarters' as such; and it must be borne in mind that there are some large 'headquarters' offices (i.e., offices whose territorial coverage is Great Britain-wide or UK-wide and not regional or local) in many 'provincial' locations – for example, the huge DHSS complex of central records offices in and around Newcastle upon Tyne in the north of England. However, if there were any dramatic change in the relation between the field strength of a department and the HQ strength over a period, that ought to show up as a change in that department's *concentration index*.[3] A high number indicates that staff are concentrated in one or a few regions, a low number, relatively even dispersion: cutting field staff more than HQ staff would increase the concentration index number. Similarly, if in Whitehall as a whole there had been significant sacrificing of field staff in preference to HQ staff, the concentration index for civil servants generally should show an increase.

In fact, between 1977 (the earliest year for which we have figures) and 1986 the concentration index for all departments taken together went down (see Table A3 in Appendix II). The hypothesis is not supported. Another crude measurement would simply compare change in total staff in the London region (the area which includes most headquarters offices, even if it excludes several large central offices) with changes in the regions. For this we have data only from 1980; but between then and 1986 London staff decreased by 15.6 percent, compared with the average decrease for all regions taken together of 9.2 percent. The London decrease is in fact the largest of all over that period. Again, the evidence is consistent with the *reverse* of the hypothesis: i.e., that in retrenchment field staff numbers are maintained at the expense of headquarters staffs.

Table 4.10 summarises our observations. It reproduces the expectations about how 'Weberian' and 'Adam Smith' bureaucrats should behave during cutbacks which we laid out in Table 4.1, and shows whether these expectations were consistent with what can be observed for the spending and staffing data examined here. The ticks and crosses are a crude simplification, and leave out some of the nuances in the observed data which are discussed in the text.

What Table 4.10 shows is that the 'popular' expectations about the effect of bureaucratic cutbacks based on a stereotype of *homo bureauensis* as self-regarding and self-serving (and in particular, wielding the axe on anyone but him or herself in time of trouble) do rather less well as predictors than do the rather less popular and more prosaic 'Weberian' expectations. Whereas only two out of the seven 'Adam Smith' expectations can be said to gain any kind of support from this inquiry,

---

[3] This is explained in Appendix II.

Table 4.10. *'Weberian' and 'Adam Smith' bureaucrats: strategies in cutbacks: results*

The Weberian bureaucrat		The Adam Smith bureaucrat	
Aim: to 'subordinate himself to the chief without any will of his own'* – in this case, to bring about effective cutbacks quickly		Aim: 'to support with rigorous severity [his] own interest against that of the country which [he] govern[s]'† – in this case, to minimise his own injury in cutbacks	
Expected strategy	Observed	Expected strategy	Observed
Prune everything back equally at first	✓	Resist cutbacks by offering 'fairy gold'	×
Cut staff before budget	×‡	Cut budget before staff	✓‡
Cut capital rather than current spending	✓	Cut anything before salaries share of expenditure	×
Cut goods and services spending before grants and transfers	✓	Cut money-moving rather than salaries-heavy programmes	×
Cut central spending before local	×	Cut central spending last	✓
Cut big battalions	✓	Cut any but top echelons	×
At outset, increase temporaries and part-time staff	✓	Cut temporaries and part-time staff	×

Note: *Weber, in Gerth and Mills 1948, 208
† Adam Smith 1776, bk IV, chap. VII, part III
‡ In initial period

only two out of the seven 'Weberian' expectations are clearly inconsistent with what we found here, and one of those is only partially so. Only in the case of the blue-collar workers can it be plausibly held that a minority or underprivileged group was sacrificed in the interests of the stronger group, in line with 'Adam Smith' expectations.

Those who feel in their bones that the popular 'Adam Smith' expectations *must* fit the facts better than the unfashionable 'Weberian' expectations are thus driven back to one or more of three lines of defence against this conclusion. The first might be that though 'Adam Smith' scores only two out of seven as against 'Weber's' five out of seven in our tests, the two points on which the 'Adam Smith' expectations are fulfilled are weightier or qualitatively more important than the five points on which the 'Weberian' expectations are fulfilled. This touches on the nonfalsifiable 'hard cores' of rival research programmes, but on the face of it seems difficult to justify. A second, more telling, line of defence might be that 'Adam Smith' strategies might be shown up by a more qualitative inquiry based on different kinds of data – for example, in the possibility that bureaucrats might pass costs on to clients and customers by subjecting them to greater inconvenience (e.g., longer queues, fewer local service outlets), in order to preserve funds for activities more 'liked' within the bureaucracy. Only further inquiry, and of a different kind, could reveal the truth of that. A third line of defence might be to refine further the 'popular' idea of the 'Adam Smith' bureaucrat, as Dunleavy has done, so that expectations about bureaucratic behaviour come more closely into line with 'Weberian' expectations. It then becomes more difficult to test the relative power of 'Adam Smith' and 'Weberian' expectations with the kind of data used here, and much more fine-tuned testing becomes necessary.

Now we shift the focus away from the bureaucrat to the department, and the programme. Perhaps differences between programmes, or departments, make one more likely to be cut than another.

5 Winners and losers III: programmes and departments

In Chapter 3 we looked into the patterns of central government spending and staffing among different programmes and departments before and after changes of governing party, to see whether individual programmes, or groupings of programmes, or departments, fared better under one party than under the other – i.e., whether it was the ideological or group interest character which explained the diverse outcomes in a period of cutbacks. We had varied success: some 'man-in-the-street' expectations were better predictors than some academic theories, but much was left unexplained. Now we want to study whether it may be some other characteristic of programmes and departments which would make them particularly vulnerable to being cut sooner, or more heavily, than others.

I Programme vulnerability

By 'programme' in this context we mean what public money is spent on, a subject classification, as distinct from who is spending it or accounting for it; for the latter we use the term 'bureau' or 'department'. In neither case is there complete unanimity or clarity of definitions.[1] The classification of central government spending programmes we used earlier (Table 3.3) contained 26 items, as found in the annual Blue Book (*United Kingdom National Accounts*) up to 1984. From 1985 the Blue Book went over to an internationally agreed 'Classification of the Functions of Government' (COFOG), which has only 14 *major groups*, which can themselves be grouped into 'General Government Services', 'Community and Social Affairs', 'Economic Services', and 'Other'; and which can be

---

[1] In particular, our use of 'programme' and 'bureau' follows that of Rose (1984), rather than that of Dunleavy (1985) in his categorisation of types of budget – 'programme' budget there meaning what we call external funding plus external spending plus internal spending; 'bureau' budget meaning the latter two only; and 'core' budget meaning the last only.

further divided into a total of 61 *groups* and 127 *subgroups* (see the explanation in the 1985 Blue Book, p. 116, or the United Nations paper referred to there). We shall concern ourselves in this chapter only with the 'major groups', and call them the 'programmes' whose characteristics we want to investigate. These 14 categories are listed in Table 5.1, which shows the pattern of spending between 1977 and 1985 in 'real terms', i.e., corrected for inflation.

Two points should be made. First, the table goes back only to 1977, because that is as far as the Blue Book goes back in giving us the 'old' data in the new format. The problems of the alternative, trying ourselves to present 1985 data in the old format, would have been formidable. Second, these figures are for 'General Government' rather than for central government as before. That is, they report spending by local authorities as well as by central government. Since in this section we are trying to address differences between programmes as such, and not between spenders, and since spending on many subjects is unequally shared between central and local government, this seemed a useful way of eliminating some problems and focussing on what we want to know.

The theoretical discussion in Chapter 2 suggested that the timing and scale of programme cuts might be affected by their economic effect, their size, their *inertia* or volatility, and their visibility (clarity, specificity). Let us start on economic effects. Two of the categories into which each programme's total expenditure is analysed are 'goods and services' (which includes wages and salaries of public employees), and 'current grants to personal sector', which economists term 'transfer payments' since they do not actually purchase anything, but give purchasing (or saving) power to others. The first hypothesis (Hypothesis 42) is that programmes which commit resources directly will suffer earlier and more than programmes which mainly act indirectly. Was this true for the UK between 1977 and 1986?

There were only three programmes which always spent more than 90 percent of their outgoings on 'goods and services': Defence, Health, and Public Order & Safety. The next in line, always around 75 percent, were Education and Recreation & Cultural, with the remainder at 50 percent or less. There were likewise only three programmes which *on average* spent more than 45 percent of programme total on transfer payments: Social Security, always above 85 percent; Agriculture/Forestry/Fisheries, averaging 51 percent but always above 45 percent; and Other Economic Affairs, averaging above 45 percent but with wide variations. The next two, Transport & Communications and Housing & Community Amenities, averaged 35 percent and 30 percent respectively; none of the others

Table 5.1. *General Government expenditure by programme 1977–85 (constant prices: GDP deflator, 1980=100) (£m)*

Programme	1977	1978	1979	1980	1981	1982	1983	1984	1985
General Public Services	4,905	5,436	5,563	4,958	4,468	4,721	4,675	4,677	5,705
Defence	10,478	10,417	10,800	11,488	11,333	12,054	12,572	13,064	13,256
Public Order & Safety	3,255	3,339	3,470	3,697	3,867	4,036	4,194	4,469	4,465
Education	12,734	12,554	12,366	12,754	12,794	12,710	13,013	12,939	12,676
Health	10,417	10,745	10,866	11,629	11,949	11,712	12,608	12,713	12,916
Social Security	22,921	24,595	25,079	25,437	27,743	30,070	31,092	32,303	33,232
Housing & Amenities	8,314	8,186	8,681	8,358	6,209	5,475	5,952	5,789	4,922
Recreational & Cultural	1,238	1,288	1,362	1,460	1,402	1,396	1,538	1,594	1,651
Fuel & Energy*	1,630	363	1,463	1,593	582	869	658	1,093	1,189
Agriculture, Forestry, Fishing*	1,617	1,525	1,402	1,641	1,512	1,669	1,960	1,665	2,043
Mining, Manufacturing, Construction*	2,411	2,813	2,992	2,709	3,121	2,336	2,139	1,860	1,768
Transport & Communication*	3,702	3,711	3,888	3,412	3,696	4,044	3,843	2,492	2,967
Other Econ.*	2,582	2,204	2,126	2,248	2,453	2,304	2,482	2,818	2,774
Other Expenditure	11,392	11,731	12,247	12,676	13,252	13,530	13,134	13,832	14,543
Total	94,336	98,909	102,328	104,060	104,381	106,928	109,788	111,308	114,071

Note: Full programme titles: General Public Services (including Parliament, Finance, External). Defence. Public Order and Safety (including Police, Fire, Law Courts, Prisons). Education. Health. Social Security. Housing and Community Amenities (including Water and Sewerage). Recreational and Cultural Affairs. Fuel and Energy*. Agriculture, Forestry and Fishing*. Mining and Mineral Resources, Manufacturing and Construction*. Transport and Communication*. Other Economic Affairs and Services*. Other Expenditure (including debt interest)

* Figures represent net expenditures after repayments of loans, etc.

Source: United Kingdom National Accounts, 1986, table 9.4

spent as much as 20 percent on transfer payments. Table 5.2 shows the year-by-year percentage increases/decreases (in real terms) for these ten programmes (indeed, for all programmes except Fuel & Energy, which is highly volatile and was therefore excluded); and also their all-over fortunes – the percentage change in real spending between 1977 and 1985, and the change in their percent share of total General Government expenditure.

The programmes high on 'goods and services' (Defence, Health, Public Order & Safety, Education, and Recreation & Culture) should have suffered earlier, and more heavily, than Social Security, Agriculture, Other Econ., Transport, and Housing, if the hypothesis is to hold. But as for timing, if anything the opposite appears to be true: between 1977 and 1980, for instance, there are three minuses for the first group, and seven for the second. As for weight of cuts overall, there is very little in it: the three programmes highest in purchases of goods and services, and the three programmes highest in transfer payments, all had considerable *gains* overall. So that horse won't run, at least. It almost seems that to be extreme in either respect does you good. The only other programme which grew over this period by more than the total for General Government as a whole was 'Other' (by 27.3 percent, against 20.9 percent total overall growth) – and 'Other' (mainly debt interest) spent hardly anything on goods and services and nothing at all on transfer payments.

The next hypothesis (Hypothesis 43) was that programmes pro-portionately high in capital as compared with current expenditure will suffer early and much. Capital spending can very often be postponed or stretched without immediate harm or sacrifice, while a great proportion of current spending represents commitments already incurred one way and another. Total General Government capital spending in this period (as judged by 'gross domestic fixed capital formation' in table 9.4 of the 1986 Blue Book) fell in real terms from £7.3 billion to £4.8 billion, with a low spot of £3.5 billion in 1982. Of this, only two programmes ever took more than 20 percent: Housing & Community Amenities, starting at 45 percent but declining to around 20 percent; and Transport & Communi-cations, starting at around 16 percent but climbing to take around 25 percent for the latter half of the period. The next most capital-intensive programmes were Health, with a proportion rising from 9 percent to 15 percent; and Education, always around 10 percent. The rest (even if we lay aside the very low capital-spending figures of the economic programmes – Fuel & Energy, Mining, Manufacturing, & Construction – because of the 'net' nature of some of their figures) have very small

Table 5.2. *General Government expenditure by programme, 1977–85. Percent year-on-year change, and overall change*

Programme	1977	1978	1979	1980	1981	1982	1983	1984	1985	Overall*
Social Security	0	+ 7.3	+2.0	+ 1.4	+ 9.1	+ 8.4	+ 3.4	+ 3.4	+ 2.9	+45.0
Public Order & Safety	0	+ 2.6	+3.9	+ 6.5	+ 4.6	+ 4.4	+ 3.3	+ 6.5	− 0.1	+37.1
Recreation & Culture	0	+ 4.0	+5.7	+ 7.2	− 4.0	− 0.4	+10.2	+ 3.6	+ 3.6	+33.4
Other	0	+ 3.0	+4.4	+ 3.5	+ 4.5	+ 2.1	− 2.9	+ 5.3	+ 5.1	+27.3
Defence	0	− 0.6	+3.7	+ 6.4	− 1.3	+ 6.4	+ 4.3	+ 3.9	+ 1.5	+26.5
Agriculture, Forestry, Fishing†	0	− 5.7	−5.1	+17.0	− 7.9	+10.4	+17.4	−15.0	+22.7	+26.3
Health	0	+ 3.1	+1.1	+ 7.0	+ 2.7	− 2.0	+ 7.6	+ 0.8	+ 1.6	+24.0
Total General Government	0	+ 4.8	+3.5	+ 1.7	+ 0.3	+ 2.4	+ 2.7	+ 1.4	+ 2.5	+20.9
General Public Services	0	+10.8	+2.3	−10.9	− 9.9	+ 5.7	− 1.0	+ 0.0	+22.0	+16.3
Other Econ.†	0	−14.6	−3.5	+ 5.7	+ 9.1	− 6.1	+ 7.7	+13.5	− 1.6	+ 7.4
Education	0	− 1.4	−1.5	+ 3.1	+ 0.3	− 0.7	+ 2.4	− 0.6	− 2.0	− 1.8
Transport & Communications	0	+ 0.2	+4.8	−12.2	+ 8.3	+ 9.4	− 5.0	−35.1	+19.1	−19.9
Mining, Manufacturing, Construction†	0	+16.7	+6.7	− 9.5	+15.2	−25.1	− 8.4	−13.0	− 4.9	−26.7
Housing & Amenities	0	− 1.5	+6.0	− 3.7	−25.7	−11.8	+ 8.7	− 2.7	−15.0	−40.8

Notes: †Figures represent net expenditures after repayments of loans, etc. Fuel & Energy is omitted, because the 1977 spending total is a minus figure, and the swings up and down thereafter are so large as to be meaningless in this table.

*The changes in percentage share of total General Government expenditure are:

Social Security	+4.8	General Public Services	−0.2
Other	+0.6	Other Econ.	−0.3
Defence	+0.5	Mining, Manufacturing, Construction	−1.1
Public Order & Safety	+0.4	Transport & Communication	−1.3
Health	+0.3	Education	−2.4
Agriculture, Forestry, Fisheries	+0.1	Housing & Amenities	−4.5
Recreation & Culture	+0.1		

Source: United Kingdom National Accounts, 1986, table 9.4

shares of the capital formation total, with Public Order & Safety (between 3 percent and 5 percent), Defence (between 1 percent and 4 percent) and Social Security (1 percent to 2.5 percent) the smallest outside the Economic group.

If we now compare the fortunes of these programmes as seen in Table 5.2, we shall see that this hypothesis *is* upheld pretty well, as we might expect from the aggregate analysis reported in the previous chapter. The largest capital-former, Housing & Community Amenities, was cut early and often and heavily, losing over 40 percent in real terms of its total budget over this period. The next largest in capital-intensive spending, Transport & Communication, was cut not early, but fairly massively, ending up second worst off overall. Education, with a relatively high share of capital spending, was also cut early and often and suffered an overall cut. Only Health among the significant capital-formers is also among the 'winners' overall. Conversely, Social Security, among the lowest in share of capital spending, is the highest overall gainer, and Defence and Public Order & Safety are also among the winners.

So there is much in the idea that in a period of cutbacks, spending programmes which have as a significant part of their purpose the formation of fixed capital – buildings, plant, roads, etc. – suffer the most. Taking all the fourteen programmes, for the period 1977 to 1985, the proportion of capital expenditure predicted the degree of budgetary cutbacks with a correlation coefficient of 0.71.[2] There seems to be a fairly clear warning for sponsors out to protect budgets from cutbacks: minimise the proportion of your initial budget devoted to capital spending.

What about programmes with 'open-ended commitments' (Hypothesis 44)? These are programmes which for one reason or another are not under government's day-to-day control: they are 'driven' more than others by market volatilities, or demography, or international agreement, or the like. These characteristics are perhaps shown most by 'Other' (debt interest), Social Security, and Agriculture. Our figures will not, of course, indicate what might have been spent under these heads if the government had tried less hard, or harder, to reduce its commitments; we can only report the outcome. Table 5.2 shows that of these

---

[2] However, there is an interesting twist: for the first two years of the period (1977–9), there is no relationship at all between proportion of capital spending and budgetary cuts ($r=0.05$), and then a very strong relationship for the following two years (1980–2: $r=0.78$, $p=0.0002$). This is difficult to interpret. It might have something to do with the Conservatives coming to power in 1979 (see above, Chapter 3. p. 76), or it might reflect the way that expenditure decisions change as retrenchment pressure deepens (a question we shall tackle in Chapter 7).

three programmes only Agriculture was cut early and often, but had massive swings in the opposite direction also; all grew considerably in real terms over the period, and increased their share of total spending. Being to some degree 'open-ended' in this way seems to have given some protection against cuts.

Hypothesis 45 is built on Klein's (1976) suggestion that the absolute size of a programme would be important. To make more than a marginal adjustment in the political objectives of a large programme, he argues, requires such a massive shift of resources as to be itself politically unthinkable. There is, on the other hand, a plausible argument that a cut of a sum which could be absorbed by a large programme in its stride might altogether cripple a small programme – and that this gives a degree of protection to the small programme. So we might equally well expect that large programmes will be cut lightly but often, while small programmes will either barely survive, or disappear. Perhaps Table 5.2 can settle the argument either way. There are five programmes that can be called 'large' (each more than 10 percent of the total): Social Security (more than a quarter of all public spending) well out in front, and then, all at a relatively similar level around half that, 'Other', Education, Defence, and Health. The two smallest programmes (leaving Fuel & Energy out of account for the reasons previously given) are Agriculture, etc., and Recreation & Culture, each between 1 percent and 2 percent of total spending. Above them comes a group of 'Economic' programmes, Mining, etc., Other Economic Affairs, and Transport, with around 2–3 percent of the total; Public Order & Safety is of the same order.

Table 5.2 shows that all but one of the largest programmes is above the line – a 'winner' in terms of our chapter title. But so are the two smallest programmes and one other of the small programmes named. So absolute size is a poor predictor of incidence of cuts. Only in the case of Education does the pattern of cuts match the suggestion that large programmes will be cut little and often. Of course, our figures do not show up 'cuts' which were reductions in growth that would otherwise have occurred. It is possible that the 'winners' would have been even greater winners if their estimates had not been pruned severely. But that applies to the large and the small.

A distinction which has become quite common in the administrative analysis literature is between programmes that obtain their ends by employing people to do things, and programmes that obtain their ends by moving money around: manpower-intensive (or bureaucrat-intensive) programmes, and cash-intensive programmes. We can measure this by using the Blue Book data on wages and salaries spending (a component of 'goods and services'), for bureaucrat-intensiveness; and that on expenditure on grants, loans, and subsidies, for cash-intensiveness. The hypothesis is that money-moving programmes will take the early brunt of cutback periods, since supposedly it is easier to 'switch money off' than to sack staff (Hypothesis 46). (There is an alternative hypothesis which we shall come to later.)

There are four programmes all heavy in wages/salaries spending: Public Order & Safety, with about three-quarters of all spending going on staff costs; General Public Services (Parliament, taxation, etc.) and Education, between 60 percent and 70 percent; and Health, just above half. All the others spend less than about 40 percent on staff costs. A number of programmes have heavy expenditure on grants, etc.: 'Other' highest, about 99 percent, followed by Social Security and Mining, etc. in the eighties percent, and (leaving Fuel & Energy out again) three around the 60 percent level: Agriculture, etc., Other Economic Affairs, and Housing. The others spend less than about 35 percent on grants, loans, subsidies, etc.

Did the money-movers get hit first and hardest? Table 5.2 shows that 'Other', the most cash-intensive programme, was not cut early – indeed, hardly cut at all (once, in 1983); Social Security not at all; and Mining, Minerals, Manufacturing, & Construction, third in this league, had large increases in three out of the early four years, though it suffered heavily thereafter. Agriculture, on the other hand, fits the prediction: it had cuts in three out of the early four years, though it did well thereafter and ended up a winner. Other Economic Affairs suffered early cuts, and ended up on the positive side in real terms though by the lowest margin. Housing, etc. also had cuts early and late, and was the worst overall loser. So: three fitting the prediction, and three not. We can score that round even.

The four bureaucrat-intensive programmes ought, according to the theory, to have escaped early cuts. From Table 5.2, we can see that Public Order & Safety indeed had only one cut, very late, and was second-best overall. General Public Services, too, avoided early cuts, though it did not in the end grow as fast as the overall total. Health had only one cut, and ended a winner. Once more, Education is the only programme in this group which does not conform to expectations. It has cuts early and late, and is an overall loser, over this period. Three out of four supporting the hypothesis this time: it does seem as if bureaucrat-intensiveness gave a degree of protection to programmes, so long as the programme was not Education.

Hypothesis 47 is based on an argument which is related to the 'visibility' of programme expenditure, and to their political 'clout'. This argument suggests that spending which has specific beneficiaries and tangible benefits will be better protected than spending which is 'for the good of all in general but no one in particular'. The archetypal 'public goods' programmes in this sense are Defence, and Public Order & Safety. Conversely, the 'specific' programmes are, first, the cash benefit services (Social Security), and (as Klein suggests) the primary and secondary sectors of Education, but not Higher Education; we might add, the Recreation part of Recreation & Culture, but not the Culture part; and similarly, some sectors of Health. Unfortunately, it is not easy on published figures to subdivide programmes in this way; so we shall have to let Social Security stand for the 'clear benefits' kind of programme.

According to the hypothesis, therefore, Defence and Public Order & Safety ought to show early cuts and overall losses, while Social Security gets off scot free. In fact, all the programmes mentioned in the previous paragraph – with the exception, once more, of Education – are 'winners'; the only one with an early cut is Defence (which *is* according to prediction), but that was only a small one, in the first year of the period. The hypothesis is a poor predictor of the outcome.

Hypothesis 48 related vulnerability in programme cutbacks to 'clarity' of budget. Budgets with only a few subheads, it might be argued, indicate clearer ties between demand and provision, more specific objectives, and more visible ways of achieving them. We investigated this possibility, but to do so, we had to go to the *Appropriation Accounts* for central government spending rather than the Blue Book; and because of a marked change in presentation of programme groupings in 1981, we had to calculate the relationship between number of subheads and overall fortunes for two periods separately: 1975–80, and 1981–4. There were 16 programmes in the earlier period, and 18 in the later; and the number of subheads ranged (leaving out Government Investment in Nationalised Industries with 3 or 4) from 33 to over 300. It is not worth presenting the data here; for what it is worth, the exercise showed that there *was* a positive relationship between number of subheads and cutbacks suffered in the first period (the more complex programmes were worst hit, by and large); but that no such trend was apparent in the later period.

Summing-up on programme vulnerability: we have looked at seven characteristics of spending programmes to see whether differences between programmes in each of these seven dimensions might predict or explain differences in programme fortunes in this period of cutbacks. At least three out of these seven dimensions did not appear to relate to programme vulnerability at all, and the hypotheses building on these dimensions (Hypotheses 42, 45, and 47) therefore look doubtful, on this evidence.

However, three of the dimensions (Hypotheses 43, 44, and 46) can be said to be related. We can say without qualification (Hypothesis 43) that there is a close correlation between proportion of expenditure devoted to gross domestic fixed capital formation and overall cuts or growth in a programme. There is some evidence (Hypothesis 44) that programmes which were 'driven' by some factor over which the government had incomplete control were *less* vulnerable to cutback, rather than more as is hypothesized, suffered fewer cuts, and grew overall by more than General Government as a whole did. Third, programmes whose own staff costs (wages, salaries, pensions, etc.) were a high proportion of their expenditure suffered fewer cuts and had overall growth, with the sole exception of Education. This conforms to Dunleavy's (1985) expectation that pressures for top administrators to defend or increase budgets will be greatest when what he calls the 'core budget' (wages, salaries, etc.) is a high proportion of the total budget. Why Education does not appear to fit the expected pattern is therefore a matter of some theoretical interest, and deserves further study.

II Bureaus under pressure

We now turn from the vulnerability of *programmes* to the vulnerability of *departments*. The budget of a *programme* can be spent by two or more different *departments*; the kind of programmes we have just been discussing could be participated in by different *spending authorities* (local government as well as central government). But in this section and the next, we concentrate upon the departments of central government only as the unit of analysis; and in practice, on a selection of those – 36 with a wide range of sizes, or the 24 largest in terms of staff numbers.

In the previous section, the analytical distinction we made in Chapter 4 between a 'Weberian' approach and an 'Adam Smith' self-interested approach became blurred. Programmes as such, one might think, having no organisational or personal embodiment (except in those cases like Defence where programme and department are pretty well coterminous), do not wield power, do not react, do not take up postures, do not engage in political in-fighting among themselves or even among their component parts or Votes; whereas departments are popularly thought to do all these things (given the normal licence to personify a collective).

Table 5.3. *Increase/decrease in generalist and specialist staff, selected departments, 1975 or 1976 to 1985*

Department	% generalist staff in 1975/6	% generalist staff in 1985	% change	Department	% specialist staff in 1975/6	% specialist staff in 1985	% change
C&E	92.2	90.5	-1.7	MOD	79.8	80.4	+0.6
ECGD*	90.3†	88.8	-1.5	HO*	77.7	78.6	+0.6
DE*	86.5	88.2	+1.7	IR*	66.6	65.3	-1.3
DNS	83.4	86.3	+2.8	DHSS*	59.4†	63.6	+4.2
LR*	82.5	83.9	+1.4	DOE	68.8	63.4	-5.4
OPCS	74.2†	81.4	+7.2	SO	56.8	61.8	+5.0
LCD*	70.2	74.8	+4.6	MAFF	53.9	55.6	+1.7
WO	65.8	69.2	+3.4	TCC	46.7	50.8	+4.1
DES	70.8	64.4	-6.4				
DEn	63.9	60.8	-3.1				
ODA	53.5	60.8	+7.3				
IND	58.3	60.0	+1.7				

Notes: * Neither continuously nor deeply cut in staff, 1975–85 (see Table 5.4 for definitions)
†1976
For key to departmental acronyms, see Table A1, Appendix I, or Index
Source: HM Treasury, 'MANDATE'

But this popular understanding is challengeable on at least two grounds. First, it may well be a *programme* rather than a department that gathers round it the sort of external support and pressure to which appeal can be made in times of cutback. Second, as Dunleavy points out (1985, 300), collective departmental behaviour is an aggregate whose outcome may be desired by no individual member, and also, even if there is a collective departmental interest, that interest may be neglected because of the usual 'free-rider' tendencies that are said to beset the provision of collective goods. It is therefore particularly important to look at the departmental level as well as the programme level and to ask: how will a self-interested bureau, bent on corporate survival in a harsh environment, react to the threat of cutbacks, in spending and staffing?

As we saw when reviewing theories of cutbacks in Chapter 2, the first ideas to explore are contained in Hypotheses 54–60. These build on the expectation that bureaus will 'protect the core' of their activities (whatever they consider that is) and throw the less essential elements to the wolves first. The first aspect of this is that if a department has more people in 'generalist' grades than it has in 'specialist' grades, for example, it will end up in a period of cutbacks with a higher proportion of generalists than it started with (Hypothesis 54); and *vice versa* – 'specialist-heavy' departments will get more specialist-heavy (Hypothesis 55).

We measured 'generalists' by adding together the Administration Group and the Secretarial Group for each department, and assumed that the remainder were 'specialists'. These data are not published in *Civil Service Statistics* and we do not have complete figures, but we amassed data for 20 large departments, although for 3 of them the initial date is 1976 rather than 1975. The figures are shown in Table 5.3. Twelve departments had more than half of their total non-industrial staff in generalist grades; eight had more than half in specialist grades. If the hypothesis is to hold, the twelve should increase their proportion of generalists and the eight should decrease it, between the initial date and 1985. In fact, eight out of the twelve generalist-heavy departments did increase their proportion of generalists, and six of the eight specialist-heavy departments increased their proportion of specialists. The hypotheses hold fairly well. It is true that some of these departments were cut in staff more heavily than others, and some were hardly cut at all; but if one removes from the lists those departments which were not much cut, the picture does not change very much: the generalist departments are reduced from twelve to eight, and of those eight, five showed a rise. The specialist-heavy departments drop from eight to five; and of the five, four show a rise. It is perhaps surprising that the degree of cutback seems not to be related to the direction or amount of change in the proportion either of generalist or of specialist staff over the period. If the hypotheses hold, it is because of a climate of (or the *threat* of) cutbacks, and not the actuality.

A broad non-statistical picture of actual 'winners and losers' among the 36 departments in our survey can be obtained from Table 5.4, in which departments are referred to by their initials: the reader needs to refer to Table A1 in Appendix I, or the Index at the end of the book, for the key. Table 5.4 shows which departments were cut in staff and in budget either continually or deeply, or both continually and deeply. 'Continually' is here taken to mean cuts in more than five years of the period. 'Deep' cuts in budget are taken to be an overall cut in real terms; a 'deep' cut in staff means a reduction of more than 15 percent over the period.

Bureaus, like programmes, can be divided into those which achieve their ends primarily by 'doing it themselves' (that is, their main costs are the salaries and wages of their own staffs – their 'core budget' is a high proportion of total budget), and those who 'move money around' (external spending, and especially external funding, is a high proportion, and salaries and wages a small proportion, of the total spending). Thus if departments protect their principal resources in times of cutbacks, the salary-heavy departments should get more so (Hypothesis 57), and the proportion of the money-movers' budget which goes on salaries should decrease (Hypothesis 56).

Out of the 36 departments in the survey, six allocated more than 90 percent of their total budget in 1975 to staffing costs; and in each case, by 1985 that proportion had gone down markedly (GA: 96 to 59; CC: 95 to 65; SRO: 94 to 59; CEO: 91 to 84; RFS: 91 to 57; PRO: 90 to 31: an average of 93 to one of 59). In spite of the pressures that Dunleavy's analysis might lead us to expect in defence of the budget, in circumstances where the core budget is as high a proportion of total budget as this, this group of departments was unsuccessful in protecting its core budget in these terms. As in the previous item, there appeared to be no relation between degree of cutback generally and depth of cut in the wages item: three offices cut neither continually nor deeply in staff went down by the same as another cut continually, and the only department of the six to be cut in staff both continually and deeply had by far the smallest drop in the allotment to salaries/wages (CEO). However, these six were all among the smaller departments, and so we looked at the five departments of over 1,000 staff with at least half of their total budgets allocated to wages and salaries: C&E (87 percent), IR (81 percent), LR (81 percent), OPCS (73 percent), and OS (65 percent). They too had gone down markedly by 1985, if not by quite as much on average: to 70, 66, 69, 54, and 52

Table 5.4. *Distribution of cutbacks among UK central government departments 1975–85: spending and staff cuts, frequency and severity*

Staff cuts	Spending cuts Neither continual* nor deep†			Continual*	Deep†	Both continual* and deep†
Neither continual* nor deep‡	DE DHSS HO GA IR	IBAP LR LCD OFT RFS	CC ROS TS		ECGD	
Continual Deep ‡	DES DEn PRO SRO	WO			SO	C&E
Both continual* and deep‡	TCC MOD FCO OPCS				PCO CEO RGS COI	DOE ODA DNS NIO IND OS MAFF

Notes: * Continual: year-on-year cut in more than five years
† Deep (spending): cut (real terms) over period as a whole (1975–84)
‡ Deep (staffing): cut by more than 15 % over period as a whole (1975–85)
For key to initials of departments, see Table A1, Appendix I, or Index
Sources: Spending: *Appropriation Accounts* (GDP deflator: 1980 = 100).
Staffing: *Civil Service Statistics*

respectively, or from an average of 77 to one of 62. Clearly, the hypothesis is not upheld. Once again, there was no relation between cutback in the wages item and cutback generally.

Large (<1,000) departments with a very small proportion (under 5 percent) of their budgets allocated to salaries and wages, the 'money-movers' in our terms, numbered seven: DES, DHSS, DOE, SO, WO, DEn, and ECGD. With one exception (the Scottish Office) these all maintained the same proportion in 1985 as in 1975, or decreased it, which this time *is* in accordance with the hypothesis. Again, there is no clear relationship between this and degree of cutback as shown by Table 5.4.

Another kind of 'principal resource' is the branch office network. The hypothesis is that departments with many 'high street' offices will try to protect that network even if total staff have to be cut (Hypothesis 58). We do not have data to test this directly, but a close surrogate is the number of staff spread throughout Great Britain (in all regions), rather than clustered in only one or two regions. As explained in Appendix II, we constructed a *concentration index* to summarise this: a high figure means that staff are concentrated and not dispersed, while a low figure signifies the opposite. DHSS, DE, and IR, as even the layman would expect, come out with the lowest index. These are the departments with which ordinary members of the public have most to do, and consequently they have the largest number of regional and local offices. (The next three in degree of dispersion are MAFF, LR, and LCD.)

Between 1976 and 1986 the indices for four out of six highly dispersed departments (including DHSS, DE, and IR) all went *down* (see Table A4), supporting the hypothesis that branch-office-heavy departments would protect this resource. The two exceptions were MAFF and LCD. However, five of these six were not actually heavily cut in either spending or staffing, suffering neither continual nor deep cuts. The exception was MAFF, which was hit both continually and deeply in both spending and staffing.

At the other end of the scale, the most concentrated departments are SO and WO, TCC, DEn, OPCS, and OS (to stop at the top six again). The three most concentrated departments have an index three and a half times that of the three most dispersed departments. Hypothesis 59 suggests that highly concentrated departments will stay highly concentrated. So what happened over the retrenchment period? Between 1976 and 1986 the concentration index of the six most concentrated departments went *up* in every case. Thus the hypothesis is upheld fairly clearly. And this time, all six suffered actual staff cuts, either continually or both continually and deeply. This finding would support the hypothesis that whatever 'fringe' there was in these departments *was* sacrificed to protect the core.

A final kind of principal resource is measured by the 'functional' breakdown of staff in a department. For some years, the Treasury published a 'functional analysis' of staff by department, indicating whether they were concerned with 'central administration' or 'executive functions'. 'Central administration' covered staff at headquarters dealing with policy and professional advice; 'executive functions' were further subdivided into 'public services' (delivering services of all kinds to the public, or to industry); 'trading and repayment services' (financially self-supporting services), and 'general support services' (common services for other departments).[3] Since some common services are increasingly provided on a 'user pays' principle, the distinction between the last two is

---

[3] *Civil Service Statistics*, 1973, p. 8. The full definitions, along with a table showing the percentage of staff in each category in each of 36 departments at 1 April 1980, can be found in Appendix III.

less and less clear, so we grouped them together. Thus departments can be listed according to their concentrations of staff in, respectively, central administration (or 'policy/parliamentary work'), public services (or 'service delivery'), and trading and repayment plus general support services (or 'trading and support'). The hypothesis is that bureaus with a high proportion of staff in one of these categories will regard that as a 'core' or 'base' to be protected, and that this proportion will go up (or at least not go down) during cutbacks (Hypothesis 60).

Unfortunately, the Treasury ceased publishing these figures in 1980/1. So we can use them to test the hypothesis only for the early cutback period, in the years 1975 to 1980.

Taking only the large (> 1,000) departments, six departments had more than 40 percent of their staffs in the Central Administration category in 1975: WO (91.7 percent), DES (69.7 percent), DEn (66.5 percent), TCC (46.9 percent), SO (45.3 percent), and ODA (41.5 percent). In 1980, five of these showed an increase over 1975 by between 1 and 2 percent; only the Welsh Office showed a fall (of 23 percent), which came about by a large increase in the total rather than a fall in numbers of Central Administration staff. So the hypothesis holds. However, only two of them had had cuts in staff in more than two years in the period, and none of them were deeply cut. (This information is not taken from Table 5.4, but from a similar table covering 1975–9.)

In the Public Services category, 12 large departments had over half their staffs so engaged in 1975, ranging from IR with 93.5 percent to FCO with 51.7 percent. Of these, only four showed an increase in this category by 1980 (including both the tax-collecting departments, highest in the list); and eight lost staff to other categories. So the expectation does not work for departments high in service delivery staff. Seven of the departments had not experienced either continual or deep cuts in the period.

Only four of the larger departments had as much as half of their staffs engaged in 1975 on 'trading and support' activities as we have defined that: LR (100 percent), DNS (94.3 percent), DOE (73.8 percent), and TCC (53.1 percent). (The next was IND at 29.4 percent.) Of these four, two had increased this proportion by 1980 (by between 3 and 4 percent), for one it was the same (100 percent), and for only one had it gone down (TCC, by 1.3 percent). The two which increased the proportion had done so in the face of severe cuts in staff or budget or both. So although the numbers are limited, so far as they go they support the hypothesis. It seems, therefore, that there may be something in the argument that, in hard times, bureaus try to protect their principal resource, as measured by the proportion of staff engaged in particular kinds of work. But, from these data it seems they either did not try so hard, or else did not succeed, in respect of service delivery, perhaps because service delivery staff not engaged in commercial-type activities are highly vulnerable to cutbacks in other ways.

But when the chips are down, or the gloves off, will not departmental *power* be used when it can be to preserve empires as far as possible? Just as in the case of bureaucrats generally, considered in the previous chapter, it may be argued that when departments are in the position of axemen, they will in the end wield the axe on others, and not on themselves. We suggested several propositions that ought to be true if that *is* the case.

The first was that the position of the Treasury (the arch axe-wielder) in a 'league table' of departments ranked either by staff numbers or by spending totals should improve (if everyone else is cut): it should climb up the table (Hypothesis 61). The tables we constructed showed that the position of the Treasury/Cabinet Office grouping worsened over the period in staffing: it dropped from fourteenth place to fifteenth. On the other hand, in budget, it did improve, rising from sixteenth place in 1975 to eleventh in 1984 (the last figure available from the *Appropriation Accounts*). There might well be explanations other than power-wielding for this outcome; but the outcome is nevertheless consistent with what Hypothesis 61 would expect.

The second proposition was that the larger departments would improve their position *vis-à-vis* the smaller departments (Hypothesis 62). Table 5.5 shows some figures. If we took 'larger' to refer only to the 'giants', then there are only three departments that could come into that category in spending terms: DOE, DHSS, and MOD; and four, in staffing terms: MOD, DOE, and DHSS again, with IR. And indeed, two out of three of the giants improved their budget-share position, and two out of four improved staff-share position, DOE losing out each time, while MOD gained in budget share but lost in staff share. If we extend 'larger' to mean, say, the 'top eight or nine' in each ranking (cut-off being 2 percent of the total in 1975), then of the eight biggest spenders four had declined in share of total spending by 1984; of the nine big employers four had declined in share of total staffing by 1985. Some won, some lost. Hypothesis 62 is not upheld.

Thirdly: since central government holds the whip hand, its own share of total General Government expenditure will rise in a period of cutbacks (Hypothesis 63). 'General Government' is not merely the sum of central government spending and local government spending, because transfers between the two spending authorities are removed. Table 4.5 showed

Table 5.5. *Nineteen departments ranked by percentage share of total government budget and staff in 1975 and 1984/5*

Depart-ment	% total government budget in			Depart-ment	% total government staff in		
	1975	1984	Change		1975	1985	Change
DOE	29.61	16.03	−13.58	MOD	38.40	31.53	−6.87
DHSS	22.70	34.23	+11.53	DHSS	12.50	15.10	+2.60
MOD	14.73	16.86	+ 2.13	IR	10.59	11.17	+0.58
IND	7.66	2.49	− 5.17	DOE	10.04	7.67	−2.37
SO	5.63	5.15	− 0.48	DE	5.33	8.69	+3.36
DES	3.45	4.00	+ 0.55	HO	4.36	5.90	+1.54
HO	2.86	3.37	+ 0.51	C&E	3.91	4.12	+0.21
MAFF	2.12	0.58	− 1.54	IND	2.58	2.01	−0.57
DEn	1.84	2.41	+ 0.57	MAFF	2.19	1.81	−0.38
DE	1.61	2.74	+ 1.13	DNS	1.95	1.27	−0.68
ECGD	1.57	1.32	− 0.25	FCO	1.48	1.33	−2.81
NIO	1.36	1.27	− 0.09	LCD	1.46	1.63	+0.17
ODA	1.33	1.14	− 0.19	SO	1.45	1.59	+0.14
WO	1.17	2.17	+ 1.00	TCC	1.12	0.94	−0.18
IR	0.90	0.92	+ 0.02	LR	0.65	1.10	+0.45
TCC	0.75	1.40	+ 0.65	OS	0.65	0.48	−0.17
FCO	0.48	0.60	+ 0.12	DES	0.42	0.40	−0.02
IBAP	0.42	0.50	+ 0.08	OPCS	0.40	0.34	−0.06
C&E	0.37	0.34	− 0.03	ODA	0.33	0.25	−0.08

Note: For key to departmental initials, see Table A1, Appendix I, or Index
Source: Budget: *Appropriation Accounts.* Staff: *Civil Service Statistics*

that central government current and capital expenditure took a gradually increasing share of General Government current and capital expenditure as the retrenchment period went on. So this expectation is fulfilled.

And finally: the assumption is that government will 'save jobs' as much as possible in a period of retrenchment by doing more 'in house' and contracting out less; in particular, that as between intramural and extramural research and development work, the intramural will increase at the expense of the extramural (Hypothesis 64). The Central Statistical Office journal *Economic Trends* regularly publishes figures of expenditure on R & D, with its own deflator. From the August 1986 issue we can learn that between 1975 and 1985 intramural R & D varied between £528m and £604m at constant prices, but in the last year was at almost the same level as it had been in the first (1975, £574m; 1985, £571m). Extramural research varied between £949m and £1,187m, but showed a steady upward trend, with a rise of 23.9 percent between 1975

(£958m) and 1985 (£1,187m), at constant prices. So there is nothing at all in that theory.

By and large, however, the somewhat more cynical approach of this section, seeing bureaus as opportunistic and self-regarding, has done quite well in its predictions. Generalist-heavy bureaus protected their principal resources against the specialists, and specialist-heavy bureaus against the generalists. Although salary-heavy bureaus did not get more salary-heavy, but became less so, money-movers got more money-moving, as predicted. Bureaus with many branch offices held on to that base, and those who began very concentrated got more concentrated. Bureaus which were heavily policy- and advice-oriented increased their proportions of policy and advisory staff, and those which were commercially oriented increased their proportions of commercial staff. The Treasury and Cabinet Office *did* improve their relative position in the spending league (though not in staffing). Central government did take up a larger and larger share of total government spending at the expense of other spending authorities. Quite a number of things happened 'just as you would expect', if you go along with much of the cutbacks literature.

Of course, a large amount of variance was not explained by these hypotheses. But we cannot say that the popular conventional wisdom about the reactions of bureaus under pressure is wrong, save in one or two instances: departments with a high 'core budget' in Dunleavy's terms (spending a large proportion of their budgets on salaries) did not succeed in protecting that core resource; large departments did not noticeably squeeze out small departments, and intramural R & D was not saved by squeezing out extramural R & D.

Now we shall turn to a different approach to understanding how departments fare during cutbacks: not so much how they react, as how they are treated. Are some bureaus more vulnerable than others because of characteristics they can do nothing about?

III   Departmental vulnerability

The idea to be explored in this section is that for public bureaucracies cutback outcomes are shaped by factors other than ideology or party politics in the broadest sense, other than 'trends', other than 'bureaucratic politics' or the predilections of bureaucrats 'Weberian' or 'Adam Smith', other than the self-interested *sauve qui peut* reactions of bureaus under threat. Rather, the factors which determine vulnerability may lie in the nature of the department itself and its ways of working. The argument goes that demands for 'savings' in spending programmes, or in staffing, have to be 'operationalised' or translated into concrete measures which alter what certain bureaucrats do; and such implementation is not only itself pre-eminently a bureaucratic process, subject to the special knowledge as well as the predilections of bureaucrats, but it will inevitably take into account the characteristics of individual bureaucracies and their production processes, and perhaps require more 'savings' from one than from another accordingly.

There is a common-sense plausibility about such ideas. They certainly surface among those affected in any institution subject to cutbacks, be it a government department, a university, a hospital, or whatever: the plea is heard that *we* should not be cut back so much as *them*, because of this or that special characteristic of our processes. This is developed to some degree in the literature on cutback management (see, for instance, Levine 1978; Wildavsky 1980; Hood and Wright 1981).

Now if it is held to be something about the nature of what a department does and how it does it which makes it either 'wide open' to cutbacks or impregnable to attack, whatever party is in government, we might expect a consistency of fortune from one era of cutbacks to another, with the same departments suffering the most whenever the pressure for cutbacks rises. Table 3.7 earlier suggested that there may be some such effect for the 1970s and 1980s, and Table 5.6 offers more information on this point by comparing the fates of 14 UK government departments in terms of staff changes, in two widely separated eras of retrenchment: 1921–31 and 1975–85. As can be seen, in something over half the cases there is indeed some consistency of fate in two decades half a century apart.

On this evidence, nonetheless, the fate of a department in the 1920s is a far from infallible predictor of its destiny in the 1970s/1980s, or *vice versa*: if you used previous fate as the only predictor, you would be wrong nearly half the time, and in that sense tossing a coin would be nearly as good. For the six cases in category (2) of Table 5.6, something obviously happened in the intervening fifty years to alter their vulnerability to staff cutbacks.

Obviously, that 'something' could be a change in production methods or activities; and in any case, there is sufficient consistency of fortune to suggest that bureaucratic-process factors may be playing some part in these outcomes. What might these factors be? The literature on cutback management makes several kinds of suggestion on this point, but as we have already remarked, it has a propensity to produce catch-all lists, rather than to identify a few key factors which will predict outcomes.

Table 5.6. *Percent change in staffing totals, 14 departments 1921–31 and 1975–85*

Department	1921–31	1975–85
(1) Consistent winners (4)		
Land Registry	+ 97.5	+49.9
Ministry of Labour/Department of Employment	+180.3	+45.7
Home Office	+ 10.7	+20.8
Ministry of Health/Dept of Health and Social Security	+ 4.9	+ 7.9
(2) Win some, lose some (6)		
Scottish Office	+ 13.1	− 2.0
Inland Revenue	+ 90.1	− 5.8
Customs and Excise	+ 34.1	− 5.9
Board of Education/Department of Education and Science	+ 18.6	−13.9
HM Treasury/Treasury, Cabinet Office, Civil Service Department	+ 9.4	−24.5
Registrar-General, England/Office of Population Censuses and Surveys	+ 51.2	−25.5
(3) Consistent losers (4)		
Foreign Office/Foreign and Commonwealth Office	− 7.2	−19.6
Ministry of Agriculture, Fisheries, and Food	− 4.7	−26.2
Board of Trade/Department of Trade and Industry	− 39.1	−30.3
Ordnance Survey	− 27.6	−34.7

Note: Departmental titles and boundaries have changed considerably over the period dealt with here; figures have been constructed by taking the nearest equivalents for the earlier period of the 1975–85 departments
Source: Annual Budget Estimates

Moreover, as already noted, much of this writing mirrors general discussions of the sources of bureaucratic power (e.g., Rourke 1976) to such an extent that it raises Occam's Razor doubts as to whether there is anything special about cutbacks, requiring a theory of their own.

The Treasury's 'functional analysis' of the proportions of staff engaged in different kinds of work, introduced in the previous section, clearly provides material relating to differences between departments in what they do and how they do it. Staff of central government departments are apportioned to categories according to whether they are deemed to be engaged in 'central administration' or 'executive functions', and if the latter, whether in 'public services', 'trading and repayment services', or 'general support services'.[4] As explained earlier, because of the broad overlap between these two functions as compared with either 'central administration' or 'public services' functions, we found it convenient for

[4] For definitions and figures, see Appendix III.

present purposes to aggregate them under the label 'trading and support services', so as to produce only three categories.

Nine departments then were found to have had in 1980 more than half of their staff engaged in 'central administration': NIO, CC, ECGD, and PCO (all 100 percent); FCO and DES (over 70 percent); WO, OFT, and DEn (over 68 percent). Fifteen departments had more than half of their staff engaged in 'public services': SRO (100 percent), IR, C&E, DHSS, LCD, and RGS (over 90 percent); DE and HO (80–90 percent); OS, MAFF, PRO, RFS (70–80 percent); IBAP, ODA, and SO (50–70 percent). Nine departments had over half their staff in 'trading and support': LR, CEO, GA, and ROS (100 percent); DNS (98 percent); COI (81 percent); DOE and TS (70–80 percent), and TCC (52 percent). Two departments did not have as much as half their staff in any category, though the largest strength in each case was in 'public services' – IND and OPCS. The information is not given for MOD.

We tested whether the proportion of staff in these 'functional' categories bore any relation to the incidence of cutbacks among departments, as conveniently displayed in Table 5.4. But no pattern emerged. Table 5.4, however, covers the whole decade; another version covering the two four-year periods 1975–9 and 1980–4 was prepared. Using the second of these, it appeared that the twelve 'administration' function departments, although cut in staff in varying degrees, with one exception fell in the first column on budget cuts – cut neither continually nor deeply, by our definitions. However, eight of the fourteen 'public-service' and seven of the ten 'trading and support' departments did so also, so no very clear conclusions can be drawn.

Since it was possible that the very small departments (<1,000 staff) might be distorting the picture by being counted equally with the giants, we omitted them from the analysis. We then constructed a third version of Table 5.4 (distribution of departments by how heavily they were cut in staffing and spending) covering 1980–4 only, for the 23 departments with over 1,000 staff, using a three-by-three matrix because no department was cut deeply in those years without also being cut continually, by our definitions. The result is seen in Table 5.7.

Some interesting features emerged. None of the departments which were least heavily cut in staffing or spending, or of those which were most heavily cut in both (the top left corner and the bottom right corner) were 'central administration' by functional analysis. All of the 'central administration-heavy' departments are found in the 'continually but not deeply' category of staffing cuts, and only one suffered significantly in budget (continual, but not deep, cuts). With one exception (LR), all the

Table 5.7. *Distribution of cutbacks among 23 UK central government departments with over 1,000 staff, 1980–4: spending and staff cuts, frequency and severity; and functional category*

Staff cuts	Spending cuts Neither continual* nor deep†		Continual*		Both continual* and deep†	
Neither continual* nor deep‡	DE HO LR LCD	P P T P				
Continual*	C&E DES DEn DHSS ECGD FCO IR	P A A P A A P	ODA SO WO	P P A	MAFF	P
Both continual* and deep‡	TCC MOD OPCS COI	T — P T	OS	P	DOE DNS IND	T T P

Notes: * Continual: year-on-year cut in at least three years
† Deep (spending): cut (real terms) of at least 15 percent over period
‡ Deep (staffing): cut by more than 15 percent over period as a whole
A = highest proportion of staff is in 'central administration'
P = highest proportion of staff is in 'public service'
T = highest proportion of staff is in 'trading and support'
For key to initials of departments, see Table A1, Appendix I, or Index
Sources: Spending: *Appropriation Accounts* (GDP deflator: 1980 = 100).
Staffing: *Civil Service Statistics*

'trading and support' functional departments were continually and deeply cut in staff, two of them in spending also. On the other hand, 'public-service' departments appear in every inhabited segment of the matrix.

It would seem, first, that in spite of the popular stereotype discussed in Chapter 4 that 'top people', and generalists, will 'look after Number One', they did not succeed in protecting themselves from cutback in these years. All of the departments heavy in 'central administration' or policy staff fell into an intermediate band of 'suffering': they were neither the least cut in staff, nor the most – they were (by our definitions) cut continually, but not deeply. On the other hand, all of them save one were among the least cut financially. Being policy-heavy apparently exposes a department to taking a significant share of staff cuts but offers some protection against cuts in budget.

The pattern for 'public-service'-dominated departments is not so clear. Half of them escaped significant cuts in budget, whereas only three out of twelve avoided significant cuts in staff. But there is little warrant for holding that being notably 'public service' in orientation made a department particularly vulnerable.

The clearest finding is that those whose staffing suffered in this period most heavily as a group (with the exception of LR) were the departments predominantly engaged in trading and support services; TCC (in this category because of its computer and catering arms), COI, DOE, and DNS. Having to 'earn your living' from other bureaucracies or in competition with alternative non-bureaucratic suppliers, as distinct from delivering a service to the public or being concerned with the formation of policy or advice to Ministers, apparently left you particularly vulnerable to cuts in resources not so earned.

We introduced in Chapter 2 the sophisticated model developed by Beck Jørgensen, identifying three dimensions of bureaucratic vulnerability. He is, however, operating mainly at what we in Chapter 1 called the 'meso-' and 'micro-' levels, and we accept responsibility for our adaptation of his model to the 'macro-' level.

The three dimensions are as follows (in our own terminology):

A *invisibility* – the probability of being identified as a potential target for cutbacks

B *output effects vulnerability* – the extent to which cutbacks if imposed will cause immediate and publicly visible damage to the public services produced by the bureaucracy in question

C *political 'clout'* – the ability to mount effective resistance to cutbacks if proposed.

We looked at the 24 UK government departments with staff numbers over 1,000, and at the 12 next largest, over the period 1975–85 to see if 'suffering' under cutbacks could be related to these ideas.

A

Invisibility refers to the ease with which central allocators of manpower and spending budgets can 'see' a bureau, when looking for targets for cutbacks. One factor that clearly plays a part here is the extent to which a department finances its budget from fees and charges rather than drawing on general tax funds. It is suggested that budgets which do not require large lump-sum grants from an overstrained general tax fund will be relatively 'invisible' to budgetary allocators, even though a 'rational-comprehensive' approach to retrenchment would imply equally rigid scrutiny of all types of public expenditure, however financed (Hypothesis 49).

The picture turns out to be much more complicated than that. For the period 1975–85, in respect of the 24 departments with more than 1,000 staff, there is no significant relationship between the proportion of 1975 budget financed from fees and charges and either spending or staffing cutbacks. The relationship is very slightly stronger during the Labour government period of 1975–9 than during the Conservative government period 1980–4, but still does not amount to much. However, the importance of self-financing in relation to staffing cuts is clearly higher for smaller departments (12 departments with fewer than 1,000 staff): there the correlation coefficient between staffing cuts and self-financing for the whole period is 0.84. Being heavily self-financing confers some protection against staff cuts, if you are also small. Beck Jørgensen is to some extent vindicated (as is the hypothesis), though not precisely as predicted.

For 9 of the 36 departments fees, charges, and other income accounted for more than 30 percent of their 1975 expenditure: by their initials (see Table A1 in Appendix I for the key), ROS, IBAP, OFT, DNS, MAFF, GA, OS, LR, and LCD. In Table 5.4 (see the previous section) they fall into two very distinct groups: three of them were cut *both* continually and deeply, and six of them were cut neither continually nor deeply – and all four of the small departments among the nine (ROS, IBAP, OFT, and GA, <1,000 staff) are among the six which suffered least. This is in line with the regression analysis.

'Invisible' departments, if cut, might nevertheless be cut *later* than more 'visible' bureaus. Here the nine highly self-financing departments show no such grouping: the relative 'invisibility' of the small self-financing departments did not protect two of them from being 'seen' in the first year of the period, and the other two in the second – though it may have mitigated the frequency and scale of the cuts imposed.

It might be supposed that departmental *size* might iself be related to visibility and hence to vulnerability, as, for example, Levine (1978) seems to suggest, though he does not say so explicitly. But we found no relationship between absolute size, of either staff or of budget, and the degree of budgetary or staff cutbacks in an examination of 36 departments varying enormously in size. Neither large nor small absolute size will necessarily make you invisible by itself, it seems.

Beck Jørgensen suggests that another factor in visibility may be the *complexity* of a department's budget (complex budgets are harder for budget allocators to take in, more 'opaque' than simple budgets). This relates to Beck Jørgensen's general argument that the more 'transparent' a department's structure and production functions are, the more difficult it will be to conceal organisational slack or reserves. Complexity confers protection (Hypothesis 50). As against this, Klein (1976) suggests that more resources will go to services which can mobilise support because they offer clear benefits to specific groups; *clarity* in that sense confers protection. Can we shed light on this?

If complexity is measured by the average number of subheads per Vote in each department's budget (which produces a range between 1 and 24 and minimises any 'size effect'), there turns out to be indeed a slight positive relationship between complexity and budgetary cutbacks ($r=0.31$), and a stronger one between complexity and staff change ($r=0.51$). Perhaps a more subtle measure of complexity might bring out this relationship more sharply; but this evidence would hardly warrant advice to bureau chiefs to aim consciously at either complexity or simplicity as a counter-cutback tactic. Thus, focussing on the fates of some individual departments shows how unreliable is complexity in this sense as a protection against cutbacks. The nine most complex departments, with an average of 12 or more subheads per Vote, were: MAFF, ODA, FCO, SO, NIO, ECGD, DHSS, DE, and DEn. From Table 5.4 their cutback fortunes can be traced: three of them were cut both continually and deeply in both spending and staffing (MAFF, NIO, ODA); three of them were cut deeply in either spending or staffing, (FCO, ECGD, SO); and the three which were not cut deeply in either are the least complex of the nine (DHSS, DE, DEn).

At the other end of the scale, eight small (<1,000) departments are the least complex, as one might expect, and of these, five are found among the least cut in budget and staff. Of the four least complex larger departments (IR, LCD, LR, OS: <1,000, four or fewer subheads), three are among the least cut, but OS was 'quadruply hit' – continually and deeply cut in both budget and staff. On either assessment Klein seems to be more supported than Beck Jørgensen. Complexity confers dubious protection against the axemen and may even increase vulnerability.

These two measures of 'visibility', self-financing and complexity, show no greater relationship with budget or staff cutbacks when taken together than when taken separately – $r = 0.38/0.29$ for the decade as a whole, though again there is an interesting difference between the earlier and later periods: 1975–9, 0.45 and 0.38; 1980–4, 0.18 and 0.13.[5] As suggested in Chapter 2, 'visibility' may have a party-political aspect: when looking for candidates for cutbacks, governments may not 'see' certain services dear to their political hearts, and may scrutinise with particular care those that are dear to their opponents. But here the answer probably is that in the 'IMF' period of Labour retrenchment cuts were less discriminate and less selective.

B

'*Output effects vulnerability*', or *operational vulnerability*, meant for Beck Jørgensen a situation where, paradoxically, the more vulnerable a bureaucratic process is, the more protection it gives from cutbacks. If your technology or other circumstances are such that even small cuts in inputs have an immediate and highly disproportionate effect on outputs, axemen will hesitate to make those cuts. As noted in Chapter 2, we did not find ways to test this with our data. But another type of output-effect vulnerability, almost the opposite, was testable: what we call 'seed-corn activities' (research, staff training, plant maintenance, and the like) can very often be postponed simply because there is *no* immediate effect on output. A department where 'seed-corn activities' form a large proportion of the budget may be thought more vulnerable to cuts than others.

One measure of this is the proportion of departmental spending devoted to research and development (Hypothesis 51). For the 24 larger departments in the survey, there is some sign of a negative relationship between R & D spending in 1975 and the degree of budgetary and staff cutbacks, but it is a very weak one ($r = 0.28/0.22$). Eyeballing the data for individual departments shows that only 12 departments spent as much as 1 percent on research and development; of the seven that spent more than that, DES led easily with 22 percent, then IND (18 percent), DEn (14 percent), MOD (11 percent), MAFF (4 percent), and ODA and OPCS on just 2 percent. If we turn to Table 5.4 again, we can see that the relationship would be somewhat stronger if we left out DES (which carries all the state research councils on its budget); then five of the remaining six would be found to have been cut both continually and deeply in staff, and three of them in spending as well. R & D spending does apparently make you vulnerable to staff cuts, on this way of looking at it.

---

[5] Here, as elsewhere, where two correlation coefficients are given together, the first refers to the budget-change variable, the second to the staff-change variable.

Another 'seed-corn' measure is the proportion of departmental spending which goes on capital as opposed to current expenditure. Unfortunately, the only available data about capital spending relate to programmes for General Government, rather than central departments, and we have already discussed programme vulnerability in section 1 above, where we found a strong relationship between proportion of budget going on capital formation and incidence of cutbacks. There seems little doubt that the same effect would be found for departments if the figures were available.

A different dimension of output-effects vulnerability concerns departments whose activities are particularly suitable for hiving off or contracting out. We hypothesised that departments with a high proportion of total staff in blue-collar or lower clerical grades would answer that description, since hiving off and contracting out (as well as automation) tend to concentrate on routine functions, and would therefore be vulnerable to staff cuts (Hypothesis 52). But in fact, there is no relationship at all between the proportion of lower clerical grade staff and overall staff cuts, whether for the 24 larger or the 12 smaller departments, and only the weakest of relationships between the proportion of blue-collar staff and overall staff cutbacks ($r = 0.21$ for the 24, 0.20 for the 36).

Regressing budget change and staff change on all these 'output' variables taken together shows a fairly weak relationship overall ($r = 0.39$ and 0.30) for the decade as a whole. But as we noted in Chapter 2, Beck Jørgensen's ideas on operational vulnerability, as with visibility, are extremely rich and intuitively fruitful. More refined and in-depth study than we can offer – probably involving an interview programme – would be required to test these ideas fully.

C

Clout. One of the characteristics conferring a degree of protection against the axeman, Beck Jørgensen suggested, was 'allocational vulnerability', or what we are calling 'political clout'; and we hypothesised earlier that, if there is anything in this theory, there ought to be a difference in the fates of each 'half' of the Department of Health and Social Security, as it then was, since the Health part would appear to meet the conditions of having 'clout', while the Social Security part exhibits the marks of the 'political weakling' (Hypothesis 53). But although there *is* a marked difference, it is in the opposite sense to that hypothesised: the health services (including local authority personal social services) decreased their share of total DHSS spending between 1975 and 1984 from 54.4

percent to 40.4 percent, while the social security services increased their share from 40.7 percent to 55.7 percent; in real terms (1980 = 100) spending on health went up from £9,179.2m to £10,766.8m, an increase of 17.3 percent, while spending on social security went up from £6,860.6m to £14,846.4m, an increase of 116.4 percent, nearly seven times as much.

Clout is something of a puzzle in other ways, in that received notions of clout either do not predict retrenchment outcomes at all in our data, or predict the reverse of what might have been supposed. For instance, Levine (1978) associates frequent changes in leadership with political vulnerability. But we found no relationship between staffing and spending outcomes and the number of changes of permanent head in our departments. That does not necessarily disprove Levine's theory, since he might have had in mind political chiefs rather than top bureaucrats. And there is indeed a relationship between number of changes of *political* head in a group of 17 departments and staff reductions ($r = 0.55$). But the relationship is the opposite of what Levine might expect – namely, that the more changes of political leadership a department has had, the *lower* its staff cuts will tend to be. Economics-of-bureaucracy theorists might perhaps interpret this finding in learning-curve terms: short-service political chiefs are not there long enough to understand the bureaucracy's production function, but more stable political leadership has time to do so and hence learns how to overcome bureaucratic resistance to cutbacks. It clearly needs more investigation.

Equally puzzling is the failure of other plausible or commonly accepted ideas about the political/bureaucratic power game to serve as predictors of retrenchment outcomes. Four negative findings of our study deserve brief mention.

First, conventional wisdom (e.g., Heclo and Wildavsky 1974) holds that spending Ministers 'fight their corner' in Cabinet to defend their departments' interests and to resist Treasury pressures for cutbacks. We might therefore suppose that departments headed by a Cabinet Minister would do better in budgetary terms (at least) than departments headed by a non-Cabinet Minister. But there was in fact a slight negative relationship between Cabinet status and budgetary outcomes ($r = -0.37$), suggesting that the conventional wisdom is either wrong or out of date.

Second, as suggested in Chapter 2, the nature of the political decision process over spending cuts might be expected to benefit departments whose interests were closely related to those of other departments. Where two (or more) departments share a programme, the Ministers concerned would seem to have a common interest in supporting each other's departmental budget (a form of log-rolling). One would, therefore, expect that the departments with the highest degree of 'interconnectedness' with other departments, through shared programmes, would benefit most from log-rolling in this way. There is in fact some evidence for a link between budgetary allocations and the number of other departments with which a department was budget-linked, but the relationship is rather weak ($r=0.25$).

Third, there is no evidence for the risk-spreading 'portfolio effect' mentioned earlier. We expected that if a department has many distinct programmes, some of them will be 'glamour stocks' whatever party is in power, and pressure-group support will also be well spread; compared to the bureau with but one programme, the balanced-portfolio department ought to fare better in a period of cutbacks. Elegant as this theory might appear, it has no predictive power on our evidence. There is no relationship between budgetary outcomes and the number of different programmes contained within each department's budget (either absolutely or standardised for size).

Finally, we thought that a department which distributes a large proportion of its budget in payments to outside groups would maximise political clout, compared with the department whose budget comprised mainly salaries for its own staff. If there is anything in the logic of the political game as usually analysed, screams from disaffected groups outside government will sound louder than those of civil servants. But in our data there is simply no relationship at all between budgetary outcomes and the proportion of budget devoted to staff salaries.

It would appear that the machinations of 'political clout' operate more subtly than any of these four hypotheses suggest, or that we need different and more sophisticated measures to show it up.

Staff change regressed on all three 'clout' variables together (programme links, portfolio, and Cabinet status) shows no strong relationship ($r=0.20$). With budget change the relationship is more significant: $r=0.55$, considerably better than either collective 'visibility' (0.38) or collective 'output effects' (0.39).

On the indicators used here, taken *privatim et seriatim*, we have not scored many successes in the attempt to explain differential departmental vulnerability to cuts in budget and in staffing. Only in one item (degree of self-financing among small departments) was a really significant relationship found between the departmental characteristic and the extent of cuts ($r=0.84$). Even multiple regressions, taking each of the three departmental vulnerability dimensions as a separate group, produced only one correlation coefficient of more than 0.5. That is 'clout': a department with a small portfolio of programmes and low Cabinet status will still do well in budget cutbacks if it has a lot of programme linkages with other departments ($r=0.55$), and this may reflect the scope for successful log-rolling by spending Ministers in the Cabinet.

However, a multiple regression linking departmental budget and staffing cutbacks to ten bureaucratic-process indicators (two of which will be discussed only in succeeding chapters) suggests that those indicators may be more powerful when taken together, fighting back to back as it were, than they are when taken separately (see Table 5.8). Such a regression produced an r of 0.82 for budget change and 0.68 for staff change. This suggests that, for budget cuts, two-thirds of the variance can be explained by the bureaucratic process factors considered ($r^2=0.66$), although taken separately none of them had such high predictive capacity.

For staff cutbacks, the ten bureaucratic process factors are evidently less powerful even when taken together. Jointly they account for slightly less than half of the variance ($r^2=0.46$), and thus have little, if any, more predictive power than some of the party-political, trend, and bureaucratic politics variables we have discussed in earlier chapters.

IV Conclusions

In this chapter, we have tested a range of both 'popular' and 'scholarly' theories purporting to predict which departments and programmes will be most vulnerable to cutbacks (Hypotheses 42–64). On the hypotheses tested here, the 'scholarly' theories do not clearly do better than the popular ones in predicting vulnerability, in contrast to what we found for bureaucratic behaviour at the aggregate level in the previous chapter.

Out of the seven hypotheses tested for programme vulnerability (Hypotheses 42–8), three had some predictive power, three had none, and one was ambiguous. Out of the sixteen hypotheses tested for departmental vulnerability, seven were upheld (Nos. 51, 54, 55, 59, 60, 61, and 63), and six of those were related to the view of departments as collectivities following strategies to protect their self-interest – protecting the areas where their principal resources are concentrated and bringing down the axe on other departments and units of government. Another two of the sixteen hypotheses (Nos. 49 and 58) produced sufficiently ambiguous results in the test to suggest that testing with more refined

Table 5.8. *Correlation coefficients (r), change in budget 1975–84 and change in staffing 1975–85 with visibility, output, and clout variables: 24 departments*

Variables	Budget change			Staffing change		
	1975–84	1975–9	1980–4	1975–85	1975–9	1980–4
Visibility variables						
Self-financing	0.14	0.34	0.13	0.21	0.36	0.12
Complexity	0.31	0.19	0.09	0.51	0.03	~0
Output variables						
%Research and Development	0.20	0.15	0.05	0.22	0.19	0.21
%Lower clerical	0.13	0.04	0.08	0.08	0.09	0.25
%Blue-collar	0.08	0.03	0.08	0.21	0.13	0.29
%Public-service staff	0.04	0.14	0.24	0.05	0.03	0.33
%Staff reduction by increased efficiency	0.15	0.19	0.11	0.21	~0	0.42
Clout variables						
Budget-linking	0.12	~0	~0	0.18	0.15	~0
Portfolio	0.09	~0	0.14	0.16	0.28	0.14
Cabinet	0.37	0.34	0.14	0.08	0.08	0.14
Multiple regressions						
Self-financing } Complexity	0.38	0.45	0.18	0.29	0.38	0.13
%Research and development %Lower clerical %Blue-collar %Public service staff %Staff reduction by increased efficiency	0.39	0.41	0.32	0.30	0.33	0.53
Budget linking Portfolio Cabinet	0.55	0.35	0.29	0.20	0.28	0.30

Full model using all variables – parameters estimates

	Dependent variable	
	Budget change 1975–84	Staff change 1975–85
Constant	230.00	47.30
Self-financing	−0.31	−0.50
Complexity	−3.76	−2.48
%R & D	−4.70	−1.79
%Lower clerical	−0.69	0.04
%Blue-collar	−3.78	−2.26
%Public service staff	−0.26	−0.14
%Staff reduction by increased efficiency	−0.21	0.67
Budget linking	1.23	−0.62
Portfolio	−2.87	8.48
Cabinet	−25.93	−8.09
	r=0.82	0.68

Sources: Budget change: *Appropriation Accounts*. Staff change: *Civil Service Yearbook*

data or a variant of the hypothesis might uphold them, and one (No. 53) showed a relationship the reverse of that predicted. That leaves six out of the sixteen hypotheses (Nos. 50, 52, 56, 57, 62, and 64) which did not predict cutbacks – and even then, as we have seen, the factors identified under Hypotheses 40–53 seem to have some predictive power when taken together, indicating that some refinement might be worth while.

Outside formal hypotheses, we have examined the relationship between incidence of cutbacks and the tasks and methods of departments (as measured by 'functional analysis' and by scoring for visibility, output effects, and political clout). We had moderately interesting results from the functional analysis: two categories out of three seemed to show definite relationships. On the other bureaucratic-process indicators there were clear relationships only in two items, although taking all the indicators together rather than singly showed a significant result.

All this suggests that vulnerability to cutbacks is by no means a random or 'Act of God' process, but that it can be predicted to some degree by reference to aggregate statistical profiles of departments and programmes. Testing such as this shows the lines which seem worth developing in 'vulnerability theory', by theoretical refinement, or by more sophisticated testing. In particular, Beck Jørgensen's hypotheses are elegant and interesting, and seem to cry out for such development. The theory that high scores on invisibility, output effects vulnerability, and political clout will protect an agency from cutbacks, whereas agencies with low scores on each of these dimensions will be more defenceless against the axemen, has survived this investigation well enough to fight another day.

That concludes our discussions of 'winners and losers' in the cutbacks period 1975–85. Now, in the next chapter, we focus on cutbacks in staffing, and consider in detail how these were achieved.

6 The tactics of shedding staff

In this chapter, we turn from a general discussion of 'winners and losers' in the cutbacks period 1975–85 to focus more closely on cutbacks in staffing, and to consider in more detail how these remarkable staff reductions were actually achieved. The government handsomely beat its own plan for a reduction of 14 percent in the total civil service between 1979 and 1984, and having then set a new plan for reductions in staffing by 1988, found actual reductions running ahead of plan. In view of the conventional wisdom about the difficulty of cutting staff in public bureaucracies, this was a considerable achievement. How was it done?

Let us begin by discussing what we might expect, in the abstract, in terms not of Adam Smith and Weberian bureaucrats this time, but of Ministers, united in their drive for what they will call 'staff savings' (what union officials will call 'staff losses'), though otherwise variously motivated.

I Conviction politics versus cosmetic politics

Staff cutbacks, let us say, might be approached by Ministers by a strategy of 'conviction politics' or of 'cosmetic politics'. In this context, cosmetic politics means the achievement of staff savings by measures of creative accounting or statistical reclassification, which serve to reduce the numbers of civil servants appearing on the ministry's books. As long as the official figures show a decrease, the political end is attained. In 'conviction politics', by contrast, the only cut worth making is a 'real' cut – because retrenchment is valued as an end in itself, not just as a means to create the sort of appearance of tough, cost-cutting government designed to win votes from a tax conscious electorate.

Within these two strategies, a variety of different tactics might be followed. For example, cosmetic cutbacks might be achieved by changing management practice or by changing goals. The 'cosmetic manager' might maintain existing policy goals while at the same time showing savings of staff on the departmental books. The time-honoured tactic here is to 'export' staff to other agencies, which will carry on the business, without any real loss of employment. Hence 'hiving off' to independent public agencies, in a way that may chime with the 'bureau-shaping' ambitions of top departmental officials, in Dunleavy's (1985) analysis. Such export can be carried out with the additional cosmetic refinement of much-trumpeted demands for the 'new' agencies to act in a 'business-like' manner. Contracting out of services formerly carried out in house can also be used for publicity advantage, and can often produce dramatic estimates of probable savings – even if the promised savings unaccountably fail to materialise later. Here, then, we have 'paper savings' along with a pretence of radical change of goals.

Alternatively, cosmetic savings can be achieved by massaging goals rather than staffing figures. The 'cosmetic prioritiser' is not concerned with inputs and outputs but achieves savings by subtle alterations in objectives. This means revising economic and other assumptions, reducing expectations, off-loading work on to suppliers, clients, or regulatees, increasing waiting times, closing branch offices, and the like – in general, reducing quality of product or service where that can be done without too strong a political backlash. The process – essentially a reshuffling of costs – also lends itself to PR trumpeting in terms of 'streamlining' and a more 'managerial' approach. But real savings may well be made; the pretence is that objectives are not being altered.

When cuts are approached by a 'conviction' strategy, neither of these two approaches will do, since real changes are the aim. But the 'conviction cutter' also has a choice of 'managerial' or 'prioritising' styles. The 'conviction manager' aims to achieve 'real' savings by genuine increases in efficiency of working, following detailed 'reviews' and 'projects', or by introducing automation or computerisation; or less concretely, by progressively instilling cost-consciousness and the spirit of 'value for money' (VFM) in senior staff, so that those staff members themselves become as active in seeking for ways of achieving staff savings as the Minister.

Alternatively, the conviction cutter might achieve real staff savings by taking the language of priorities to its logical conclusion and deciding on more or less ideological grounds which services are to be continued, and which to be ended or all but ended; thus attaining two objectives at once – staff cutbacks, and the abolition of services that the government should not be providing in any case, in the eyes of the conviction prioritiser. Of a similar nature are genuine privatisations, where government divests itself of an entire agency, or sells off its interests to 'the market'.

These 'cosmetic' and 'conviction' strategies and styles could be summed up as follows:

Strategy	'cosmetic'	'conviction'
Style		
managerial	hiving off contracting out	working more efficiently instilling VFM spirit
prioritising	streamlining reducing quality	abolishing functions privatisations

II   Cutbacks under Thatcher: popular and sceptical expectations

Undoubtedly, the popular expectation about the staff cuts strategies of Ministers under the Thatcher government would be that they were of a 'conviction' kind. The Prime Minister and her government carefully cultivated the public relations image of a 'new' style of government, going beyond the messy compromises and cosmetic political management of previous governments since 1945, talking a sharper language of priorities and committed to a genuine 'rolling back of the state'. If we follow this popular image (reflected also in much 'serious' writing about the Thatcher style), we would expect that cuts in staffing derived from 'working more efficiently' and 'abolishing functions' would predominate, and that cosmetic manipulations would be positively frowned upon.

Within that, however, this view does not tell us what expectations to have about the mix of 'managerial' and 'prioritising' styles by which the staff cutbacks were achieved, or how that mix might change over time. If we follow the government's own rhetoric, we might expect 'prioritising' approaches to predominate. Mrs Thatcher probably shared the received 'public-choice' view that the well-known inefficiency of government agencies is rooted in the property-rights structure of public bureaucracy (no incentive to negotiate optimal employment contracts or to monitor 'slacking' closely), thus needing a good infusion of 'managerial' methods; but in her statement of 13 May 1980 (quoted on p. 18 above) she put 'concentrating on essential functions' before 'making operations simpler and more efficient' – suggesting that she put 'conviction prioritising' even before the 'conviction managerial' style, in the categories we are using.

As to change over time, on the one hand we might expect a

government's major priorities to be in place after a few years in office (particularly in the case of a government as purposeful and single-minded as the Thatcher government is painted in the popular image). On the other hand, we might expect the effects of 'managerial' changes to achieve increasingly high savings, as the new managerial gospel spread and the 'VFM spirit' more and more animated the workings of government. Mrs Thatcher clearly believed that firm and resolute leadership of the bureaucracy from the top could create an employment discipline within the public service that would substitute for the 'profit motive' in achieving efficiency.

Not everyone would take the popular image of Thatcherism at face value, however. The world-weary sophisticate, or sceptic, might take an alternative view, that the Thatcher government cannot be all that different from any other government in a democracy, that Ministers would find required cuts by the easiest possible means, that 'conviction cutbacks' would be confined to the early years of government, as the victorious party used cutbacks to settle old political scores and wind up the previous party's pet creations; that real 'managerial' savings would prove to be as illusory as they have always done over half a century of mostly unsuccessful attempts to change government by more 'business-like' methods; and that in practice cosmetic cutbacks would play a large and probably increasing part in the government's strategies.

One body which perhaps took the latter view of the probable style of cutbacks, and which took a keen interest in just what sort of cutbacks were coming, was the House of Commons 'watchdog' committee in this area, the Treasury and Civil Service Committee. In their report of 22 July 1980 they complained as follows:

The major policy statement made by the Prime Minister on 13 May 1980 [already quoted – see Chapter 1, p. 18] contained no hints of the services to be cut, and in evidence to us, Sir John Herbecq proved incapable of elaborating further, other than by pointing to efficiency studies already undertaken by the CSD, Departments, and Sir Derek Rayner. Indeed this inability to state which Government services are to be affected by the cuts is reflected in the inability to produce a figure for the net saving in cost, or even to estimate how many tasks will be given to the private sector, what the effect will be on industrial as opposed to non-industrial staff, on headquarters or regional staff, or on grades within the Civil Service.

Moreover, we have seen no assessment by the Government of the social and economic effects of ending or reducing services that make up the Government's action list. It is impossible to come to any view of the impact of the cuts in Civil Service numbers until the Government has detailed the services which are to go and given some assessment about the effects of their abolition. [*Fourth Report,* 1979–80, HC 712–I, paras. 12 and 13]

The government had in fact given some information on the ways in which staff ('manpower') savings were expected to be made, in a list accompanying a statement to the House on 6 December 1979. Ministers had conducted an initial examination of the activities of their departments, to identify where cuts were feasible, whether through increased efficiency or by the abolition or curtailment of functions. It was the results of this examination that were set out in the list. All major departments were mentioned: the flavour can be gained from a few of the entries:

Department	*Approximate staff saving*
MINISTRY OF DEFENCE	
Various economies and placing some work currently done in-house out to contract (in particular cleaning and catering); administrative economies from such measures as changing the arrangements for paying salaries and wages and for bill paying; further changes in arrangements for quality assurance, involving greater reliance on industry	7,500
FOREIGN & COMMONWEALTH OFFICE AND DIPLOMATIC SERVICE	
Closure of some overseas posts; reduction in the size of the largest overseas missions and in staff numbers in the United Kingdom	425
OFFICE OF FAIR TRADING	
Extension of validity of consumer credit licences	70
MANPOWER SERVICES COMMISSION	
Reductions in employment and training services	3,400
INLAND REVENUE	
Savings from measures in the 1979 Budget and Finance Act; the cancellation of rating revaluation; changes and simplifications in administration and procedures including reduced checking of repayments of tax, a reduction in statistical work, the abolition of continuous referencing for rating purposes, reduced spot checks of local authority valuation work, less information passed to local tax districts, changes in PAYE procedures	5,515

[HC 712–II, App. 1, pp. 170–2]

(There is some hint here of the 'bleeding stump' ploy – if cut, bleed where it shows – but that is another story.) The Treasury and Civil Service Committee acknowledged this list, but pointed out that it covered only the first tranche of staffing cuts. They therefore asked the Civil

Service Department for quarterly progress reports of actual cuts made, saying that they would be monitoring:

(i)   the split between the industrial ['blue-collar'] and non-industrial ['white-collar'] Civil Service
(ii) the extent of transferring tasks to the private sector, and the net savings that result
(iii) where the cuts are made in the non-industrial Civil Service, by region and by rank
(iv) how far savings result either from ending or curtailing services, or from increased efficiency
(v)   the total financial saving to the Exchequer.   [HC 712–I, para. 16]

Now, we have already dealt with numbers (i) and (iii) on this list in earlier chapters. Here we are principally concerned with (ii) and (iv), and we shall have a look at (v) at the end of the section. As a result of the Committee's request, the Civil Service Department produced reports from which we derived all the figures we have used in this chapter, covering the five years 1980/1 to 1984/5 inclusive.

With its first annual report to the Committee, on staff reductions in 1980/1, the Civil Service Department sent the following letter:

As promised, this includes an attribution by departments of the manpower reductions into broad categories. Some departments have had difficulty in attributing all their savings in this way. That is because some savings have not been brought about by reduction in functions or any major change in method, but have instead been made possible by general streamlining and other minor changes. As you will appreciate, any change which results in better value for money implies increased efficiency. In this broad sense that term embraces most of the categories of savings in Note 5. Thus increases in efficiency are not confined to any one entry in that Note. A sizeable number of savings have therefore been attributed to the general savings category. [HC 423, Appendix, p. 1]

The categories used are set out in note 5, and are standard for all of the five annual reports being considered here:

(a) (i) increases (ii) decreases arising from change in workloads (including revised economic assumptions)
(b) carrying out work more efficiently by a major change in method
(c) general streamlining (including lower standards of service) and other minor changes
(d) increases arising from major new activities
(e) dropping or materially curtailing a function
(f) privatisation, including contracting out
(g) hiving off to new or existing public body
(h) [from 1982/3] contracting-out.

There were three categories into which *increases* of staff might fall: (a)(i), (c), and (d). Many departments had increases under these headings over the five years, but in few did they lead to net increases overall. In what follows we lay aside staff increases, and concentrate on how savings were made.

If the government really followed a 'conviction' strategy in cutting staff, it should presumably have aimed for 'managerial' cutbacks under (d), 'change in methods' and for 'prioritising' staff cutbacks under (e), 'dropping functions'. We would expect cuts under (e) to be especially large in the early years of the government, as the new priorities were put in place; and cuts under (b) to remain high or even increase over time as the new managerial style took root. We would expect the government to avoid tactics of staff savings that might be characteristic of the 'cosmetic' strategy, which could achieve 'managerial' cuts under (g), 'hiving off' and 'prioritising' cuts under (a), 'change in workload' and (c), 'general streamlining'. Those would be the marks of the ordinary politico, not of the 'conviction politics' that is attributed to the Thatcher government in popular imagery.

III   The observed pattern

Table 6.1 gives the basic data on sources of reductions for the civil service as a whole.[1] We can use this to test the 'outsider' expectations of the cutback style of the Thatcher government, as against the more sceptical expectations of the 'insider'.

From Table 6.1 we can make the following observations:

(i)   *'cosmetic' cuts form a large proportion of the total.*

Adding together the percentages of savings in each year for 'conviction' and 'cosmetic' strategies as described above produces the following:

	1980/1	1981/2	1982/3	1983/4	1984/5	1980–5
'conviction' (b)+(e)	40.1	37.8	44.6	45.0	18.2	36.4
'cosmetic' (a)+(c)+(g)	54.1	42.9	41.7	47.7	75.5	53.3

[1] 'Contracting out' was only distinguished from 'privatisation' after 1982/3, but the table shows that privatisation after that date (within this period) accounted for negligible savings, so perhaps we would be entitled to guess that the bulk of the savings from the combined category in the first two years came from contracting out and not from privatisation as such. However, since there is an ambiguity (and since in any case the heyday of Thatcherite privatisation was after 1985), we will not use the figures in either row (f) or row (h) in what follows.

Table 6.1. *Staff reductions by source category 1980–5: total civil service: numbers of staff (and percent of total)*

	1980/1	1981/2	1982/3	1983/4	1984/5	Total
(a)(ii) change in workload	1,746.5 (6.5%)	3,845 (12.3%)	4,716 (16.1%)	7.348 (20.2%)	4,563 (11.9%)	22,218.5 (13.7%)
(b) change in methods	3,966.5 (14.8%)	4,640 (14.8%)	5,404 (18.5%)	4,447 (12.2%)	3,385 (8.8%)	21,842.5 (13.5%)
(c) general streamlining	12,188 (45.4%)	8,526 (27.3%)	6,831 (23.4%)	6,891 (18.9%)	5,216 (13.6%)	39,652 (24.5%)
(e) dropping functions	6,787.5 (25.3%)	7,184 (23.0%)	7,632 (26.1%)	11,933 (32.8%)	3,582 (9.4%)	37,118.5 (22.9%)
(f) privatisation	1,571 (5.8%)	6,046 (19.3%)	304 (1.0%)	0 (0.0%)	11 (0.02%)	16,725 (10.3%)
(h) contracting out			3,725 (12.7%)	2,655 (7.3%)	2,413 (6.3%)	
(g) hiving off	601 (2.2%)	1,008 (3.3%)	600 (2.1%)	3,162 (8.6%)	19,061 (50.0%)	24,432 (15.1%)
Totals	26,860.5	31,249	29,212	36,436	38,231	161,988.5

Note: The distinction between (f), privatisation and (h), contracting out was made only from 1982/3

Sources: Seventh Report from the Treasury and Civil Service Committee, 1980–81, *Civil Service Manpower Reductions.* HC 423. 13 July 1981

First Special Report from the Treasury and Civil Service Committee, 1982–83, *Civil Service Manpower Reductions.* HC 46. 15 November 1982

Report on Manpower Reductions in 1982–83 to the Treasury and Civil Service Committee. Third Annual Report. Management and Personnel Office. 207. No date

Fourth Annual Report ditto. 1983–84. 207. No date

Fifth Annual Report ditto. 1984–85. 207. No date

There seems no doubt that in spite of the 'conviction' image of the Thatcher government, the 'cosmetician' predominated both at the start of the period and overall. The 1984/5 figures show 'cosmetics' at its height, reflecting enormous 'hiving-off' activity in that year, due entirely to the transfer of nearly 19,000 staff of the Royal Ordnance Factories out of the Ministry of Defence into a public corporation. Only in one year (1982/3) did 'conviction' savings outweigh 'cosmetic' ones. Clearly the popular view of Thatcherism as single-minded 'conviction politics' is difficult to reconcile with these results. Nor is it even true that 'conviction' savings predominated in the first flush of Thatcherism, giving way to 'cosmetic' savings as initial zeal waned and scores had been settled. 'Cosmetic' cuts never dropped below 40 percent of the total, and in that sense a sceptical 'insider' interpretation of the Thatcher cutbacks cannot be eliminated.

(ii)   'conviction prioritising' does not predominate in the early years and 'managerial' cuts are not sustained.

At the same time, it must be conceded that a substantial minority of staff savings in every year was indeed achieved by 'conviction' methods in the senses described above. In each year a rather larger proportion of cuts was achieved by 'conviction prioritising' (i.e., dropping functions) than was achieved by 'conviction managerial' styles (i.e., changing methods of work in the bureaucracy). A hypothesis drawn from the popular image of the Thatcher government was that savings in the principal 'managerial' category, (b), 'change in methods', would increase over the years as the 'VFM' discipline began to bite and the new hard-headed Marks and Spencer-style bureau management made itself felt. There is not much evidence of this from the data shown in Table 6.1, which in fact shows the proportion of cuts achieved by this means falling away after a peak in 1982/3. But the time-period is admittedly short, and (to those of the faith) may not give a long enough run to test the hypothesis carefully. To those not of the faith, who know the long and disappointing history of attempts to achieve dramatic savings in public bureaucracies by the introduction of 'business method', it is exactly what would be expected.

Fig. 5 shows the data in Table 6.1 in graphical form, which dramatises the differing importance from year to year of the various sources of staff savings. Two categories, (a)(ii), 'change in workload' and (e), 'dropping functions', peak in 1983/4; (b), 'changes in method', peaks in 1982/3; (f) with (h) peaks in 1981/2; (c), 'general streamlining', peaks in the first year, accounting for almost half the total in 1980/1, as if savings could be made most easily under this head at first, but only up to certain limits; while (g), hiving off, shoots up in the last year, accounting for half of a much-increased total in 1984/5. This pattern may show 'learning', or 'stages' of retrenchment; but that is the subject of the next chapter, so we shall not pursue it now.

Table 6.2 shows the estimated financial saving per person cut, in real terms, for each of the seven categories of cutbacks shown in Table 6.1. These figures are calculated from aggregate estimates produced by the Civil Service Department (later, by the Management and Personnel Office).

(iii)   'cosmetic managerialism' saves less than other styles of cutback

What Table 6.2 shows is that, though the 'cosmetic managerial' approach ('contracting out') can produce large reductions in the staff

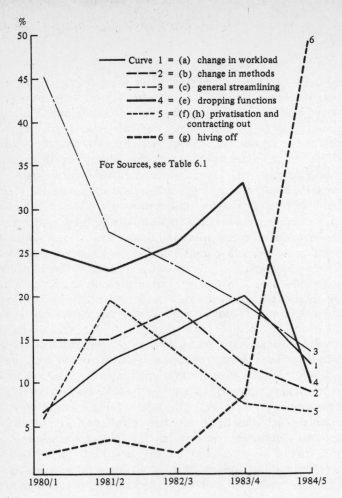

Fig. 5. Civil service staff reductions, 1980–5; proportions from each
source category, year by year.

numbers on a ministry's books, the estimated savings per person cut are
very much smaller than those achieved by categories (a) to (e). What this
indicates is that contracting out cuts very low-level staff in comparison to
the other categories of cutbacks, as might have been predicted from the
early emphasis on cleaning and catering services as candidates for
contracting out. It is interesting – particularly for those inclined to be

Table 6.2. *Civil service staff reductions 1980–5: average saving per person by source category in each year (£ at constant prices: GDP 1980 = 100)*

		1980/1	1981/2	1982/3	1983/4	1984/5	1980–5
(a)(ii)	changes in workload	5,390	4,903	4,972	5,306	6,034	5,321
(b)	efficiency through change in methods	5,238	6,111	4,983	5,737	5,537	5,521
(c)	streamling and lowering standards	3,680	7,853	6,082	6,332	6,766	6,143
(e)	dropping or curtailing functions	5,449	6,017	5,732	6,030	5,826	5,811
(f),(h)	privatisation and contracting out	344	1,032	1,217	1,020	1,149	952
(g)	hiving off	6,076	102	*	*	*	
	Overall average*	4,020	5,183	4,597	4,885	5,062	

Note: *Financial savings 'cannot be quantified' (*source*). Category (g) omitted from calculation of overall average
Sources: As for Table 6.1

suspicious of this kind of accounting – that for some mysterious reason the central management agencies in government could not quantify the financial savings accruing from the other 'cosmetic managerial' approach to cutbacks, namely, (g), 'hiving off', for three of the five years. This perhaps reinforces the suggestion that the real savings achieved for such 'cutbacks' are of a rubbery nature. But financial savings under the 'cosmetic prioritising' approach of (a), 'change in workload', were quite respectable – indicating that the 'cosmetic' nature of this approach lies more in the pretence that goals and service levels have not changed than in the registering of only 'paper' savings.

IV Departmental analysis

The totals for the civil service as a whole are naturally made up of the sum of the totals for the individual departments, so that unless all of at least the larger departments showed the same distribution of proportions among sources year by year as did the civil service as a whole, the figures in Tables 6.1 and 6.2, and the lines on Fig. 5, may merely represent the accidents of aggregation of widely differing departmental savings and attributions to categories. We have already noted this in respect of the rocketing of (g), 'hiving off' in 1984/5, and it applies also in respect of the marked decline of (e), 'dropping functions', between 1983/4 and 1984/5, which is largely accounted for by the performance of the three largest departments. Together these provided cuts of 10,920 staff in 1983/4, over 90 percent of the total (e) savings in that year, whereas their collective cutback in 1984/5 was only 2,617 staff.

There were in fact great variations among departments as to where they found their staff cuts from, and great variations for any one department from one year to the next, which it would be tedious to record even in tabular form. As illustration only, Table 6.3 gives the picture comparatively for the three giants MOD, DHSS, and IR (which collectively accounted for over half of the total civil service manpower savings in each year, and for 80 percent in 1984/5, thanks to the ROF transfer, even though they were by no means the most heavily cut in proportional terms).

It can immediately be seen, for instance, that DHSS had no savings at all under (f) or (h), 'privatisation' and 'contracting out', while IR had none under (g), 'hiving off'; (c), 'general streamlining', was much more salient for MOD than for the other two departments, until the end of the period, when it leaps into importance for IR. And so on: explaining such differences at length would require rehearsing the special history and circumstances of each department, in the way that is indeed done by Note 7 (Explanatory notes on Changes in Departments) in the Annual Report to the Treasury and Civil Service Committee of the House of Commons, but in even greater detail, and with numbers.

Yet some departments *appeared* to adopt similar strategies in finding staff cuts. We applied techniques of cluster analysis to see if distinct 'families' of cutback strategies could be identified.[2] We found seven main groupings sorting themselves out fairly clearly, for which our interpretation was as follows.

(1)   Four departments (FCO, OS, TCC, DTI) formed a family in that their staff cuts were drawn mainly from category (a), 'changes in workload'. FCO and TCC are the departments generally considered of highest status in Whitehall, very policy-oriented, with wide horizons; DTI is also such a department, if not of quite such high status. But OS is an odd member of the family, being a largely executive department, fulfilling commissions. Perhaps the link is that they are all 'reactive' departments, whose workload more than most is determined by changes in their environment, or what others require of them.

(2)   Five departments formed a grouping achieving staff cuts largely by category (b), 'changes in methods'. This grouping (ECGD, LR, DNS, C & E, MAFF) is perhaps easier to understand: all are notable for processing

---

[2] This exercise is described in Appendix IV.

Table 6.3. *Staff reductions by source category, 1980–5: Ministry of Defence, Department of Health and Social Security, and Inland Revenue: numbers of staff and percentage of total*

		1980/1	1981/2	1982/3	1983/4	1984/5	Total
(a) change in workload	MOD	1,077	1,592	1,344	1,373	518	5,904
		10.3 %	12.4 %	13.8 %	12.7 %	2.0 %	8.5 %
	DHSS	0	161	100	70	1,200	1,531
		0	7.0 %	2.9 %	1.2 %	38.6 %	9.3 %
	IR	0	350	148	1,164	500	2,162
		0	14.3 %	6.2 %	30.8 %	23.3 %	17.1 %
(b) change in methods	MOD	301	500	286	138	185	1,410
		2.9 %	3.9 %	2.9 %	1.3 %	0.7 %	2.0 %
	DHSS	99	490	1,500	700	700	3,489
		5.7 %	21.3 %	41.9 %	11.9 %	22.5 %	21.1 %
	IR	1,000	450	298	980	248	2,976
		37.2 %	18.4 %	12.6 %	25.9 %	11.5 %	23.6 %
(c) general streamlining	MOD	7,848	5,034	3,075	3,516	3,857	23,330
		75.4 %	39.1 %	31.7 %	32.4 %	15.2 %	33.7 %
	DHSS	0	278	600	300	66	1,244
		0	12.1 %	17.2 %	5.1 %	2.1 %	7.5 %
	IR	488	148	298	368	706	2,008
		18.1 %	6.0 %	12.6 %	9.7 %	32.8 %	15.9 %
(e) dropping functions	MOD	875	2,982	3,345	4,853	881	12,936
		8.4 %	23.2 %	34.4 %	44.8 %	3.5 %	18.7 %
	DHSS	1,624	1,370	1,297	4,802	1,040	10,133
		92.8 %	59.6 %	37.1 %	81.8 %	33.5 %	61.3 %
	IR	1,200	700	1,197	1,265	696	5,058
		44.7 %	28.6 %	50.5 %	33.5 %	32.4 %	40.0 %
(f), (h) privatisation and contracting out	MOD	304	2,599	1,570	891	1,026	6,390
		2.9 %	20.2 %	16.2 %	8.2 %	4.0 %	9.2 %
	DHSS	0	0	0	0	0	0
		0	0	0	0	0	0
	IR	0	0	427	0	0	427
		0	0	18.0 %	0	0	3.5 %
(g) hiving off	MOD	0	156	89	65	18,933	19,243
		0	1.2 %	0.9 %	0.6 %	74.5 %	27.8 %
	DHSS	26	0	0	0	100	126
		1.5 %	0	0	0	3.2 %	0.8 %
	IR	0	0	0	0	0	0
		0	0	0	0	0	0
Totals	MOD	10,405	12,863	9,709	10,836	25,400	69,213
	DHSS	1,749	2,299	3,497	5,872	3,106	16,523
	IR	2,688	1,648	2,368	3,777	2,150	12,631

Sources: As for Table 6.1

large numbers of individual cases – perhaps this is particularly conducive to 'work study' types of improvement in methods; three of them collect a high proportion of their budgets in fees and charges, and could possibly offload work on to their customers.

(3)   A third group (WO, DEn, MOD, and NIO) found their savings largely from category (c), 'general streamlining'. Perhaps we can explain this by the fact that WO, DEn, and NIO are first, second, and fourth or fifth in two 'league tables' measuring 'complexity' (number of Vote Heads per 1,000 staff, and number of Vote Subheads per 1,000 staff). But in each table MOD is bottom marker – huge in staff for not an extraordinary number of subheads. Still, perhaps MOD counts as 'complex' for this purpose; and the next most (c)-dominated department, DTI, is also high in these league tables. This would lead us to suppose that there is more scope for 'general streamlining (including lower standards of service)' in complex departments which deal with a large number of different subjects. Two of these departments are 'territorial' (WO and NIO), and may well be subject to the 'small country effect' – each senior official on average covers a larger number of distinct subjects than does his or her opposite number by rank in a large country. If five officials are dealing with twenty subjects between them, perhaps if one goes four officials can cope with one extra subject each, at an acceptable drop in quality of service. It is interesting to note that the Scottish Office (SO), the other territorial department, takes third place in both of these league tables, though it is not particularly (c)-dominated.

(4)   A fourth group (DHSS, OPCS, COI, LCD, IR) forms a family in that staff cuts were achieved principally in category (e), 'dropping functions'. This grouping is more difficult to interpret. OPCS and COI are 'central services', and LCD could be pressed into that mould; all three of these raise a fair proportion of their budgets in fees and charges (ranked 7, 6, and 5 in that regard). It might be feasible for them to save staff by not offering so many services. But DHSS and IR are quite different from these, and from each other, except that they are both highly dispersed around the country – it is not easy to see how that relates to 'dropping or materially curtailing a function', unless closing local offices has been so designated. This one remains a bit of an enigma.

(5)   Only one department (DOE) is in the fifth group, comprising departments where staff cuts were achieved mainly in category (f), 'privatisation and contracting out'. DOE was where the 'value-for-money' doctrine was first most assiduously preached, under Mr Michael Heseltine – perhaps the archetype of the 'conviction manager'; it also embraces the Property Services Agency, the Crown Suppliers, and many

technical services and research stations, many of which might lend themselves to a degree of contracting out.

(6) Likewise, there is only one department (DTp) in a 'group' of departments with cuts predominantly in category (g), 'hiving off'. DTp used to provide highways engineering and regional road construction units, now hived off to local government.

(7) The seventh and final grouping (DE, DES, HMSO, SO, HO) comprises departments which did not follow a strategy of achieving cutbacks predominantly from one of the seven categories described earlier ('predominantly' being defined as having 40 percent or more of staff savings drawn from a single category). The common characteristic of the grouping is that they all have substantial savings in several categories; and what is otherwise common to them is that they all run several major functions. SO, DES, and HO are high in the league table of 'number of Votes'; DE looks after several large agencies in the employment, training, and conciliation fields; HMSO is a grouping of large publishing and printing consultancy 'firms'. We should probably find on closer investigation (for which the data are, however, not available) that different sectors of these departments were dominated by different categories of staff saving.

We naturally wondered whether the source of staff cuts, as so analysed, is connected with the degree or incidence of staffing cuts. But the possibility can be dismissed. If one looks back at Table 5.4, which sets out groupings of departments according to the frequency and severity of spending and staffing cuts, none of the seven groupings we have just found corresponds at all to the distributions in Table 5.4.

Nor, although we have interpreted these seven groupings of departments in terms of the kind of work that these departments do, do the seven groupings in fact match up with the groupings of departments in the 'functional' categories we discussed in the last chapter – that is, departments concentrated in staff terms into 'administration', 'public service', and 'trading and support'.[3]

[3] In formal terms, there was no significant correlation between percentage of staff in either the 'public-service' category or the 'trading and support' category and percentage of staff reductions in any of the staff reductions categories described in Table 6.1. The one slight exception is a weak negative correlation between percentage of staff in the 'public-service' functions and (c), 'general streamlining' staff cuts ($r = -0.41$, $p = 0.007$), indicating that the higher the proportion of staff in 'public-service' functions, the less likely was a department to adopt a 'general streamlining' strategy in staff cuts. This is curious, since we might have expected exactly the opposite in markedly 'public-service' departments, where there might seem to be most scope for off-loading costs on to clients by reductions of service quality.

However, when we group departments in a slightly different way, we can relate the 'functional' analysis of departments to their cutback strategies. First (anticipating something we shall explain in the next chapter), we aggregate cutback strategies into three rather than seven categories: (a), 'changes in workload', goes with (c), 'general streamlining' as being *incremental* in nature; (b), 'change in methods', is taken with (f), 'privatisation', (g), 'hiving off', and (h), 'contracting out', considered together as *managerial*; and (e), 'dropping functions', becomes a category labelled *strategic*. If we then relate departments grouped according to the three functional analysis categories (administration-heavy, public-service-heavy, and trading-and-support-heavy) to these groupings of cutback strategies, a pattern does begin to emerge, as is shown in Table 6.4. That is, there was a strong propensity for 'admin-heavy' departments to choose cutback strategies which are labelled *incremental*, i.e., a mixture of (a) and (c), rather than what we called *managerial* or *strategic* categories. 'Public-service-heavy' departments, however, achieved their greatest cutbacks in the *managerial* category of (b), (f), (g), and (h). In the case of departments which are 'trading-and-support-heavy', there is a more even spread across the cutback categories.

This finding does map more closely on the explanations given above for the seven groupings of departments by cutback category, and confirms the pattern which we suggested there. Departments with a high policy profile seem to have a tendency to cut back staff through changing workload and streamlining, presumably because there is less 'routine work' lending itself to hiving off or privatisation or change in methods. Departments with a high public-service profile, on the other hand, may have little scope for changing their workload, but may have more scope for privatisation, contracting out, and change in method. Departments which engage in trading and common service activities seem more able to spread their cutbacks across the whole range of strategies, perhaps because many of them are conglomerate in the types of activity that they perform.

V   Conclusion

In this chapter we have been investigating how the major cuts in civil service staffing which have been such a feature of the Thatcher approach to retrenchment were found; using mainly the figures produced for the appropriate watchdog committee of the House of Commons, for the period 1980–5, in terms of savings derived from changes in workload,

Table 6.4. *Staff of central government departments: functional analysis of tasks 1980/1, and categories of cutbacks 1980–5; 22 departments with more than 1,000 staff*

	Categories of cutback								
	Incremental			Managerial			Strategic		
Functional analysis									
Administrative	73.9	FCO	94.6	100.0	ECGD	51.3			
	69.1	WO	83.0						
	68.7	DEn	69.6						
	70.4	DES	45.0						
Public service	77.2	OS	67.6	93.6	C&E	58.6	92.7	DHSS	61.7
	37.4	IND	71.2	84.7	HO	55.3	92.0	LCD	40.6
	56.5	ODA	46.5	76.3	MAFF	62.8	94.4	IR	40.1
				52.3	SO	43.4	41.9	OPCS	57.5
				87.0	DE	43.1			
Trading support	51.8	TCC	100.0	77.1	DOE	57.8	81.5	COI	50.3
	98.1	DNS	47.2	100.0	LR	48.6			

Notes: Figure before departmental acronym is percentage of staff in given functional category
Figure after departmental acronym is percentage of staff in given cutback category
MOD is absent because no functional analysis data are available
For key to departmental acronyms see Table A1, Appendix I, or Index
Sources: As for Table 6.1

increases in efficiency, general streamlining, dropping functions, privatisation, contracting out, and hiving off. With those we tested some hypotheses drawn from popular stereotypes of policy style under Thatcherism, and found that although the 'cosmetic' approach did provide much of the cutbacks throughout the period and dominated at the start, 'conviction' strategies provided a large part of the overall staff savings. And Mrs Thatcher's own declared priority, for 'concentrating on essential functions' rather than 'making operations simpler and more efficient' (translated here into 'dropping functions' before 'change in methods'), was delivered in the event, 'dropping functions' producing just under a quarter of total savings over the period, compared with just over an eighth for 'increased efficiency through change in methods'.

We found, however, that knowing where the staff cuts came from did not tell us anything about where the staff cuts would fall: there was no relation between the pattern of sources and the incidence of light, medium, or heavy staff cutbacks, whether at the overall civil service level or department by department. In a cluster analysis (reported in detail in Appendix IV), departments did fall into groupings which were probably based on the degree to which their staff savings had come from one source rather than others, but it was not always easy to produce an explanation of *why* that should be – what departments which derived the bulk of their staff savings from (e), 'dropping functions', for example, had in common to make them likely to achieve their cuts that way.

But when we put these data, on how the staff cuts were found, alongside another set of categorisations of departments, by 'function', some interesting results appeared. This categorisation gave the numbers of staff in each department engaged in 'central administration' functions, 'public services', 'trading and repayment' services, or 'general support' functions, from which departments could be classified according to the predominance of one function in their staff make-up. It transpired that departments mainly involved in 'policy matters' were considerably more likely to find their staff cuts through 'change in workload' and/or 'general streamlining' rather than other attributions; the 'public service', 'trading', and 'general support' departments were more evenly spread over the cuts categories. Departments which had lost a lot of staff through 'dropping functions' were almost all in the 'public-service' functional category.

Now we go on to consider the *time dimension* in more detail.

7 The dynamics of cutback management

In this chapter, we consider whether, as is sometimes averred in the literature, the approach of government to the need for cutbacks changes as the crisis deepens, or as the period of fiscal restraint lengthens. Are some programmes, or departments, or groups of personnel, or regions, or economic categories, or spending authorities less vulnerable, or more vulnerable, as time goes on? Do axe wielders move from being 'Weberian' to being 'Adam Smith' bureaucrats as pressure for cuts rises? Do the tactics of saving staff change over the years? We shall not try to answer all of these questions now, although the material for answers to many of them has already been given. Rather shall we explore the application to our data of one of the more sophisticated theories of the dynamics of the cutback process, and suggest an alternative theory which better explains what we have found.

First, however, let us consider what may seem a prior question. Is cutting back on expenditure the only way out of fiscal crisis? After all, at an individual level, if one does not have enough money to buy what one wants, there is an alternative to going without it, or without something else: one can try to earn more, or acquire more by other means. Governments can raise more income rather than retrench expenditure. Do governments try first one way, and then another, as crisis persists?

I Raise income rather than cut spending?

Gladstone and later Chancellors of the Exchequer, as we saw in Chapter 1, felt it imperative that public expenditures should be balanced by public income. Long before Gladstone, Adam Smith was much concerned about the 'crippling burden' of the national debt, and favoured reducing that burden by raising more revenue – finding new things to tax; only very briefly did he consider reducing expenditure to match income. War has always been a great augmenter of 'unavoidable' spending, and throughout history has usually been financed mainly by borrowing, rather than by raising all the required income by increased taxation. In

Table 7.1. *Total government expenditure (Appropriation Accounts) and appropriations-in-aid, 1971/2 to 1984/5 (£m at constant prices) (GDP Deflator, 1980 = 100)*

Year	Gross actual expenditure (current cash) 1	Gross actual expenditure (constant prices) 2	Actual appropriations-in-aid (cash) 3	Actual appropriations-in-aid (constant prices) 4	Column 3 as percentage of column 1 5
1971/2	16,168.5	54,623.3	1,325.3	4,477.4	8.2
1972/3	17,954.6	56,623.3	1,453.2	4,541.2	8.1
1973/4	20,416.3	59,696.8	1,750.1	5,117.2	8.6
1974/5	27,818.8	70,785.8	2,333.7	5,938.2	8.4
1975/6	37,156.7	74,313.4	3,064.9	6,129.8	8.2
1976/7	41,547.8	72,257.0	4,535.5	8,808.0	10.9
1977/8	43,850.1	66,946.7	3,840.4	5,863.2	8.8
1978/9	50,149.9	68,792.7	4,410.9	6,050.6	8.8
1979/80	58,785.9	70,486.7	4,971.7	5,961.3	8.5
1980/1	73,602.5	73,602.5	5,965.6	5,965.6	8.1
1981/2	81,193.4	72,558.9	6,900.5	6,166.7	8.5
1982/3	87,960.6	73,178.5	7,355.3	6,119.2	8.4
1983/4	95,135.7	75,325.2	8,501.6	6,731.3	8.9
1984/5	102,704.7	77,924.7	9,116.3	6,916.8	8.9

Sources: Annual Appropriation Accounts presented to House of Commons

peacetime, Labour Chancellors have been marginally less reluctant to raise taxes and to borrow to match increased public spending than have Conservative Chancellors.

Fiscal crises have occurred precisely when the tax base would not expand enough (in economic recession) to balance rising spending and when the cost of external borrowing became prohibitive. Whether in the 1920s or the 1960s and 1970s, it was because external lenders would no longer finance spending at current levels (especially any attempt by government at 'spending its way out of the crisis') that cutting back was resorted to, when 'taxing your way out of crisis' was not a feasible alternative. During the IMF crisis of the mid 1970s *both* large cuts in spending *and* increases in taxation were demanded.

We might conclude that the dynamic in the first half of the century, therefore, went as follows: raise expenditure as long as tax income is buoyant; borrow 'temporarily' to match spending if tax income declines; cut spending if borrowing fails. With the advent of the Thatcher government in 1979, however, the ideological atmosphere was decisively altered. There was a manifesto commitment not only to reduce taxation and borrowing but also to reduce public expenditure and public employment. Increasing income, therefore, is not an alternative to reducing spending. Both must be reduced. From 1979 to the time of writing, cutbacks have been only partly (if at all) driven by external pressures: they are a product of the government's commitments to 'rolling back the state', and will persist as long as these commitments remain. We have already seen that the Thatcher government, though notably successful in reducing civil service employment, did not actually reduce public expenditure: but the measure of policy here depends upon a counterfactual (by how much might public expenditure have risen if there had been no pressure for cutbacks?).

But of course there is another way of increasing revenue to match 'unavoidably' rising expenditure, without increasing taxation, or borrowing: that is, by raising more revenue in fees and charges and shifting costs on to users rather than taxpayers. It has been part of the Thatcher platform to do this also: to convert 'free' (paid for out of taxation revenue) public provision into goods and services subject to 'commercial' charges per unit consumed (where provision cannot be, or has not yet been, privatised altogether). In the *Appropriation Accounts* much of that kind of revenue is entered under the mysterious head of 'appropriations-in-aid'. So we might expect that the amount listed under that head would increase after 1979. And indeed it did: as Table 7.1 shows, at constant prices the appropriations-in-aid for total government expenditure went

Table 7.2. *Actual appropriations-in-aid (applied) as percent of actual gross expenditure: 24 departments (staff more than 1,000: ranked in order of actual gross expenditure in 1980/1), 1971/2 to 1984/5*

Department	1971/2	1972/3	1973/4	1974/5	1975/6	1976/7	1977/8	1978/9	1979/80	1980/1	1981/2	1982/3	1983/4	1984/5
DHSS	10.3	9.7	10.1	10.5	9.8	12.3	12.0	11.9	10.8	10.4	9.6	9.6	8.9	9.1
DOE	1.9	1.8	1.8	1.5	1.5	13.4	1.9	2.6	1.6	1.4	1.7	1.9	1.7	1.7
MOD	10.5	13.7	14.4	11.8	10.3	10.7	10.6	11.1	9.7	10.2	11.0	9.8	9.5	8.6
IND/TR	3.4	2.6	7.3	2.5	3.3	31.7	8.1	4.4	6.2	5.5	6.0	7.4	12.0	9.9
SO	3.8	5.3	5.4	4.4	4.7	5.9	6.0	5.7	6.1	5.6	6.5	5.0	33.7	8.4
DES	14.9	15.1	16.1	14.7	15.4	17.0	18.2	19.9	19.2	18.7	21.2	19.8	19.8	22.2
HO	4.8	5.0	3.3	2.9	2.2	2.3	3.0	24.4	18.9	19.4	1.5	2.1	2.2	3.4
DTp	0.4	0.4	1.1	1.7	1.8	13.5	5.6	5.7	3.3	3.0	4.9	3.4	5.3	4.2
DE	2.5	3.3	5.6	8.2	7.1	5.5	4.6	11.8	12.1	11.3	13.4	15.6	11.2	9.9
WO	6.6	5.8	0.1	4.6	8.7	5.8	6.1	6.0	5.9	5.3	3.7	4.3	4.7	6.3
ODA	0.3	0.5	0.2	0.2	0.4	0.5	0.6	0.7	0.4	0.6	0.6	0.5	0.5	0.7
DEn	52.7	48.6	64.1	8.6	10.8	23.6	28.5	23.2	22.6	25.0	21.4	16.4	31.3	15.1
ECGD	100	100	8.6	11.7	12.8	15.4	54.3	49.1	63.4	40.1	38.4	33.3	37.3	41.1
MAFF	1.8	2.2	2.2	37.4	37.3	41.2	4.8	5.5	5.0	7.3	7.0	3.9	12.8	7.6
IR	3.0	3.3	2.8	3.4	3.9	4.2	14.9	5.0	4.9	3.9	5.4	5.2	4.5	4.4
TCC	3.4	3.1	14.1	14.6	13.6	16.1	19.7	16.0	15.8	28.3	13.3	9.8	21.4	29.5
FCO	15.2	9.2	7.9	6.9	8.9	10.2	10.6	12.2	11.6	11.7	10.0	8.8	8.0	6.1
LCD	39.4	32.3	31.1	30.4	31.3	33.0	30.9	29.6	29.0	23.1	19.0	18.2	19.4	20.1
C&E	7.1	5.5	4.7	4.9	3.4	3.9	6.4	6.2	5.5	5.0	5.1	4.9	4.4	2.0
DNS	59.0	58.8	53.2	57.0	54.3	51.7	52.9	56.3	57.3	51.9	45.2	0.4	0.6	0.9
LR	100	100	100	97.8	100	100	100	100	0.0	0.2	0.0	0.1	0.0	0.1
COI	16.6	10.4	8.7	11.3	13.3	16.1	28.0	24.3	18.4	16.0	14.1	17.0	20.6	0.0
OS	32.6	34.8	43.2	35.2	33.8	43.3	48.6	52.0	50.6	51.7	51.5	56.4	59.9	65.2
OPCS	10.7	22.0	25.4	24.7	21.1	26.8	26.4	28.6	27.8	20.9	11.3	22.8	23.0	22.7

Sources: Annual Appropriation Accounts presented to House of Commons
Figures underlined are highest in row, 'peak year'
For key to departmental acronyms see Table A1, Appendix 1, or Index

up from £5,961 million in 1979/80 to £6,917 million in 1984/5, from 8.5 percent of total expenditure to 8.9 percent. But it had been at £6,129 million (8.2 percent) in 1975/6, and at £6,051 million (8.8 percent) in 1978/9. So there is perhaps not as much as one would expect in the 'party-political' explanation of these variations. Indeed, the highest figure for appropriations-in-aid, and the highest percentage of total expenditure, was reached in 1976–7 (£8,808 million, 10.9 percent), during the IMF crisis. Perusal of the departmental breakdown of these totals shows that appropriations-in-aid percentages for several departments leapt up in that year by several points, sometimes quite unaccountably; some of them stayed near the higher level for a few years, but most dropped back immediately. Still, the constant prices figure for appropriations-in-aid, and the percentage of gross expenditure, was at its highest in 1983/4 and 1984/5 other than in that exceptional year; so perhaps policy *is* biting.

Departments vary greatly in the degree to which they raise their own revenue in this way, as we have already found, and as is shown in Table 7.2. Conventions of recording also change, so the significance of time-series of appropriations-in-aid has to be interpreted with caution. For example, the Land Registry went from having its entire spending accounted for by appropriations-in-aid (100.00 percent), before 1978/9, to having none of it so accounted for, in 1979/80. DNS, having had percentages in the fifties until 1980/1, dropped to 0.4 percent in 1982/3.

Changes also occur with hivings-off and transfers of functions: MAFF had percentages in the thirties around 1975/6, but dropped to 4.8 percent in 1977/8, and varied between 3.9 percent in 1982/3 and 12.8 percent in 1983/4. The group we label TCC (Treasury, Cabinet Office, and Management and Personnel Office taken together) had percentages varying between 3.1 percent in 1972/3 and 15.8 percent in 1979/80, and then varied between 28.3 percent in 1980/1 and 9.8 percent in 1982/3, rising again to 29.5 percent in 1984/5. Appropriations-in-aid accounted for 64.1 percent of total expenditure in the Department of Energy in 1973/4, and 8.0 percent in 1974/5, varying then between 10.8 percent in 1975/6 and 31.3 percent in 1983/4 – clearly a matter of net outcomes rather than growth or decline in the same set of fees or charges. Changes in this percentage also hang on changes in the department's total expenditure, of course. So not too much weight can be put on changes either in the amount of appropriations-in-aid (even if inflation-adjusted) or in the percentage which that is of total departmental expenditure, without careful and detailed investigation.

Only perhaps Ordnance Survey comes up to 'Thatcherite' expectations. From an a-i-a percentage of 50.6 percent in 1979/80 it rises steadily to 65.2 percent in 1984/5. DES, too, shows a rising proportion of a-i-a in that period, from 19.2 percent to 22.2 percent. Others are: MAFF, TCC, WO, SO, IND, by varying degrees – and so long as one ignores their earlier history. Most of these show a dip in percentage around 1982/3, so that the climb in the last two years is quite marked, corresponding to the rise in appropriations-in-aid percentage for government expenditure as a whole (Table 7.1), from 8.4 percent to 8.9 percent. This just might be evidence of a 'learning curve' of J-shape: it could be that shifting to user charges on a new and more 'commercial' basis actually reduces revenue initially, until the 'marketing operation' takes over fully. That, however, is pure speculation; and how are we to account for the great variation in earlier years?

In the rest of the chapter, we shall concentrate (as in the rest of the book) on reductions in expenditure and in staffing: that is, on the *cutback* approach to dealing with fiscal crisis, rather than on the revenue-increasing approach. In this chapter, it is the overall dynamics of the process on which we particularly focus.

II   Decremental and quantum cutbacks

We have already introduced (in Chapter 2) the familiar broad distinctions to be found in the cutback management literature, between 'equal misery' (percentage cuts all round) and 'selective cuts' or priorities (Hartley 1981, 143), or between equity and efficiency (Levine 1978, 320). Crecine (1969, 203), Schick (1971, 67 – quoted in Glassberg 1978) and others consider that when cuts are inevitable, they will be made arbitrarily, but always in such a way as to maintain existing power relativities among departments and programmes. Equal sacrifice all round may be felt fairer, or simpler, or easier to conceal. These distinctions do not contain the implication of a necessary progression from 'equal misery' to 'selectivity'.

Glassberg (1978, 327), however, suggests a slightly different distinction, between 'incremental' and 'quantum' cuts. He quotes Dahl and Lindblom's classic argument for incrementalism ('men cannot rationally choose among alternatives drastically different from present reality' – 1953, 83), but notes that they also formulated an alternative approach, for when existing reality is clearly so unsatisfactory that 'to continue existing policies is a greater risk than to discard them in favor of an alternative calculated risk' (85–6). Where a budget decline is substantial, Glassberg suggests (and his examples indicate that budget decreases of

15–20 percent are 'substantial'), the disadvantages associated with repeated decremental cuts – build-up of detrimental effects, Levine's 'paradox of irreducible wholes' (1979, 180), earlier thresholds of collapse for some organisations than others, and so on – will lead decision makers to calculate the alternative risks of 'quantum' cuts – eliminating a programme altogether, closing down a facility, withdrawing a service.

The crucial distinction between incremental and quantum cuts for the purpose of his analysis, he says, is

the extent of leadership expectation that cuts might be restored if proper strategies were undertaken. If there is some expectation that they might be, then Wildavsky's catalogue of 'defending the base' strategies, mentioned at the beginning of this paper, becomes appropriate. If, however, the overall fiscal environment is such that these expectations can no longer be held, then 'defending the base' strategies become increasingly less useful. (Glassberg 1978, 327)

Here there *is* an inference of 'phasing': different tactics as the crisis deepens.

Wildavsky's classic treatise on *The Politics of the Budgetary Process* has a section entitled 'Defending the Base: Guarding Against Cuts in the Old Programs' which begins by arguing that 'a major strategy in resisting cuts is to make them in such a way that they have to be put back' (1964, 102 – quoted in Glassberg 1978, 325). The climate of the spending cutbacks of the 1950s and 1960s was precisely that: cuts could be survived, good times would come again, the rational way to keep the fabric in being for when it would all be needed once more was to offer 'fairy gold' (cuts in growth), if you could get away with that, or if not, then use 'bleeding stump' ploys, or make sure that it was the most squeaky wheel that was denied the oil, and so on. At worst, prune off a twig or two, but never allow the axe near the trunk itself. Demands for 20 percent cuts, however, severely test such strategies and present a quite different context. One may be obliged to move to non-reversible types of cutback.

The Geddes Committee in 1922 were invited to aim at economies in government expenditure of nearly 30 percent – £175m, at that time. Their approach was selective, but 'arbitrary' at the same time: they targeted the biggest spenders, because only from them could money of that order be found. Defence cuts of a drastic order were recommended, which would substantially and permanently affect Britain's standing in the world – just as in a later decade Britain withdrew from 'east of Suez' as (at least in part) an economy measure. Meriam and Schmeckebier

(1939, quoted in Schaffer 1973, 94) made a point of the same kind, though in another direction, in a review of the report of the (US) President's Committee on Administrative Management (the Brownlow Committee, 1937), who advocated full-scale reorganisation of the executive branch, in the interests of greater efficiency. They demonstrated by an analysis of federal expenditure that significant reductions in expenditure could not come from structural reallocations. Only about 17.6 percent of the Federal budget was spent on the running of government agencies, and the great bulk of that went on salaries. Substantial savings, they showed, could only come from curtailment of services, and to a lesser extent from reductions in staff; they cannot come from reorganisation (Meriam and Schmeckebier 1939, chap. 2).

Here we have three kinds of response to cutback pressures being discussed in the literature: first, decrementalism; second, reorganisation and demanning; third, curtailment. It is sometimes explicit, more often implicit, in these formulations that axe-wielders will be obliged to move from the first to the second as pressure increases, and then (as cutback demands continue or keep rising) from the second to the third. The most elegant model of this process is again owed to Torben Beck Jørgensen (1982, 1985, 1987a, 1987b), and will be set out in the next section.

III   Incremental, managerial, and strategic cutbacks

The Beck Jørgensen model begins from Glassberg's observation about the 'climate' of the cutbacks situation. Historically, cutting back comes after a period of sustained growth, as in the 1950s and 1960s. At first, psychologically, people are still living in the 'climate' of growth. The conscious or unconscious expectation is that cutbacks are a temporary phenomenon, and that though belt-tightening and delayed gratification must take place, growth will eventually be resumed. People think in terms of 'weathering the storm', or even 'waiting for Spring to come round again'. This is the first phase. The time-scale is a short one, and the kind of cuts that are made have three main characteristics: they are quick to find, they are easy to put into effect, and they maintain the existing power relationships as far as is feasible – minimising conflict and doing no lasting damage.

In more formal terms, because the search process is superficial the decision costs are low; because implementation is simple the process costs are low; and because the cuts are reversible the costs of restoration of the *status quo* are low. We have already noted the kind of cutbacks that meet those specifications: make percentage cuts all round, prune budgets at the edges, clamp down on recruitment, defer expenditures (especially maintenance and capital expenditures). This is the *incremental* style.

After a while, two things begin to be noticed: first, the amount saved from the cuts begins to drop off quite rapidly, and second, other costs are introduced, arising from distortion in bureaucratic structure and operations. The effects of the piecemeal, unplanned cuts and postponements of expenditure begin to show (to 'send in their bill') in minor collapses of many sorts. Lack of maintenance brings its nemesis in the need for major repairs and replacements, and the like: a build-up of detrimental effects means that not only is a cheap return to the *status quo* less and less possible, but that the current situation cannot be maintained for much longer.

Clear-sighted people begin to recognise that it could be a long haul, that although growth will eventually return it will be in years rather than months, and that piecemeal opportunistic cuts are not a rational way of approaching the situation. In fact, such cutting is *wasteful*. Consciousness of the organisation as a *production system* increases, and even in the classic bureau, people begin to search for ways to provide services at lower cost, to think in terms of *productivity*. More effort has to be put into finding ways of reducing inputs that will not just put off an evil day, but will result in real, reproducible, and lasting savings.

The change in psychological climate is marked by an acceptance that this kind of 'cut' may be costly in the short run, in research and in disruption and in conflict; but that, once these installation and start-up costs have been borne, the rewards in increase of efficiency will be high. In this second phase authorities are often preoccupied with organisational restructuring and 'reform', including 'privatisation' and hiving-off tasks to bodies outside the mainline bureaucracy; with rationalisation of procedures, bringing in outside experts and consultants to 'streamline production'; with retraining staff, and introducing machinery or computerisation.

Also, Beck Jørgensen says, authorities attempt to *regulate the boundary between the organisation and its environment*: to smooth out inputs (formalising access by clients, standardising forms and treatments, establishing quotas, raising prices), to level down outputs (reducing variety of service tasks, fixing quality of treatment, reducing frequency of inspection, reducing number of service outlets), and to export costs to clients and suppliers (increased waiting times, delayed payments, item charges for service). This is the *managerialist* approach.

These more sophisticated (and costly) forms of cutback management have their limits also, however, and pay decreasing dividends. Greater productivity can only deliver a certain amount of savings, and this typically decreases over a year or two, as ways around the rules are found, slack habits reassert themselves, and unforeseen consequences begin to emerge. Reorganisations may have a brief 'honeymoon effect' in increased task-orientedness and corporate-consciousness, but this too wears off as the system settles down again. The environment changes and requires continual experimental readjustment of the boundary-regulating devices.

Meanwhile, the increased degree of built-in conflict which was initially 'acceptable' becomes less so as it goes on, as opposition regroups and learns the new ropes, and as continued calls for more cuts exacerbate the situation. The abundance of 'slack' resources that formerly 'paid for' lack of co-ordination and tight control have now gone, and the internal shake-up discloses the nature of the zero-sum game that has taken their place (Jørgensen 1987a, 26). The organisation dissolves into its competing interests. Awareness of the detrimental effects overcomes appreciation of the decreasing savings. Scepticism about 'efficiency' allies with a waning belief in eventual regrowth. It becomes obvious that the required cuts cannot be achieved by greater efficiency and shifting burdens at the margin.

The cutback process enters its *strategic* phase. People begin to talk of goals, not methods; the language of priorities, not of efficiency; of the costs and benefits of one object of expenditure rather than another. The attempt at rationality in choosing between activities (that is, which programme to end, which service to abandon, which agency to close down), and in ordering priorities on a defensible basis, hoists the search costs to previously unscaled heights. The collection of social and economic data on which to base decisions involves more surveys, more time, more expertise by an order of magnitude, than in other phases. Demands for documentation are prodigious. Comprehensiveness is the unattainable *sine qua non*. And historically, these tools of macro-rationality appeared just as the preconditions for their use were disappearing.

Beck Jørgensen points to four 'paradoxes' of this situation.

1. The demand for rationality, the ubiquitous use of management information systems and techniques of cost-benefit analysis in the drive to justify spending on one object rather than another, is at its highest precisely when the demand for prioritisation has stepped up the politicisation of all budgeting. Similarly, the need for increased flow and accuracy of information is at its greatest as the supply of it becomes unreliable, highly subjective, in the competitive atmosphere.

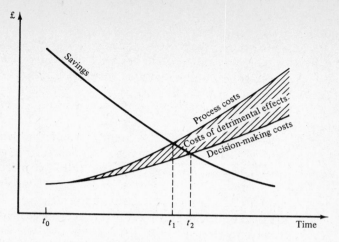

Source: Beck Jørgensen (1987) as modified

Fig. 6.   The Beck Jørgensen model: savings, decision costs, and process
costs.

2. The greatest demand for high-cost research in priority-analysis
arrives when resources are getting scarcer and scarcer.

3. The need for innovative and creative thinking is at its peak just
when the mood of pessimism is at its most dispiriting. And

4. The organisation behaves more and more like an arena of warring
vested interests at the very moment when fiscal survival dictates the
strongest need for comprehensive integrated evaluations.

The elegant lines of the Beck Jørgensen model are represented in Figs. 6
and 7. The vertical axis counts 'costs' in pounds or relative utilities; the
horizontal axis measures time. Fig. 6 displays the typical curves for
'decision-making costs' (costs of search for what to cut, of obtaining
agreement, and of formal authorisation), and for 'process costs' (the total
costs of the cutback process, including implementation and enforcement,
and including also the costs of secondary or 'detrimental' effects). At
whatever level the start-up costs begin, as time goes on they increase, the
total process costs faster than the decision costs themselves – a large part
of the difference in rate being due to the rise in 'detrimental effects'. The
'savings', or value accruing from making the cuts, starts at a relatively
high level in relation to the costs, but falls off with time, as argued above.
Although, of course, the precise length of time it takes for the savings
curve and the process costs curve to intersect, and the precise value

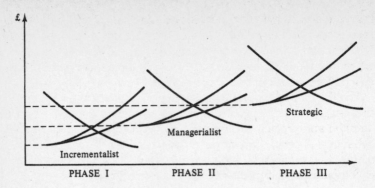

Source: After Beck Jørgensen (1987), as modified

Fig. 7.　The Beck Jørgensen model: incrementalist, managerialist, and strategic phases.

(vertical measurement) at which they do, are empirical matters, different in each case, if the logic of the argument is accepted they will eventually do so; and after that time it will cost more to make cuts than is gained by making them.

As argued in the text, at any particular time the start-up costs of 'incremental' cutbacks are lowest, while those of a 'managerialist' style are higher, and (according to Beck Jørgensen) those in the 'strategic' phase are higher still. This is portrayed in Fig. 7 by the three dotted lines crossing the vertical axis at progressively higher points. The value of the respective savings are correspondingly higher – though not, of course, necessarily higher by the same amount, as the diagram suggests: that too is an empirical matter.

The dynamic of the model is explained thus: beginning at time zero (t_0), incrementalist cuts are made. At time 1 (t_1) the falling efficacy of the cuts has combined with the rising costs of incrementalist pruning to make it no longer sensible to continue – though the fact may not be immediately apparent, if the detrimental effects are not correctly attributed to the cuts or are not easily measured, and so on. However, by t_2 the pure decision costs are clearly prohibitive; a change in approach is needed. At some point in time, whether around t_1 or t_2 as the diagram suggests, or earlier, the need to keep up or even increase the level of savings has made the start-up costs of the managerial approach worth incurring. The switch of approach is rational, rewarded in considerably higher savings, and Phase II has begun. Phase II continues until such time as the falling returns, perhaps combined with yet more fierce demands for cutbacks, induce consideration of the high start-up costs of 'strategic' cuts, with their promise of even more substantial savings to compensate, and Phase III is entered. (The 'doomsday problem', in the sense of what happens when not even Phase III cuts can deliver the necessary savings in expenditure of resources, is not explored in the model.)

This is a richly suggestive, subtle, and sophisticated model, and even at this length we have not exhausted its subtleties. It is designed to describe and predict (on the assumptions of economic rationality) the behaviour of people in a single organisation. However, its very richness makes it the more difficult to test against empirical experience. It encompasses variables dealing with psychological set and time-horizons, intra-organisational politics and assumptive worlds, as well as with the economics of search and transaction costs, intended and unintended consequences, and diminishing returns. Every additional variable brings it closer to a recognisable picture of reality, makes it more plausible and perhaps enlightening, but less easy to test.

In that regard, such a model includes too many variables of quite different kinds, some of them not fully quantifiable. It is impossible, in applying to a real-life situation, to stop enough of them from varying simultaneously. And even then, as Beck Jørgensen acknowledged in a private communication, apparently supportive empirical material might not in reality be so. Public organisations are open to other external influences than demands for cutbacks: the introduction of new technology (at any time) can equally threaten basic power distributions and distort bureaucratic symbiotic patterns. Again, different organisations are differently vulnerable (as we saw in Chapter 5) and so react differently to general pressures for cutback. Yet again, some purely bureaucratic factors may inhibit perceptions of a 'rational' response to diminishing returns: for example, the short time-horizon built into the ordinary budgetary process, and the asymmetrical distribution of benefits and costs in non-selective cuts, might keep an organisation in the incrementalist phase longer than would be rational by concealing the development of detrimental effects – and some such effects are more 'visible' than others. The model might, he concludes, be a useful tool for analysis, but one should not too blithely hope to test it empirically, or be disappointed by finding discrepancies between model and reality.

Above all, Beck Jørgensen warns, it is not designed for application at the macro-level, the level of Cabinet discussion of government programmes in general: it is therefore not testable with data about changes in overall spending and staffing, even department by department.

Before tackling the problems of testing for phasing at macro-level, however, there are perhaps some queries about the logic of the model itself. These principally concern the scope and placing of 'strategic' cutback behaviour. First, strategic cuts, meaning prioritisation among activities and abandoning some, are identified with high search- and transaction-costs and high savings benefits. That 'strategic' is intended to signify 'important' or even merely large cuts is plain both in the original paper and in Beck Jørgensen's private communication, where he explains that the model can be used independently of the 'phasing' dynamic, to predict how an organisation under norms of rationality will react to demands for cuts of any particular size. Very large cutbacks in resources may cause behaviour of the strategic sort directly, without going through the preceding phases. But surely an organisation can prioritise among *minor* activities, and drop some, at small cost and with relatively small benefit? If so, *a priori* one might as well expect a 'strategic' phase to precede the 'managerial' one as to follow it; or, in the non-phased use of the model, for it to predict 'strategic' behaviour at the middle range of required savings, and possibly the lowest one.

The question is whether preserving one programme, service, or agency within a bureau, at the expense of abandoning another, need necessarily involve high search and transaction costs. It seems at least as plausible to argue that the very first phase of cutback management might well include a degree of 'prioritisation'. We might expect to see the elimination of easily identified 'undefended' targets unpopular with bureaucrats, or attacks on particular services by a newly elected Minister with political scores to settle, which can be pursued without the high search and transaction costs that the managerial style will inevitably involve – costs which have to be incurred before any saving whatsoever can take place. Only when the scope for this kind of opportunistic dropping of functions begins to diminish – when politically or bureaucratically unpopular targets are exhausted – will it be worth while to undertake the weary process of managerial cutbacks, with all the conflicts they generate within the bureaucracy as a result of any attempt to disturb its internal organisation and power distribution, and with their sometimes unexpectedly low returns.

In the light of such observations, a reconstruction of the Beck Jørgensen model (even at the meso-level of cutback management for which it was designed) would have to accommodate a division of the 'strategic' type of cuts into, on the one hand, those curtailments and prioritisations which are either minor, or relatively cheap, or politically opportune (or perhaps all three); and on the other hand, those cessations of activities which are major, costly in search and wind-down costs, and above all politically painful to the axe-wielders. We would argue that minor, cheap, and opportune closings-down are likely to be found in the first phase of the cutbacks management dynamic; that cessations of activities which are more important and costly to implement, but still politically (or ideologically) ordained, are quite liable to be undertaken in the second phase, contemporaneously with managerial cutbacks; and that only the abandonment of services the organisation's leaders would really like to retain falls into the third phase.

Such a restructuring would require at least the redesignation of the model's three phases; but we fear that it may rather impugn the logic of the phasing itself to such an extent as to destroy the elegance of the entire model. We shall come back to the point in section v.

Leaving that aside for the moment, let us return to the question whether it is plausible to apply the insights of the Beck Jørgensen phased model of cutback management to the 'whole government' level, rather than to the individual organisation. The first argument is that, as section II of this chapter showed, the earlier literature on cutback management in general prefigured a structure of phases of a similar kind (incremental and quantum, reorganising and curtailing), although with nothing of Beck Jørgenson's comprehensiveness. Second: the discussion of successive 'climates' of psychological disposition is also foreshadowed in earlier literature, and seems as directly applicable to 'national' mood or civil-service-wide attitudes as to those within a single organisation.

Third: an impressionistic review of the historical situation in the UK since 1975 does indeed seem to corroborate the suggestion of a shift from 'incremental' attitudes at the time of the 'IMF' cuts and before, to a more 'managerialist' temper after 1979, and it is quite illuminating to see a 'strategic' phase of cutbacks being triggered by the recognition of 'secular decline', or a reduced role in the world – as Adam Smith explicitly suggested in the final sentence of The Wealth of Nations (quoted in Chapter 1, p. 3). A third phase, 'demand for more rationality', might emerge as a wish for a comprehensive strategy of national priorities in the face of an uncertain future, warring with the realistic appreciation that priority-setting is of its nature conflict-engendering and divisive just when you want national unity. One faction may seek the solution in mutual accommodations, reciprocal acceptance of sacrifices in the building of a consensus-for-survival: to another, the solution may lie in a strong lead in a definite direction, embodying a consistent view of what had 'gone wrong' with the national economy in recent decades, and instituting radical target-setting with authoritarian implementation of firm measures towards these targets. Both 'solutions' would call for legislative changes, deregulations, cessations of some activities, drastic prioritisation – all accurately characterised by Beck Jørgensen's 'four paradoxes'.

There does, then, appear to be good ground for supposing that Beck Jørgensen's model, used with due care, might well provide enlightenment at the macro-level of cutback management, as it does at the meso-level. In any case, the challenge of the earlier literature remains: can we find any evidence for 'phasing' in response to cutback pressures, on the basis of what happened to staffing and spending in British central government departments in the decade 1975–85? If so, does it correspond in any way to a succession of the three cutback styles, incremental, managerial, and strategic?

IV Cutback phasing in Britain, 1975–85

Given the argument in the foregoing paragraphs, it will be appreciated that in what follows we are not really 'testing the Beck Jørgensen model'. To do so adequately we should take the relatively small number of central government departments which were most heavily cut (both continually and deeply, by the definitions in Table 5.4, and in both spending and staffing) over the period (or, desirably, a longer period), and investigate closely the *internal* dispositions made in those departments. This would require a quite different research project from the one we carried out.

Nevertheless, we found that some of the insights of the Beck Jørgensen model were quite plausibly applicable to the whole-government level, and that in any case the suggestion of 'phasing' in cutback management precedes that model. So what we are setting out to do here is to see whether the data on government spending and staffing for the period since 1975 show any evidence of the 'phasing' of 'styles' – that is, moving over time from one style of cutback management to another; from behaviour that is recognisably 'incremental' to behaviour that is 'managerial', and then to 'strategic' cuts (to retain Beck Jørgensen's terms and descriptions).

Even then, it is not easy to find data for the whole decade that can be made to represent incremental, managerial, and strategic styles of cutback management. Plenty of data on spending and staffing exist, as has been shown in earlier chapters, for each year of the period, for central government as a whole, and for each of the departments. But changes in total expenditure or total staffing, or even differential expenditures between programmes or differential cutbacks among categories of staff, and the like, do not readily lend themselves to being classified as incremental, or managerial, or strategic, without a lot more information than we have about what precisely was sacrificed to make the cut possible.

However, the literature is in general agreement that deferment of capital expenditure is typical of the first or *incremental* style, and there are readily available figures for fixed capital formation as a proportion of total programme expenditure, by programme (although not by department). Similarly, a change to the imposition of fees and charges for services rendered, instead of 'free' delivery, is recognised as a characteristic of the *managerialist* style; and we can provide figures for 'appropriations-in-aid' for the whole decade. It is harder to think of a similar use of generally available figures which would indicate 'strategic' behaviour – the abandonment of functions, the significant curtailing of services. The best surrogates are perhaps the proportion of total programme spending represented by 'transfer payments' and grants, loans, and subsidies, which can be gleaned for the period 1977–85 from the *United Kingdom National Accounts*, 1986.

Let us look at capital expenditures first. If the 'phase' theory of cutback management is right, we should be able to detect the start of a period of public-sector cutbacks by noting a drop in the incidence of capital expenditure, followed after a few years, perhaps, by a gradual climb upwards again as nemesis sends in its bill and the consequences of capital expenditure deferment begin to cost more than the savings. Table 7.3 presents the figures for Gross Domestic Fixed Capital Formation as a proportion of total spending for each of the thirteen major programmes of General Government for the period 1977 to 1985 (the fourteenth, 'Other Expenditures', had no expenditures on capital formation; the period was chosen for technical reasons, the method of presenting data in the *National Accounts* having changed). 'Peak' and 'trough' years are indicated in the table.

There is certainly evidence of a common pattern: eight of the thirteen programmes have their 'trough' year in 1981, and two more in the year preceding or following. The years 1980 to 1983 are free of 'peak' years. The question is what these figures tell us about when the period of cutbacks began. Closer inspection of the figures hints at a dip followed by a rise just before the 'trough' year; and this pattern is confirmed by analysis of Table 7.4, which presents the year-on-year percentage change in the figures for capital spending (converted to constant prices). Counting the pluses and minuses in each column gives the following

Table 7.3. *General Government expenditure by programme 1977–85: Gross Domestic Fixed Capital Formation as percent of total programme spending*

Programme	1977	1978	1979	1980	1981	1982	1983	1984	1985
General Public Services	9.0	7.1	6.9	7.7	6.8	8.9	7.1	8.1	7.8
Defence	0.9	0.6	0.7	0.6	0.4	0.6	1.1	1.2	1.5
Public Order and Safety	6.7	6.1	4.6	5.0	4.5	5.0	5.0	4.9	5.3
Education	6.4	5.1	4.7	4.5	3.9	3.3	3.4	3.5	3.7
Health	6.2	5.9	6.1	5.3	5.2	5.8	5.4	5.6	5.6
Social Security	0.3	0.4	0.4	0.4	0.3	0.3	0.3	0.3	0.3
Housing & Amenities	39.9	33.8	28.5	22.7	13.8	n/a	15.1	19.8	17.1
Recreation & Culture	14.4	14.3	15.3	15.3	15.4	15.7	16.5	18.9	15.1
Fuel & Energy*	n/a	7.5	2.0	1.9	4.5	2.4	4.7	2.4	3.0
Agriculture, Forestry, Fishing*	7.5	8.9	11.7	9.8	8.9	10.0	5.5	5.0	3.6
Mining, Manufacturing, Construction*	2.3	2.0	2.3	2.3	1.6	1.6	2.0	2.4	3.6
Transport and Communication*	32.1	28.6	28.4	31.0	25.9	28.0	30.5	48.2	41.4
Other Econ.*	6.6	5.8	6.9	6.7	4.4	4.4	5.0	5.0	3.7
Other Expenditure	0	0	0	0	0	0	0	0	0

Note: *Figures represent net expenditures after repayments of loans, etc.
Figures underlined are highest in row, 'peak year'
Figures in italics are lowest in row, 'trough year'
Source: United Kingdom National Accounts, 1986, table 9.4

result, for the number of minuses (out of thirteen) in each successive year:

1977/8	1978/9	1979/80	1980/1	1981/2	1982/3	1983/4	1984/5
8	5	8	10	5	5	2	4

What we are probably seeing in these years is the tail-end of the Callaghan government's 'IMF' cuts, followed by a brief and slight recovery in 1978/9, then a renewed attack on capital spending under the Thatcher government, reaching its trough in 1980/1 and thereafter easing off again. A longer run of consistently presented data might show these patterns up more clearly; so far as they go, the figures are consonant with the predictions of phasing theory, provided we accept *two* distinct periods of cutbacks, the first ending just before the end of the Labour government in 1979, the second beginning then with a renewed 'incremental' attack on capital spending.

The *managerialist* style is typified by a shifting of financial burdens on to clients, the imposition of fees and charges. If we can detect a clear rise

Table 7.4. *General Government expenditure by programme 1977–85: Gross Domestic Fixed Capital Formation at constant prices and year-on-year percentage change (GDP deflator, 1980=100)*

Programme	1977	1978	1979	1980	1981	1982	1983	1984	1985
General Public Services	441	385 −12.7	385 0	383 − 0.5	302 −21.1	421 +39.4	334 −20.7	379 +13.5	442 +16.6
Defence	99	66 −26.1	79 +19.7	69 −12.7	46 −33.3	68 +47.8	141 +107.3	158 +12.1	195 +23.4
Public Order & Safety	218	196 −10.1	161 −17.8	184 +14.3	173 − 6.0	203 +17.3	201 − 1.0	219 + 8.9	237 + 8.2
Education	812	642 −20.9	585 − 8.9	574 − 1.9	503 −12.4	417 −17.1	439 + 5.3	458 + 4.3	470 + 2.6
Health	641	630 − 1.7	665 − 5.5	616 − 7.4	626 + 1.6	680 + 8.6	676 − 0.6	717 + 6.1	728 + 1.6
Social Security	79	103 +30.4	92 −10.7	92 0	86 − 6.5	85 − 1.2	79 − 7.1	93 +17.7	113 +21.5
Housing & Amenities	3,321	2,768 −16.6	2,475 −10.6	1,895 −23.3	854 −49.5	n/a	879 + 5.0	1,147 +27.9	843 −26.5
Recreation & Culture	179	184 + 2.8	209 +13.6	224 + 7.2	215 + 7.6	219 + 1.9	254 +16.0	302 +18.9	251 −17.2
Fuel & Energy	26	27 + 3.8	30 +11.1	30 0	26 −13.3	21 −19.2	31 +47.6	26 −16.1	36 +38.5
Agriculture, Forestry, Fishing	121	136 +12.4	164 +20.6	160 − 2.4	134 −16.2	167 +24.6	108 −35.3	83 −23.1	74 −10.8
Mining, Manufacturing, Construction	56	56 0	69 +23.2	62 −10.1	50 −19.3	37 −26.0	43 +16.2	45 − 4.6	64 +42.2
Transport & Communication	1,189	1,060 −10.8	1,105 + 4.2	1,059 − 4.2	957 + 1.1	1,150 +20.2	1,173 + 2.0	1,201 + 2.4	1,231 + 2.5
Other Econ.	171	129 −24.6	147 +13.9	150 + 2.0	108 −28.0	102 − 5.5	125 +22.5	142 +13.6	101 −28.9

Source: United Kingdom National Accounts, 1986, table 9.4

in the proportion of a department's income arising from such sources in
particular years, we might be seeing the onset of the managerialist style
of coping with cutbacks. Here we do have a longer run of figures, and we
have already seen (Table 7.1) that for central government as a whole
there certainly are changes in the proportions of total government
expenditure accounted for by appropriations-in-aid (mainly fees and
charges) from year to year. Between 1971 and 1985 there was a sudden
rise in 1976/7, followed by a decline until 1980/1, and then the beginning
of a rise which might not have peaked by 1984/5.

As usual, breaking down total government expenditure into departmental expenditure produces a more complicated picture. But a 'peak
year' analysis of Table 7.2, which presents appropriations-in-aid as a
percentage of gross expenditure for 24 departments, rather confirms the
overall pattern. If one eliminates the Land Registry (for which the figures
are either 100 percent or virtually nothing), and picks out for each of the
remaining 23 departments the year in which appropriations-in-aid
reach their highest proportions during this period, the clusterings are in
1971/2, 1976/7, 1978/9, and 1984/5, with a scattering in other years. If
one then nominates for each department a second year, not necessarily
the year of the second highest proportion but one which seems to
represent the peak of a different cycle, the clusterings are in 1978/9 and,
quite strongly, in 1983/4 and 1984/5. Adding these two distributions
together gives the bottom line below, which (leaving aside the clustering
at the very beginning of the period) seems to suggest a phase peaking in
1978/9, and a second one around the end of the period, 1984/5:

	71/2	72/3	73/4	74/5	75/6	76/7	77/8	78/9	79/80	80/1	81/2	82/3	83/4	84/5
1st	5	0	1	0	1	5	2	3	1	0	0	1	1	3
2nd	0	0	0	1	0	0	1	3	1	1	4	0	6	6
	5	0	1	1	1	5	3	6	2	1	4	1	7	9

If, therefore, an increase in the number of departments deriving a higher
proportion of their revenue from fees and charges rather than from
central taxes indicates a cutback management strategy of the 'managerialist' kind, then there were such phases in the UK around 1978/9
and 1984/5 (the latter possibly continuing).

So this finding, too, though somewhat weakly, is consistent with the
phasing theory: the first cycle peak year for 'managerialist' cuts is later
than the first cycle peak year for 'incrementalist' cuts, and the
'managerialist' peak year in the second cycle is likewise later than the

Table 7.5. *General Government expenditure by programme 1977–85: spending on grants, loans, and subsidies as percentage of programme total spending*

Programme	1977	1978	1979	1980	1981	1982	1983	1984	1985
General Public Services	34.9	43.7	45.6	38.6	34.7	33.4	34.9	37.3	44.0
Defence	0.5	0.5	0.4	0.4	0.5	0.7	0.4	0.5	0.4
Public Order & Safety	2.8	3.0	2.7	2.7	2.1	2.0	1.9	1.8	1.6
Education	18.1	17.8	17.6	18.2	18.4	18.0	18.0	17.9	17.8
Health	0.4	0.4	0.4	0.4	0.3	0.5	0.5	0.6	0.7
Social Security	87.3	87.8	87.8	87.3	88.0	88.4	88.5	88.5	88.6
Housing & Amenities	43.4	48.5	53.9	67.3	61.3	70.9	56.8	51.2	47.3
Recreation & Culture	9.7	10.1	9.9	12.2	10.8	8.9	9.2	8.9	12.9
Fuel & Energy*	—	55.1	89.7	86.8	75.7	88.5	70.6	80.8	80.9
Agriculture, Forestry, Fishing*	62.7	60.7	60.5	59.7	66.0	58.8	62.7	81.4	58.6
Mining, Manufacturing, Construction*	87.1	87.1	91.1	99.2	87.9	84.7	82.2	72.8	76.3
Transport and Communication*	33.9	37.3	38.3	30.3	37.5	37.1	33.8	0.5	14.5
Other Econ.*	61.5	51.5	48.1	50.3	58.0	58.2	58.0	58.5	57.6
Other Expenditure	99.9	99.5	99.6	99.4	99.7	99.5	99.5	99.1	99.7

Notes: *Figures represent net expenditures after repayments of loans, etc.
Figures underlined are highest in row, 'peak year'
Figures in italics are lowest in row, 'trough year'
Source: United Kingdom National Accounts, 1986, table 9.4

'incrementalist' peak year, as measured by the representative objects of expenditure we have used. But the cycles are quite short, and the gaps between the first and second phases surprisingly shorter than the language of the phasing theory ('deepening crisis', etc.) might suggest.

For 'strategic' behaviour, involving abandonment or significant curtailing of services, it is more difficult to nominate representative objects of expenditure for which comparable figures across programmes might be available. It is, however, perhaps reasonable to assume that if curtailing and closing down services is the order of the day (or year), then this will be reflected in expenditure on transfers and subsidies – for which figures are available in the *National Accounts.* Table 7.5 shows these expenditures as percentages of total programme spending, and again, peak years and trough years for each programme are highlighted. The figures for five programmes in the table are unreliable, since they represent net calls on budget after receipts are taken into account. So we performed the additions shown below with and without these programmes – for either 14 or 9 programmes – to give an overall impression of 'trough year' percentages.

| Numbers of programmes with 'trough years' in each year 1977–85 | | | | | | | | |
	1977	1978	1979	1980	1981	1982	1983	1984	1985
Subsidies,									
14 programmes	1	1	3	1	1	2	0	3	2
9 programmes	1	0	2	1	1	2	0	1	1

There is very little evidence here of significant bunching. If one includes the dubious 'net expenditure' programmes, more troughs appear in 1979 and 1984 than in other years, but the differences are small, and the only judgement on the figures as a whole must be that 'strategic behaviour', as measured by this representative type of expenditure, is spread throughout the period.

A similar analysis of 'peak years' (when spending on subsidies, etc. was at its highest during the period) produced a similar result: for 14 programmes one of the years with most 'peaks' was also 1979, and the other was 1985 (as it was for 9 programmes).

If this is evidence for anything, it goes to reinforce our theoretical doubts expressed in the preceding section about identifying 'strategic' or third-phase behaviour with prioritising as such, abandoning functions or curtailing services; not all prioritising need be associated with high search and transaction costs and large benefits. We argued that curtailment might just as easily be a low search and transaction costs activity producing relatively low but quick (and politically desirable) benefits. If there is such a cutback management style as the 'strategic' to be identified, characterised by high decision costs and high benefits, and phased so as to begin when the managerialist phase runs out of steam, we have not managed to capture it by logging changes in spending on subsidies.

A more impressionistic overview of the UK situation since 1979 may yield empirical support at the macro-level to these theoretical doubts about the phasing model. The cutback management approach of Mrs Thatcher's government, certainly not markedly incrementalist, has incorporated much managerialist behaviour, but has also (and perhaps dominantly) shown a strong reliance on prioritisation, deregulation, and dropping activities – from the beginning, and throughout the decade since she became Prime Minister, not merely after the exhaustion of managerialist economies. The theory that prioritising behaviour is forced on cutback managers by the realisation that greater efficiency in operating existing functions will simply not deliver the savings in inputs required by the deepening crisis, or by the reluctant recognition of a diminished role in the world, and so on, just does not explain this. Mrs Thatcher is no pessimist, and she professes to be establishing the conditions for future growth, not accepting the inevitable consequences of secular decline. Nor does it appear to be the size of the cuts required that triggers off 'strategic' behaviour in this case; certain kinds of activities are dropped even when savings demonstrably cannot or are most unlikely to result. Nor do these curtailments necessarily involve high search and transaction costs, or even any high detrimental political effects, if the winning of a third General Election in 1987 is any measure.

Similar puzzles attend many examples of Mrs Thatcher's 'managerialist' behaviour, if we consider it as a style of cutback management. Policies on returning public agencies to the private sector, requiring agencies which remain public to launch commercial activities and find their own revenue, obliging others to buy in services they have been providing for themselves in house (even if no clearly demonstrable 'economies' result), and so on, are not to be justified only by the effects they may (or may not) have on the spending or staffing figures. In some cases at least they would not stand up to a test of rationality on that basis any more than would some of the prioritisations. They are clearly linked with some set of objectives going beyond retrenchment and fiscal restraint altogether.

The explanation of these apparent contradictions was already mentioned at the beginning of the chapter, when it was noted that since 1979 in the UK government cutbacks in spending and staffing have been only partly (if at all) driven by fiscal crisis and external pressures, and have rather been a product of the government's commitment to 'rolling back the state'. Now this is such an obvious and well-appreciated feature of the ideological make-up of 'Thatcherism' (and comparable doctrines in other countries) that it may seem odd to produce it here with a flourish of revelation, as it were. Yet it is the case that most, if not absolutely all, of the discussion about cutback management in the literature has been in the context of fiscal crisis, of externally imposed and ever-deepening financial troubles, of overload of government, and of reluctant (and even recalcitrant) compliance with *force majeure*. As we have demonstrated, models of cutback management dynamics devised in that context may not fit well, or illumine revealingly, the situation where the 'cutbacks' are deliberately sought, done on principle, and pursued regardless of outcome in terms of efficiency or even economy. Perhaps the dynamics of the cutback management process at macro-level need rethinking, to distinguish between cuts which are in practice imposed by external pressures, as were the 'IMF cuts' under the Labour government in 1976, and cuts which are the result of a 'new Right' government's efforts to 'roll back the state'. Let us in the concluding section re-examine the received theories with this in mind.

V   Dynamics of cutback management: a conclusion

From some points of view, a cutback is a cutback, and the 'problem of cutback management', which we identified in Chapter 1 as 'how to wind back bureaucratic spending and staff with least damage to whatever is held dear (including one's hold on power)', is present whether the impetus for the cuts comes from ineluctable external pressure or the relentless drive of the political leaders' inner convictions. One such point of view would be that of the official whose budget is slashed, or whose job disappears. Another such might be that of the senior bureaucrat whose own job or budget is secure enough, but who is charged with wielding the axe on others. He may belong to either the Adam Smith or Weberian tendency and yet see the task as one imposed on him, whatever the motivations of his political bosses. So by no means all (indeed perhaps not much) of the elucidation and analysis of vulnerability to cutbacks, or of tactics of shedding staff, which we have carried out in the preceding six chapters need be re-evaluated in the light of the distinction between 'IMF-type' cuts and 'new Right-type' contraction just made in the previous section. But we have seen the need to think afresh about theories of the *dynamic* of the cutback management process.

There are two main elements of these theories, whether of the simple and partial kind like that of Glassberg (1978) or of the more sophisticated and comprehensive kind like Beck Jørgensen's: an aggregation of 'molecular' cutback management behaviours into distinct 'molar' *styles*, and a non-reversible temporal ordering of these categories of cutback behaviour. If in such a theory cutback management behaviour changes, it changes from one style to the *next*: never backwards, and never mixing bits of one management style with bits of another, because it is an evaluation of the costs and benefits of one molar category of actions-in-pursuit-of-cuts measured against the current demand for cuts that triggers off the switch to the next category. The two elements of the theory of the dynamic are not separable except analytically. (It is true that Beck Jørgensen allows for a non-phased use of his model to predict style from size of cutback demanded; but by the same token that is then not a *dynamic* model.)

The logic of the model thus hangs on the integrity of the aggregations of individual behaviours into a 'style' as much as it does on the aetiology of the phasing. If the same molecular behaviour can with equal plausibility be attributed to two or more different styles then the whole model is impugned, because the causality of the temporal ordering is also affected. If abandoning a service can equally well be seen as a low-cost low-benefit activity, a low-cost high-benefit activity, and a high-cost high-benefit activity, then the integrity of all three aggregations is damaged, and one cannot sum the costs or benefits of each 'style', or reckon when it would be worth while moving to the next. One can attempt to save the theory by separating out 'incremental', 'managerial', and 'strategic' kinds of abandoning a service. But if then the same challenge comes in respect of other forms of selectivity and prioritisation, and later in respect also of molecular privatisation and contracting-out activities (designated 'managerial' in the model but also potentially low-cost low-benefit or high-cost high-benefit in nature, given an alternative rationale), it surely becomes questionable whether the theory is salvable.

That is what the introduction of an alternative rationale for cutting back, in the shape of a new-Right orientation rather than (or on top of) a response to external pressure, does to the received theory of the dynamics of cutback management, as epitomised by Glassberg or Beck Jørgensen (except, of course, that Beck Jørgensen would say that *inside* the bureaucracy, a new-Right orientation among Ministers *is* external pressure). The basic assumption of a phasing model, that cutback methods will be adopted and discarded according to the size of the cuts they deliver compared with the size of the cuts required, is knocked away if some cutback methods are adopted irrespective of the size of the cuts they deliver: the edifice built on that assumption falls down.

Does anything of the phasing theory remain? It might seem so, since our empirical testing of a simple version by means of investigating one molecular item taken as typical of each of the three molar styles of cutback management behaviour did appear to result in confirming that the peak of activity in the 'incremental' item did precede the peak of activity in the 'managerial' item, though nothing much could be said about the 'strategic' item. But the phasing was suspiciously rapid, and in any case the peakiness was by no means striking, and the methodology very weak. No great confidence can be placed in the exercise. Improving the exercise so that it became one in which one could place more confidence (whatever its results) would require another research project.

We cannot say that the possibility of a phasing dynamic in the cutback management process is ruled out by our work. But we would point to two difficulties that any revised theory would have to surmount. The first is that observations of the cutback process in the UK from 1975 to 1985 and later does show a different 'climate' operating in the early years and in the later years of the period; but (a) the difference is not associated empirically with deepening recession or fiscal crisis, and (b) in the later years particularly, different kinds of molecular cutback methods (which would probably be assigned to different aggregates or molar categories in almost any conceivable model) are found operating together. Maintenance is postponed, efficiency drives are mounted, and functions are closed down, in the same year. If a phasing theory is to take this into account, it will have to be a very sophisticated one.

The second difficulty that a revised phasing theory will have to deal with is what we in passing called earlier the 'doomsday problem'. This refers to the need to account in the theory for what happens *after* the third or seventh or whatever is the final phase in the theoretical dynamic. Especially if the model is driven by successive types of response to an ever-increasing demand for retrenchment in staff and restrictions of budget, the theory should incorporate a treatment of one or both of two contingencies: the conditions in which the system collapses altogether (the capacity to respond disappears), or the conditions of reversibility (how the steps are retraced if the demand for cuts slackens off and disappears). We have remarked several times that some theories of cutback management are very similar to theories of government growth run backward; in the same way, a phasing theory of cutback management which can turn into a theory of regrowth is, by Occam's Razor, to be preferred to one that does not even contemplate what happens after cutbacks stop.

It may be that the whole issue of 'cutback dynamics' could be academic in the slighting sense of 'irrelevant to practical policy', if renewed government growth is just around the corner. But as it happens, we ourselves think that staffing cutbacks may go on for a long time yet, for reasons that we shall set out when we gaze into the crystal ball in the final section of the next chapter.

8　The consequences of cutbacks

The cutbacks which we have described in this book have become an international landmark in public-sector management – a landmark seen by some as an awful warning, and by others as a model to be emulated. It is important, however, to keep the cuts in historical perspective.

I　A reprise

As we saw earlier, the lean decade of 1975–85, which saw civil service staff numbers in the UK fall by about 15 percent (by 20 percent if we start the decade with 1976), was not the first or even the most dramatic instance of bureaucratic retrenchment in this century. Rather larger proportionate cutbacks were in fact achieved in the 1920s, when white-collar staffs were cut by over one-third in ten years; and in the demobilisation decade after the Second World War, the total civil service went down between 1945 and 1955 by 35 percent. Fig. 8, drawn from *Civil Service Statistics*, summarises the whole picture.

What is more: the total cut in the 1976–86 decade of 153,600 was made up of 70,500 white-collar staff out of 568,500, or 12.4 percent, together with 83,100 blue-collar staff out of 179,100 – proportionately nearly four times as many (46.4 percent). As *The Economist* pointed out (2 March 1985), Mrs Thatcher's civil service cuts were mainly at the expense of the industrial staff in the dockyards and Royal Ordnance Factories. If the white-collar 'non-industrial' civil servants are regarded as the 'real bureaucrats', the cutback in that decade of 12.4 percent should be compared with the 35 percent white-collar cuts of 1920–30 and the 23 percent white-collar cuts of 1945–55.

Another way to put these staff cutbacks into perspective is to express them in relation to the size of the UK population, as Fig. 9 does. What this shows is that the decade of civil service cutbacks from 1976 to 1986, frequently seen as drastic by both their apologists and their critics, succeeded in winding back the number of white-collar civil servants per thousand population in the UK by only the equivalent of half a decade of

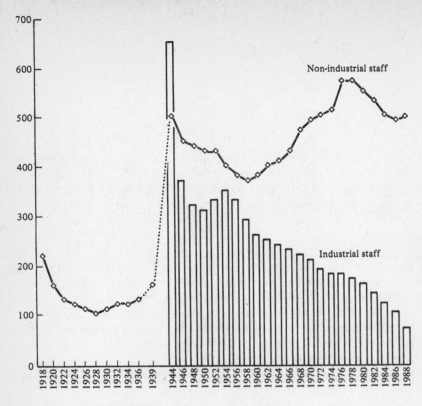

Source: *Civil Service Statistics*, 1988

Fig. 8. UK civil service staff, industrial and non-industrial, 1918–88
(thousands).

growth – to approximately the 1971 level. There would have to be
cutbacks of at least *double* the magnitude of the last decade to bring down
this ratio to the 1961 level, let alone to pre-Second World War levels.
Seen in such a perspective, Mrs Thatcher's espousal of 'Victorian values'
(Daly and George 1987, 121) stopped a very long way short of recreating
nineteenth-century ratios of civil servants to citizens. As Fry (1986, 539)
puts it: 'In its dealings with the main body of the civil service . . ., the
Thatcher government has talked harshly but . . . it has not really
wielded the big stick' (see also Fry 1988).

All that said, however, the UK civil service cutbacks of the 1970s and
1980s are certainly not to be seen as insignificant; and they stand out

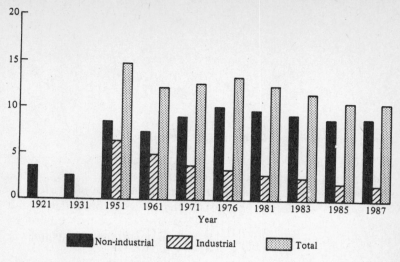

Sources: *Annual Abstract of Statistics*
           Social Trends (annually)
           Civil Service Statistics (annually)

Fig. 9. Civil service staff per thousand population, selected years
          1921–87.

from the earlier periods of cutbacks this century in that they are not
linked to a post-war adjustment, or 'civil demobilisation'. No other major
advanced country has made such dramatic reductions in the staffing of
its core central government bureaucracy in recent years, though some
have been more successful at winding back real public spending per head.

Up to now, we have been describing who and what were cut back,
exploring ways of explaining why some parts of the bureaucracy were
cut heavily while other parts came off with hardly a scratch, and others
again actually obtained substantial extra resources; and investigating
the dynamics of the cutback management process. 'Vulnerability', we
saw, is more difficult to explain than commonly accepted ideas would
lead us to think; 'what everybody knows' is an unreliable guide to actual
outcomes, and even quite refined logic sometimes fails to explain what is
observed.

Now, however, we turn from a focus on the causes or predictors of
bureaucratic cutbacks to discuss instead what people believe the
consequences of such cutbacks will be. It is too early, and there is no
adequate data, to try to evaluate the effects of the recent staffing cuts on

the quantity or quality of public services, in objective terms. But we can survey what commentators believe are 'bound' to be the consequences of such cutbacks. This is what we do in the next section and the succeeding one. In the final section of the chapter we hazard a look into the future of the civil service bureaucracy in the UK, towards the turn of the millennium, based on the trends already in evidence.

II   The consequences of cutbacks: three credos

Like vulnerability, the consequences of cutbacks in bureaucracy are more commonly asserted than demonstrated. 'Evidence' is offered rather in the classical rhetorical form of *enthymeme* – chop-logic, often involving a cumulation of selected examples – than by systematic survey (cf. Aristotle 1932, 150ff.). Here we will consider three 'credos' or positions on the consequences of bureaucratic slimming, designated as follows:

the *lean and fit* credo;
the *anorexia* credo; and
the *gattopardismo* credo.

The 'lean and fit' credo

This is, of course, the official religion. It embodies the optimistic belief that financial and staffing pressures on public bureaucracies will make them more efficient and effective in the long run – indeed, perhaps that cutbacks are the *only* way of making public bureaucracies more efficient.

Those of this belief may well concede that a host of ills may need to be faced before the desired configuration is attained. These ills may include initial bureaucratic responses to cutback pressures, comprising defensive and unimaginative strategies of damage limitation (equal misery, cosmetic cuts), or, worse, a strategy of deliberate damage maximisation designed to achieve the restoration of resources by channelling cutbacks into the most politically embarrassing areas. But as cutbacks continue, the argument goes, such strategies will be exposed as irrational, and persistent squeezing will eventually force bureaucracies out of lassitude or complacency, oblige more radical and imaginative restructuring of methods and activities, and expose bureaucrats to the painful but salutary process of prioritisation and close-in trade-offs. Those of this persuasion also hold that the quality of the bureaucracy will rise as it shrinks in total size, as a lower volume of recruitment drives up entry standards and as reduced opportunities for promotion force ambitious bureaucrats to lift their performance well above what might have been needed in the 'fat years'.

The latter argument has been put by Self (in Wright 1980, 126), who argues:

A reduction in the intake of staff should improve the quality of those appointed, given the growing competition for jobs – especially jobs carrying a good deal of security. The explanation would not be simply or primarily a slightly higher possibility of the sack, but the keener competition for promotion which occurs when rapid growth ceases, and possibly some shift in the climate of social psychology about work behaviour.

This is the corollary of Self's later argument that:

Public expenditure growth has largely been negatived through declining levels of efficiency and performance . . . a rapid expansion of staff under conditions of full employment . . . can be expected to lead to some dilution in the quality of staff and also (though more arguably) to some decline in work incentives or motivations. (Self 1980, 132)

Such a belief rests on an ultimately rational view of organisation. It is, of course, espoused by those who believe that public bureaucracies are amenable to greater efficiency through the use of business methods, for example in Lord Rayner's well-known view that talent is grossly wasted in the UK civil service because of traditional management techniques which fail to harness the ideas of staff that could lead to higher efficiency levels (see Bray 1987, 33–5). The view also has some academic adherents, notably Hartley and Lynk (1983), who have offered some evidence of increasing rationality of resource use in UK defence expenditure in the context of continuing cutbacks; and also Beck Jørgensen (1985), whose ideas we have discussed earlier in the book and who sees a process of bureaucratic responses to cutbacks which reflect increasing 'realism' over time.

The anorexia credo

Contrary to the beliefs of the 'leaner (eventually) means fitter' school are the views of those who see bureaucratic slimming as in general profoundly damaging to the quality of public-service provision and as tending to make those bureaucracies even less effective and efficient than they were before. An elegant early statement of this viewpoint was made by Glennerster (1981). If 'leaner means fitter' is the official religion, 'leaner means anorexia' is the commonest form of dissent.

Far from visualising the immediate disruption, conflict, and damaging 'sore thumb' tactical responses to cutback pressures as temporary ills leading eventually to glowing health and efficiency, this school of thought sees such ills as the symptoms of more deep-seated diseases, presaging only increasing debilitation. The obsessive desire for leanness is seen as *anorexia bureaucratica*, which in the long run has the unintended consequence of bringing on chronic weakness or even death. Such a pathology is so far removed from the conventional stereotype of bureaucratic dysfunctionality – chronic waste of resources through excess demands on the public budget to finance overconsumption and overproduction – that it rarely figures in lists of bureaucratic diseases (it is, for example, little discussed by Hogwood and Peters 1985 in their catalogue of policy pathologies).

Such a belief may have several grounds. First, it may be held that the scope for 'efficiency' gains in public bureaucracies is generally quite small, contrary to widespread popular myths of inherent wastefulness and 'slack'. From this point of view, exercises in promoting efficiency and cutting waste are like looking for the crock of gold at the end of the rainbow – we search for something that simply is not there, however conditioned we may have been to believe in it. So, the argument runs, efficiency drives will inevitably lead to disappointment in terms of real results achieved (Schaffer 1973, 100), or else achieve spurious economies by sacrificing quality. Several outsider accounts of the efficiency programme in the UK civil service in the 1970s and 1980s put the results down to simple cost-cutting without regard to outputs, rather than to genuine gains in efficiency (see for example Thomas 1984); this is probably the dominant academic interpretation.

Second, and rather more radically, it may be held that cutbacks, far from promoting efficiency, will actually tend to have the opposite effect. It is a common experience for people on a diet to find that the weight that is shed is not always in the places that they expect or desire; bureaucratic slimming, it is argued, often has a similarly unfortunate effect, in several possible ways. Legal and other constraints often mean that eating their seed-corn is the only feasible strategy for bureaucracies faced with demands for immediate cutbacks. Given that the basic wage bill has to be paid and that services required by law or by political pressure cannot be quickly scrapped, the only options lie in cutting maintenance, training, research, or capital spending; so that efficiency is progressively reduced by increasingly dilapidated or out-of-date equipment and obsolete skills.

Similarly, it is argued from this viewpoint that – in spite of brave talk about purposive management drawn from private-business management textbooks – public bureaucracies often have no other feasible method of coping with staff cutbacks than by a hiring and promotions freeze. Such a policy denies youthful talent to the bureaucracy and results in disproportionate cutbacks at the bottom and the top of the bureaucracy, which tend to be the groups with the highest turnover, and also in those areas where the bureaucracy is competing most actively with the private market, for example, the tax avoidance industry (for evidence of this, see *Civil Service Statistics*, 1987, 31).

The result of such processes, it is claimed, will be anything but rational or efficient. They mean a middle-ageing body of bureaucrats increasingly concentrated in grades where turnover is lowest and occupying positions that are nominally senior, managerial, or advisory but who in fact have fewer subordinates to supervise, and who are increasingly depleted in key strategic areas such as tax-collection and data-processing skills. In other words, the bureaucracy develops an increasingly out-of-date and inappropriate resource mix just at the time when it is under greatest pressure to raise its efficiency.

Nor does the efficiency-lowering effect of cutback end there, to this way of thinking. Cutbacks are also held to have deeply negative motivational effects on those who are left working within the bureaucracy. Squeezes on promotion may cause some bureaucrats to opt for an easy life rather than try to raise their performance level sufficiently to compete successfully in a promotions pool that has all but dried up. Job satisfaction may decline because cutbacks are perceived as attacks on the worth of public bureaucracies, particularly since such cutbacks tend to be much trumpeted and often exaggerated by governments in order to please the financial markets and party zealots. Further, it is often said that the increased stress, frustration, and bureaucratic in-fighting associated with deepening cutbacks have a devastating effect on bureaucratic morale. In this credo, therefore, there is a 'pincer movement' consisting of reduced motivation on the one hand and increasingly out-of-date or inappropriate resources on the other hand, which drives the bureaucracy to test new lows of inefficiency.

The gattopardismo credo

Heretical to both the creeds mentioned above is the belief that cutbacks in bureaucracies make hardly any difference to bureaucratic working. Bureaucratic slimming is like the person who does not diet or exercise but wears 'more slimming' clothes – vertical stripes rather than horizontal, and so on. Nothing changes underneath. Cutbacks in this view are seen as just another instance of a phenomenon commonly

196 The consequences of cutbacks

observed in organisational and bureaucratic life, the 'deck chair shuffle' or superficial reform for appearances' sake, which changes nothing of substance. The Italian term, applied to the frequent government reshuffles, is *gattopardismo*: the *gattopard* is the leopard, who as everyone knows, cannot change his spots.

In this heresy, the dancing of the bureaucratic corps on the policy stage – their manoeuvres, their victories and defeats in their balletic battles for 'turf', access to the throne, treasure, followers – bears little if any relation to real life, to wider social outcomes. To this way of thinking, the idea that government departments (indeed, any organisations) do or ever could act rationally is dismissed as fantasy, wishful thinking of the first order, a sly joke by Max Weber. *Gattopardismo* heretics would not expect levels of bureaucratic efficiency to have any relationship to changes in resource inputs, or bureaucratic outputs to have any save quite accidental relationship to observable social changes. Aaron Wildavsky (1980) sometimes shows heretical leanings of this sort, as in the chapter 'Doing better and feeling worse'.

But there is a sect which, starting from *gattopardismo*, takes the credo a stage further, and believes that there *is* sometimes a relationship between bureaucratic action and social outcomes – a perverse one. These adherents have their guru in Ivan Illich (1977), who pointed out that schools diseducate and doctors make you ill. They like to cite off-beat instances showing how problematic, to say the least, is the relationship between bureaucratic outputs and social outcomes: for example, the reduction of death-rates during doctors' strikes in Israel in 1973 and Bogotá in 1976, the tendency for police staffing levels to be positively rather than negatively related to crime rates, the fact that during the three-day working week imposed during the 1974 coal strike in the UK, industrial output was 80 percent and not 60 percent of normal; and so on. For such ultra-heretics, we are lucky if the relationship between what bureaucrats do and what happens to us is a random one; they are more likely, in this view, to make any social situation worse than if they had left it alone. In that respect, indeed, the fewer civil servants, the better – but not on any belief that a slimmer bureaucracy is a more efficient or effective one.

III A trialogue

Which of these three credos (presented in tabular form in Table 8.1) is closest to the truth about bureaucratic slimming? There can be no definitive answer. What we should try to do is to clarify the issues, to

Table 8.1. *Effect of cutbacks on bureaucratic performance: three perspectives*

	The 'lean and fit' credo	The anorexic credo	The *gattopardismo* credo
Believed effect of cutbacks on bureaucratic performance	STRONG	STRONG	WEAK
Believed effect of financial pressure on bureaucratic motivation	POSITIVE (pressure to perform better, increasing quality through stiffer competition in recruitment and promotion)	NEGATIVE (promotion cuts reduce incentive to raise performance and cuts have symbolic effect)	INDETERMINATE
Believed effect for efficiency gains from efforts to cut waste	HIGH (waste through poor management)	LOW (cuts may reduce efficiency)	INDETERMINATE

bring out some of the ambiguities which confront any simple interpretation of the consequences of bureaucratic cutbacks and to refer to the kinds of evidence that each of the three viewpoints just described might base themselves on. The traditional device of exposition for such a purpose is to present a dialogue between protagonists of each point of view; and that is the means we have chosen to use here. The matters at stake are rather less profound than those treated in the classic dialogues of political thought, such as *Crito* or *The Republic*, but perhaps the presentational device will serve the same purpose.

Our imaginary 'trialogue' involves three stereotype characters, each representing one of the credos set out in the previous section and trying to construct arguments in support of his or her views about the consequences of cutbacks. The names we have given to the trio are Orthodox Believer (as the embodiment of the 'leaner is fitter' credo); Dissident (as an embodiment of the 'anorexia' credo); and Heretic (as an embodiment of the *gattopardismo* credo). 'Dissident' opens the discussion.

Dissident: It is easy to see that cutbacks in the UK civil service over the decade of the middle seventies to the middle eighties had a very damaging effect. The earlier chapters of this book contain much of the evidence that is needed. The government's own figures on the sources of staff cuts which were discussed in Chapter 6 (and which are summarised

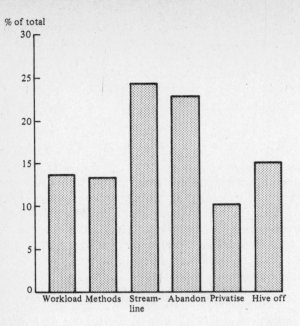

Sources: Management and Personnel Office
(as for Table 6.1)

Fig. 10. Sources of civil service staff savings, 1980–5.

here in Fig. 10) show that a quarter of the civil service staff losses over the period 1980–5 came from 'general streamlining', which is obviously a bureaucratic euphemism for reduced levels of service, and another 23 percent came from dropping functions. So even on the official figures we can see that half of the staff cutbacks came from simply chopping services, not raising efficiency, and it is plausible to suppose that the true figure must be well above that when the creative accounting is stripped away.

Orthodox Believer: Is it quite as clear-cut as that? There is a loose but still intelligible sense of the word efficiency in which you can say that it is inefficient to retain services for which demand is low and provision is very costly – to offer a Rolls-Royce service when a Ford or a Toyota will do. I don't accept anyway that 'streamlining' simply means reduction in service quality and nothing else: the official definition of the category to which you are referring is 'general streamlining (including lower standards of service) and other minor changes', which implies that lower standards are only a minor part of the category as a whole. I think that these figures show considerable evidence of increased efficiency, in that fewer than a quarter of the jobs were shed by abandoning functions *simpliciter*, and that therefore three-quarters of the cutbacks must have resulted from increased efficiency. Notice that more than a quarter of the cuts were made by changing methods or as a result of changes in demand.

Heretic: Another quarter of the staff cuts came from hiving off, privatisation, and contracting out, which conveniently got the civil service staff numbers down, particularly when the Thatcher government failed to make any real cuts in aggregate government spending (as this book shows), and therefore needed to show bureaucratic scalps on the wall to convince the voters that it was keeping its election promises. But are these shifts to contracting out, private ownership, or other public bodies really *cutbacks* at all, or just creative accounting involving ever more subtle kinds of quangos? I'll need some convincing that they are not just cosmetic, shuffling the deck-chairs on the *Titanic*. And that goes particularly for these numbers about sources of staff cuts that Orthodox Believer and Dissident are arguing about. How real are they? To my mind, they are just the quirky product of yet another meaningless exercise in bureaucratic form-filling. How carefully did departments make the returns which form the basis of these figures? Or was it just one of those exercises in which no one understands quite what the categories that have come down from on high are supposed to mean, but it's too much trouble to sort out, and the inevitable result is incomprehension at compound interest?

Dissident: Well, let's move on to something that rests on a more objective basis. Just look how much more middle-heavy in structure the UK civil service bureaucracy became over the period 1976–86. This is something that this book has also shown, and it is summarised here in Table 8.2. As you can seen, the highest and the lowest ranks were in proportionate terms cut more severely than the middle ranks. It's the usual political story of those at the bottom of the heap getting hit the hardest, at the expense of those with more clout. Now this squares exactly with Martin's (1983) examples of the same phenomenon in various bureaucracies undergoing cutbacks in the USA. It shows that staff imbalances of just the sort described by Beck Jørgensen (1985) and other theorists of bureaucratic cutbacks did develop in this case.

Table 8.2. *Percent changes in civil service staff 1980–5: full-time equivalents*

Top	
Grades 1, 2, 3 (Under Secretary and above)	−19.3
Middle	
Grades 4 to 10 (Assistant Secretary to Executive Officer or equivalent)	− 9.2
Bottom	
Grades 11 to 13 non-industrial civil service	
(Clerical Officer and below) plus industrial civil service	−18.2

Source: Management and Personnel Office

Orthodox Believer: I don't agree with that at all. If you read the earlier chapters on vulnerability carefully, you see that not all 'bottom of the heap' groups were hit harder than those which have traditionally been more entrenched. For example, UK civil service staff during these cutbacks became distinctly less, not more, London-based; less, not more, male; less, not more, concentrated into the five largest (or nine largest, if you prefer) government departments. You have only achieved your Table 8.2 result by lumping industrial staff together with lower-grade non-industrial staff. I admit that bracketing the two categories together is accurate in terms of the salary levels of the non-industrial civil service, but it is still a rather contrived result. If you leave the industrial civil service out, you can no longer say that the lowest ranks were cut much more heavily than the middle ranks. The suffering was more or less equal between them.

But even if I accept your argument that the bureaucracy really became more middle-heavy over this period, I would personally explain that by the pressure imposed by cutbacks for more efficient methods of operation, and that generally means using more complex technology, with consequently rising labour skill requirements – for example, computer-controlled robots to inspect the drains rather than gangs of labourers with picks and shovels trying to find leaks. The tendency is anything but irrational, and actually is associated with rising efficiency levels, not the reverse.

Heretic: You have both just committed the familiar logical fallacy of *post hoc ergo propter hoc*. What your arguments ignore is that there is a generic trend in the direction of middle-heaviness in modern bureaucracy everywhere, mainly because of the production style-changes to which Orthodox Believer refers. But does this trend have anything much to do with cutbacks? And does it necessarily mean more efficiency? Or is

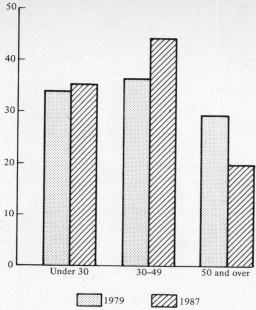

% of non-industrial staff

Under 30   30–49   50 and over

☐ 1979   ▨ 1987

Source: HM Treasury ('MANDATE')

Fig. 11. Percentage of civil service staff under age 30, 30–49, and over 50 years, 1979 and 1987.

it just a bureaucratic imperative, like police preferring to work with specialised high-tech units rather than pounding a beat?

Dissident: There might be something in that, Heretic, if it were just grade changes that we were seeing. But take a look at what happened to the age distribution of the bureaucracy over the same period (Fig. 11). The civil service may have become less, not more, male, but it became distinctly more, not less, middle-aged. The proportion of staff in the 30–49 age-bracket rose markedly over the period. It's not just a drift to middle-heaviness but a drift to middle-age as well, and that just proves my point. It's linked with the fact that resignation rates tend to be much higher in the under-30 age-band of the civil service in all grades than among the over-30s (*Civil Service Statistics*, 1987, 31, gives the evidence for this).

Orthodox Believer: Now you really are twisting the facts to suit your argument. The civil service bureaucracy was only 'middle-ageing' over that period in one special sense, as Fig. 11 shows. The increase in the proportion of the 30–49 age group comes at the expense of the over-50s (who have markedly fallen back as a proportion), not of the under-30s, who as a proportion of the civil service actually rose over this period. Now I would say that this means that the bureaucracy actually became more *youthful* over the period. And though it is true that resignation rates are much higher in the under-30 age-group than among the over-30s, don't forget that the same goes for *recruitment* rates (see *Civil Service Statistics*, 1987, 30) – and recruitments exceeded voluntary resignations for every year but one over 1977–86.

Even to the extent that the bureaucracy did become more 'middle-aged', I certainly couldn't agree with your implied point that the reduction in the proportion of over-50s is necessarily conducive to reduced efficiency. I suggest that it is just the reverse, since the over-50s are the group which are most likely to have obsolete skills and to have the greatest difficulty in adapting to new methods and technology.

Heretic: You have both committed the *post hoc ergo propter hoc* fallacy again. The relationship between these age changes and cutbacks is highly problematic. It could well be explained by long-term social trends such as increasing female participation in bureaucratic work (making for middle-ageing with fewer interrupted female careers and a reduced turnover of young females) and by a general society-wide trend towards earlier retirement.

Dissident: Well, you can't deny that the seed-corn was eaten, and that is a pretty good indicator of cumulative inefficiency. When cutbacks come, capital spending is always the main casualty, and that means increasing inefficiency over the long run.

Orthodox Believer: Actually, capital spending fell back by less than 1 percent (0.67 percent) of central government spending over the period 1978/9 to 1985/6 (see *UK National Accounts*, 1986, tables 7.2 and 7.3) – and that was out of a total spending which was *increasing* in real terms, remember. And spending on research and development changed very little as a proportion of the total. I think that both of these facts indicate that this period of cutbacks was relatively well managed, so that reductions didn't create inefficiency.

Heretic: What exactly are these figures supposed to prove? Overall levels of expenditure say nothing about the efficiency with which the resources are used, which is what you two are trying to argue about. What matters is not the *level* of spending but the *quality* of that spending and the way that the capital items are actually used. Neither of you has produced any evidence about that.

Dissident: There isn't any systematic evidence on it, though I could tell you plenty of stories. But I would confidently expect the level of efficiency in the use of resources to fall dramatically when people are as poorly motivated as public bureaucrats became during a period of severe cutbacks. That's because the cutbacks mean that opportunities for bureaucratic promotion dry up, and job satisfaction declines as harassed bureaucrats find themselves being attacked by clients (sometimes physically, especially if they are working in the front line of the welfare bureaucracy) for declining levels of service. As massive public discontent builds up against collapsing public services and the short-staffed bureaucracy becomes increasingly creaky and inefficient, civil servants take the blame, and at the same time feel reduced self-esteem because the cutbacks are saying that the government doesn't value their services and believes that the bureaucracy is wasteful and self-serving. That's a climate in which efficiency goes backwards, not forwards.

Orthodox Believer: What exactly *is* the evidence that civil servants were demoralised by the cuts? I haven't seen any reliable opinion polls which show that. Simple assertions by obviously self-interested parties such as public-service labour unions can't be accepted as reliable evidence, any more than assertions from farmers can be accepted as evidence that the price of grain is too low. Now, if the public bureaucracy has really become much less attractive a place to work, as you argue, we should expect the incidence of departures from the bureaucracy to increase. March and Simon (1958, 84–8) and Barnard (1938) before them say that any organisation needs to maintain some balance of inducements and contributions for its members if it is to survive, and if that balance changes unfavourably for employees, we can expect an increased rate of exodus. That's only common sense. In fact, if we look at the rate of voluntary resignation from the civil service bureaucracy over the period 1977–85 (Fig. 12), we can see that *exactly the opposite* happened. Now, this suggest to me that the civil service bureaucrats became *more*, and not less, satisfied with their work, and that even civil servants respond enthusiastically to discipline and better management methods. Moreover, as I mentioned before, for every year between 1977 and 1986 except for 1979 (Fig. 13) there was more than one new recruit to the civil service for every civil servant who voluntarily resigned, which doesn't suggest that the inducements–contributions balance got any worse.

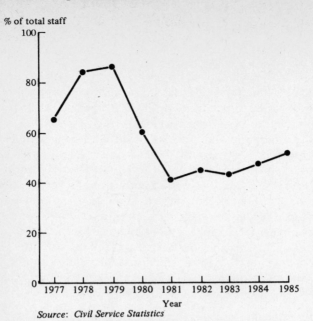

Source: *Civil Service Statistics*

Fig. 12. Voluntary resignations from the civil service: percentage of total staff, 1977–85.

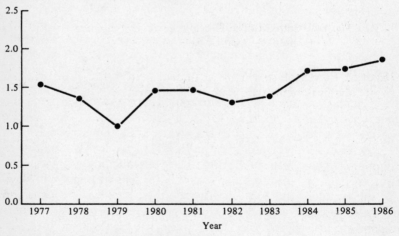

Source: *Civil Service Statistics*, 1977 and 1986

Fig. 13. Number of civil service recruits for each voluntary resignation, 1977–86.

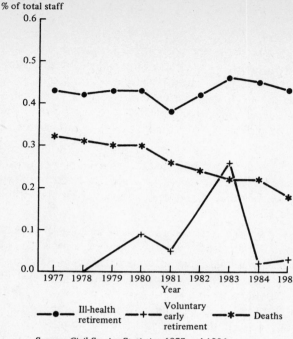

% of total staff

——●—— Ill-health retirement   ——+—— Voluntary early retirement   ——*—— Deaths

Source: *Civil Service Statistics,* 1977 and 1986

Fig. 14. Deaths in office, ill-health, and early retirements as percentage of total civil service staff, 1977–85.

Dissident: Pure sophistry. Your argument ignores the most important point, namely the sharp rise in unemployment rates in the labour market over the period, which narrowed the opportunities for disgruntled ex-bureaucrats seeking alternative employment, and this only served to increase levels of discontent by removing the safety-valve. And look at the incidence of voluntary early retirement (Fig. 14), which *did* show an increase for years in which early retirement schemes were available. If, as I argue, morale in the civil service was reduced by cutbacks, but did not manifest itself in mass resignations because of the unfavourable general job market, that should not affect departures due to early retirement to the same extent, and therefore this is the better index of discontent in the bureaucracy.

Heretic: But the greater incidence of voluntary early retirement (actually a very slight one) simply goes back to my earlier point that this is a generic social trend and it is difficult to show that it has much to do with cutbacks in the civil service. And if bureaucrats were really being subjected by cutbacks to intolerable and life-shortening levels of stress, we might expect that to show up in increased incidence of ill-health retirement, or even a greater incidence of deaths in office. In fact, there is no real change in the incidence of these types of departure at all, as you can see from Fig. 14. So if cutbacks exposed bureaucrats to greater stress and pressure, the effects were evidently not fatal in a literal sense. Neither Dissident nor Orthodox Believer can draw much comfort from these indices.

Dissident: Even so, these cutbacks damaged the capacity of the bureaucracy to operate efficiently and to provide the levels of service that people in an advanced country ought to have a right to expect. The dismal evidence is all around us.

Orthodox Believer: Did service deteriorate markedly in quality? Was this the general perception? If this was obvious to everyone, why wasn't Mrs Thatcher's government summarily voted out of office in 1983 and 1987? Why did the incidence of complaints to the Parliamentary Commissioner for Administration about maladministration by the civil service (and of complaints which were found to be valid by the PCA) actually decline between 1976 and 1985, if the cutbacks reduced competence and efficiency as you suggest? Why did rates of emigration from the UK actually fall back over this period and rates of immigration increase if, as you suggest, public services were worsening to such an extent that the country was becoming a much less attractive place to live in? Look at *Social Trends,* 1987 (table 1.15, 37) if you don't believe me. Does this signify widespread discontent with deteriorating public services? I think it is just the reverse.

Dissident: That is completely beside the point. The election landslides of 1983 and 1987 were engineered by cynical vote-buying ploys such as the sale of nearly a million publicly owned houses to tenants at knock-down prices between 1979 and 1985, not by maintaining high-quality public services. In fact, when public-service quality deteriorates year after year, despair starts to set in and expectations decline, and that is how I would account for the falling incidence of complaints to the PCA. What you really have to look at is the basic quality of life in the UK, which was profoundly damaged over this period as a result of these cutbacks. They turned the UK into a nastier, more crime-prone, more unequal, and above all more unemployed society with steadily declining levels of service in health care and education. I rest my case.

Orthodox Believer: I simply can't accept that. Levels of reported crime may have risen, but police and law enforcement was one area in which cutbacks were not made in either staff or spending (see Chapter 5), which hardly supports your argument. And you are on shaky ground in arguing that society became more unequal. It is true that in his discussion of this, Halsey (1987, 17) shows that in terms of income, the share of the lowest quintile of households slipped back slightly and the share of the highest quintile slightly increased between 1976 and 1984 (though the changes in share of final income were very small), but for holdings of wealth he shows just the opposite picture. The percentage of marketable (and also of non-marketable) wealth in the hands of the richest 1 percent, 5 percent, 10 percent, 25 percent, and 50 percent of the population all declined between 1976 and 1984. Is that rising inequality? Unemployment rates may have risen as a result of the second wave of post-Second World War 'baby boomers' coming on the labour market, but the absolute number of people in employment scarcely fell at all after 1976. As for declining levels of service in health care and education, I'd like to point out that death rates per 1,000 population slightly fell between 1976 and 1985, mean expectation of life at birth rose (see *Social Trends*, 1987, 1.14, 36) and participation in the non-compulsory sector of education (higher education and public-sector schools for children under 5) actually increased between 1975/6 and 1984/5. In fact, the civil service cutbacks were associated with increased levels of performance. I rest *my* case.

Heretic: Does any of this have any demonstrable relationship to the numbers employed in the civil service? Death rates and crime rates reflect generic social trends which bureaucrats can affect very little. Anyway, I think you'll find much the same trends in countries which have not had civil service staff cuts. And I rest my case also.

This imaginary trialogue reflects fairly closely, we think, the terms in which the debate over the consequences of bureaucratic cutbacks in the UK (and elsewhere) has been conducted over the past decade. It is for the reader to judge what weight is to be put on the arguments put forward by the three protagonists; but each of the trio has a point to make and can find some corroboration within the (severe) limits of the available public-record evidence. We can confidently predict that future historians are likely to be pondering the effects of the 1970s/1980s civil service cutbacks for years to come.

The one thing that Orthodox Believer, Dissident, and Heretic probably could agree upon is that their debate is important, but that at the point where each participant wants to inflict a knock-out blow on the others, the data run out. Clearly, if such debate is to be sustained and to move beyond the confident assertions of first principles which our trio exchange, further and much more detailed monitoring of this landmark experiment in bureaucratic staffing reduction is needed.

IV   Crystal gazing

Only future historians are likely to know the answer to the question whether these civil service cutbacks will appear as a temporary hiccup in a long-term development of government growth in staffing and spending (call that Scenario One); whether they will 'bottom out' relatively soon into a new lower plateau (in a reversal of Peacock and Wiseman's (1967) famous 'peak and rising plateau' account of UK public-spending growth from the 1890s to the 1950s) – Scenario Two; or whether they presage a continuing process of cuts in the central civil service well into the twenty-first century (Scenario Three).

Predictions in public administration have a notoriously short shelf-life. But in this final section of the book we shall marshal such evidence and arguments as are available, based on trends that are already apparent, to let us look into the crystal ball and discern which of the three foregoing scenarios is the most likely.

Scenario One

There are a number of reasons for supposing that the present era of cutbacks may be a phase that will come to an end. First, sustaining the momentum of serious cuts takes a great deal of commitment and political energy; in the long run, politicians and their advisers will usually find more advantages in spending more money and doing more things than in doing less. At one time, not long ago, there was a great passion among Conservatives in the UK for abolishing 'quangos' (non-departmental agencies of various kinds); but it proved more difficult than was at first appreciated, and after two largely cosmetic purges had taken place in the early 1980s the issue was quietly allowed to drop. It is not impossible that the drive for cutting back the civil service will follow the same course; when enough political capital has been made, when party zealotry has found a new kind of target altogether, when all the easy pickings have been gathered in and further cuts get harder and harder to find – then, perhaps, efficiency in management will be considered to have been achieved, the honours will be distributed, and the issue laid to rest. There came such a time, after all, in the earlier period of retrenchment in the 1920s, when 'Geddes' Axe' was put away and recruitment began again.

A second argument for supposing that the civil service cutbacks are bound to come to an end, and sooner rather than later, hangs on a turn-around of government policy – either under a new majority party or coalition, or even under a Conservative government. It takes no great imagination to envisage circumstances where even Tory backbenchers may begin to fear the consequences of continuing cutbacks, and where public protest (built up by long frustration and triggered into media outcry by some particular death or disaster) is focussed on staffing deficiencies: a spate of battered babies or hypothermia deaths, a surge in illegal immigration or smuggling, massive corporate swindles or trans-port disasters, if linkable with staffing cuts or the 'lean government' philosophy, might perhaps jerk the retrenchment engine out of forward gear and into reverse. Not on quite the same argument, but turning also on a change in policy, it is not wholly inconceivable that a government would once more use public employment as a job-creation machine; perhaps as a prophylactic against renewed inner-city riots, enrolling jobless youngsters by the thousand into a civilian army or National Urban Renewal Force. Perhaps a British government may one day adopt an 'Indian policy' on machine-substitution, maximising human labour rather than economising on it.

Any such changes in policy might halt the slide in public-service numbers. However, it is difficult to imagine many disaster-linked policy recoils which would bring much comfort to the central bureaucracy as such. Perhaps we lack imagination, but it seems to us that the likeliest sites for such a recoil in the civil service would be in the customs and immigration fields, or perhaps in defence procurement. In most cases of plausible policy recoils, staff replacement would seem likely to occur in local government services, or in grant-funded independent bodies, in public corporations, or at best in the industrial civil service.

It is one thing to show how the slide in public employment might conceivably be halted; but it is another to demonstrate that renewed secular growth in government staffing is likely to resume. The argument for that rests essentially on projection of past trends for a century and more, and on explanations for the growth of government in the decades up to the 1980s. But the weight of evidence and argument today is on the other side. The cutbacks we have been elucidating fit into what can be seen as a long-term shift in administrative style, from classic public bureaucracy (direct service delivery) to a 'contract state'. Too narrow a preoccupation with what is seen as 'Thatcherism' can blind one to the fact that, as we have shown, 'monetary' policies and cutbacks began before the Thatcher government came to office, and the administrative changes which came into sharp focus in the decade from 1976 to 1986 were merely an accentuation of trends which have been in operation for some time – i.e., continuing high levels of aggregate real government spending, particularly in the welfare area, but by a policy-delivery style switching markedly towards 'money-moving' and contracting out (hence the long sunset of the blue-collar civil service, shown in Fig. 8). Nor are these trends unique to the UK.

Scenario Two

Putting a probability approaching unity on the likelihood of an eventual diminution of the political head of steam behind cutbacks, coupled perhaps with some modest changes in policy leading to renewed staff recruitment, but setting those factors into the long-term trends in policy-delivery style discussed above might persuade us that the cutbacks will indeed 'bottom out' but that no return to anything like the 'fat years' is at all likely – the 'lower-level plateau' scenario painted in at the beginning of this section.

There are administrative as well as political reasons for believing that civil service staff cutbacks cannot long continue at their present rate. The pool of blue-collar civil servants, who as we have shown took the brunt of staff cutbacks in the 1976–86 decade, is now so depleted that it could only sustain about another decade of cuts on the same scale before drying up altogether. Conventional marginal analysis in economics would tend to support the expectation that although the first 10 or 20 percent of cutbacks may be quite feasible, the costs in other values (policy objectives, compliance, comfort) of each succeeding 10 percent will escalate rapidly until at some point the cost of the next marginal 1 percent cut is just not worth paying. Even for those who firmly believe that in any bureaucracy you can *always* find a 10 percent cut once a year (because the 'cushions of fat' regenerate themselves), a 10 percent compound decrement will mean a decreasing scale of absolute numbers cut (a 'bottoming-out' effect). That is, if a bureaucracy of 500,000 is cut by 10 percent each year, 50,000 jobs will go in the first year, but in the fifth year only 32,800 jobs will go, and so on.

Moreover, there are practical and transactional limits to what we might call the robotisability, contractability, and corporatisability of government operations, if only in terms of the size of the core bureaucracy needed to manage an extended contract business and to regulate an expanded network of quangos and firms. Administration of the public domain through a plethora of special-purpose authorities and through myriad contract arrangements has its drawbacks, as the historical record shows (particularly for services where it is not easy to specify the product or level of service required, or where there are many possible contingencies for which the contract ought to provide, or where the number of potential contractors is low).

The United Kingdom may be about to enter another cycle of the secular swing between fragmentation and integration, which saw the nineteenth-century invention of the ministerial department to gather under one roof (and so render more accountable) the host of *ad hoc* bodies (Schaffer 1973, 3), and which now decrees that the executive arms of these ministerial departments be released from such direct account-ability and made into free-standing 'agencies' on the Swedish pattern, eventually employing their own staffs on their own conditions, leaving only small policy ministries close to the parliamentary centre (Jenkins, Caines, and Jackson 1988). It takes not much sense of history to predict that in considerably less than another hundred years there will be a call to swing back again towards greater co-ordination, and to create 'a single civil service' in order to maximise the use of available talent, ease transferability from one agency to another, and regularise account-ability to Parliament for executive action. But in respect of the total size of the central government service, such changes are in themselves 'cosmetic', rather than basic: the numbers of those called 'civil servants' may go down markedly, but the executive agencies will still have to be staffed. It is true that there was at least one well-known case (medieval Iceland) of a government system which survived for three hundred years with a developed legislative branch and judicial branch but with no executive branch at all (apart, significantly, from the 'King's Spies' or political police); but that was a long time ago, and in another country.

Other arguments for thinking that nevertheless, although there may be limits to the degree of staffing cutbacks possible, the long-term trends are against any resumption of growth, have been led by one of us elsewhere (Hood 1989). The long-term change in administrative style discussed under Scenario One may be related, firstly, to social changes such as an increasingly middle-class society (in terms of lifestyle and educational attainment) making 'subsidiarity' in service provision more feasible; secondly, to changes in bureaucratic production methods, with new electronic information technology, and the shift to a 'service' rather than a 'manufacturing' economy generally, making contracting out of government functions easier; thirdly, to a rising sensitivity of the population at large to bureaucratic waste – brought about by a sharp rise in direct tax demands from average earners over the past thirty years, and by greater exposure of families to direct taxation as more married women took paid jobs outside the home; fourthly, to a general hegemony in public administration of ideas drawn from private business management. These exogenous, contextual changes which seem to be associated with the changing administrative style link with what Dunleavy (1985) identifies as the interest of top civil servants in 'bureau-shaping' (making bureaus smaller in total size, but containing more high-status staff and more discretionary budgets), and provide an opportunity for such interests to be realised. This clock, if not irreversible, seems unlikely to be turned back soon.

Such a change in administrative style for 'classic' bureaucracies is not, of course, incompatible with a large and even increasing public sector in other forms. Today, the police and the school teachers in the UK together outnumber the civil service by quite a lot, and although there is talk of 'privatising' both to some extent, that is a reversible policy decision and not a matter of long-term change in administrative style. But perhaps there are other factors in the mix today which we are not yet bringing into play, and which together with this change in administrative style might overwhelm these brakes on staffing cutback rates discussed in this section, and lead us to favour Scenario Three.

Scenario Three

What are the grounds for believing that the recent cutbacks are not a mere blip in the upward trend, not even the painful descent to a new plateau of less direct state action, but the early harbingers of a continuing contraction in central government staffing extending well beyond the immediately foreseeable future? We see three kinds of such grounds: the now-entrenched 'managerialism' of civil service culture; the flowering of the electronic revolution; and a profound shift in popular expectations of the role of state and government.

Although (as we and others have repeatedly said) Mrs Thatcher did not invent or inaugurate 'managerialism' in the UK civil service, there is no room for doubt that her enthusiastic espousal of the VFM philosophy, and perhaps her selective appointments to senior civil service posts over the past decade, have gone far to bring about the process of culture change called for by the (Fulton) Committee on the Civil Service (1968) and, even before that, by the (Plowden) Report on the control of Public

Expenditure (1961). The result may well be that at the helm of decision in the UK civil service today there is a whole generation of bureau heads and chief executives who have made their bureaucratic pile on bureau-shrinking rather than policy expansion; who are programmed to do nothing other than think in cost/benefit and value-for-money terms; to consider 'labour' as a businessman does, as an on-cost to be minimised in the interests of productivity; and to see personal and corporate advantage lying in the direction of continual 'saving' of staff.

This behaviour pattern would contradict not only the conventional self-regarding 'empire-building' stereotype of the economic theorists of bureaucracy (whose assumptions about bureaucratic motivations we never thought very realistic in any case – at least as applied to the UK civil service), but also the conventional in-bred 'power-wielding mandarin' image of much native writing on top civil servants, and even, perhaps, the 'public-service ethic' tradition that was built into the constitutional doctrine of civil service loyalty to the Minister of the day, under which programme ends rather than managerial means were the ruling criteria.

Be that as it may, we see no good grounds for believing that these older behaviour patterns somehow persist underneath the newer manageria-lism, that they are inherently stronger and more entrenched, and that they will 'out' once more when the régime changes and/or the current fads fade from memory. It may be the case, of course, that the 'business model' of managerial behaviour which the modern civil service has adopted in its culture shift is one which in several respects is quite archaic in modern business; perhaps the really advanced corporate executive in the contemporary multinational conglomerate looks more and more like the 'mandarin' and less and less like his or her cost-cutting successor. But that is a totally different point. We believe that, with great *angst* and self-questioning over two decades, but with final determi-nation and conviction, a managerialist bed has been made in Whitehall, and we shall all lie in it for some time to come even if the political climate begins to change radically in this regard – and there are no convincing signs of that even in the non-Conservative parties.

From this point of view, then, the drive behind the recent cutbacks in the UK civil service (which could not have been made by Ministers on their own, without the – yes – enthusiastic co-operation of senior civil servants) is in many ways self-reinforcing rather than self-limiting. We may be locked into a process which would escalate, but for the braking effects of the factors discussed under Scenario Two.

The second main ground for believing that Scenario Three may be the appropriate one is that we are only at the beginning of a technological development with a momentum of its own, quite apart from its importance as a staff-saving managerialist tactic. The electronic technology is now available (never mind the amazing speed with which the latest capability is made obsolete by an even more incredible development) to revolutionise utterly the relationship between official and citizen we have come to think of as the bureaucratic norm: mediated by forms and files, formal correspondence, across-the-counter interviews, more forms and signatures, vouchers, permits, warrants, girocheques. Already in a building in Washington, Tyne and Wear, payments of child benefit for the whole country are printed and dispatched by post automatically at the end of a process where for the bulk of the cases the only human input was right at the beginning, with roomfuls of young women keyboarding basic data from the claimant's original application form. Approximately 65 percent of the time the computer itself deals with the case, with no human involvement – and the computer picks out the difficult or anomalous cases for human perusal and discretionary decision. It only requires the initial keyboarding to be performed remotely by the local office interviewer to complete the automation of the routine.

The same applies now, or soon may, to a large number of citizen/official transactions. Further, the rapidly advancing computerisation of records of all kinds can enable the integration of many currently distinct financial transactions between state and citizen, and cut out entirely a number of procedures. Now, these developments are still a little 'scary' to many people, and certainly they present dangers to civil and human liberties and require many safeguards to be devised and entrenched. Nor is one obliged to accept that, because something is now possible (like Electronic Funds Transfer at Point of Sale in ordinary supermarket shopping), it must inevitably be installed and made compulsory. That is not our argument here. It is simply that, without a conscious and deliberate decision to *prohibit* these developments, to adopt an 'Indian policy' of turning one's back on such job-eating technologies, they will indeed spread and intensify – because they offer other advantages than mere job-saving and lower transaction costs, such as increased accuracy and avoidance of human error, enormous increases in speed, greatly enhanced provision of management information, and better control of the process generally (albeit with enormous 'downside' problems when the system malfunctions or 'crashes', or is paralysed by strike action).

On that understanding the prognostication for civil service numbers is clear and unambiguous. There are many services and aspects of services where human contact between performer and consumer is recognised to be of the essence, even if some potential for greater use of machines exists, as for example in education, counselling of all kinds, protective services and justice, recreation and entertainment. But there are many services where great numbers of officials work on routine tasks behind closed doors and never see members of the public at all as part of their duties: tax collection agencies, social security headquarters offices, savings bank headquarters, land and property administration, many aspects of defence. It is by and large in these services where the large numbers of lower-grade civil servants are found, and these are the groups which are vulnerable to being superseded by electronic devices. In the absence of a deliberate job-creation policy, the only argument for continuing to employ large staffs of lower-grade machine operators or clerical workers in social security headquarters offices, for example, when they could be by-passed electronically, would be that it was cheaper to do so than to install and maintain the advanced technology.

A decade or two hence, accordingly, we might confidently expect to see a considerably smaller and perhaps much more dispersed central civil service, but with each member on average wielding more discretion and undertaking more responsible tasks than the present average. Already one in four of the UK white-collar civil service is an Executive Officer in grade – what one might think of as the lowest rung of the middle ranks. By the turn of the century that proportion may well have risen to a half, with the virtual elimination of the battalions of clerical officers engaged on computerisable routine operations.

Finally, a less concrete and perhaps more contentious ground for believing that Scenario Three may be more likely than Scenarios One or Two: a secular, long-term, societal plate-tectonics shift of basic assumptions, understandings, and expectations about what the state is for. The literature on 'Thatcherism' is by now voluminous (see, e.g., Jessop *et al.* 1984; Marquand 1987), though by no means unanimous in its interpretations of the phenomenon, and we do not intend to enter these lists. But it would be generally agreed (a) that Margaret Thatcher is working with the grain of history rather than single-handedly altering its course, and (b) that one of the principal elements in her success is her turning of the fairly general disillusionment with Keynesian methods in the middle seventies into a positive programme (more fully articulated as the years went on) of re-education in reduced expectations of what the government should and can do.

One side of this concerns industrial non-intervention, encouraging enterprise rather than subsidising failure, abandoning protectionism; a second side concerns the more blatant aspects of 'rolling back the state' – privatisations, the 'return to the market', the selling off of public assets; and yet another side concerns what she may think of as 'Victorian values' (self-help, the duty of charity, family responsibilities, etc.), more post-Beveridgean politics than post-Keynesian economics. It cannot be said that this programme of re-education has wholly succeeded, at least not yet. But it is frequently acknowledged that Mrs Thatcher has 'shifted the centre of politics to the Right', and that even the main opposition party, Labour, no longer hopes simply to put the programme into reverse.

But Mrs Thatcher's campaign has not just been to capture 'hearts and minds'. A commitment to 'the disciplines of the market' rather than to the allocations of bureaucracy in determining 'who gets what, when, how' (Lasswell 1936) by no means rules out strong government; Mrs Thatcher's has been perhaps the most centralising government this century. In true radical fashion she has used brute legal force and financial weight to break up existing power structures, in local government, in the trade unions and the tripartite institutions of neo-corporatism, in the universities and the secondary education system – all in the interests of freeing up the logjam of habitual responses to stereotyped problems, of (in a most unConservative way) breaking the crust of custom.

But Mrs Thatcher did not engineer what is possibly the most significant shift in gradual popular appreciation of underlying social change, the notion of passage from one era to another in production technology: the ideas variously named post-industrialism, deindustrialisation, post-Fordism, each of which has its own precise references but with a common thread, the close of the age of the factory and the assembly line as the paradigmatic workplace for both males and females. It is not that there are no longer any large concentrations of 'labour' in manufacturing plants, but fewer of them are in the UK, and the trends are widely seen to be in the other direction: the *small is beautiful* credo, the computer revolution, the growth of 'knowledge-based' rather than 'skill-based' industries, the great increase in speed of communication and transport, the shift from a heavy-manufacturing to a services economy – these and other such developments combine to persuade both theorists and ordinary people that industrial capitalism is moving into a new phase.

These historical trends, these Thatcherite campaigns and policies, and deeper technological changes, do not inherently or inevitably entail civil service cutbacks. But we believe that they create a climate in which it might very plausibly be argued that the central bureaucracy is much more likely to shrivel than to blossom. Government will still be needed, to fulfil the 'defining functions of the state' at the least; but 'the state' may not remain as we know it now, even territorially – it may very well be both larger (Europe) and smaller (Scotland, Wales, Northern Ireland, East Anglia, etc.) than the present London-governed United Kingdom.

Our crystal-gazing has shown us three scenarios of possible futures. Readers can make up their own minds about which of them is most probable. For ourselves, we think that elements of all three scenarios are quite likely to occur. As in the first scenario, the passion very probably will go out of the drive for staff cutbacks (there are signs of that already: the government in February 1987 announced that no new manpower targets were to be set after that for 1 April 1988); public employment may well be used as a prophylactic against urban unrest, or, with a change of governing party, to eliminate the dole queue. The forces leading to a retarding of the present rate of cutbacks described in the second scenario are certainly operating. But we think that the three tendencies outlined in the third scenario will together prove more powerful in the long run. Our crystal ball tells us that by the turn of the millennium, the civil service cutbacks of the 1970s and 1980s will be only one chapter of a developing story. The heyday of public bureaucracies will be seen, world-wide, to have been the third quarter of the twentieth century. The study of cutback management, in classic public bureaucracies at least, will continue to have relevance.

A new science of politics is indispensable to a new world. This, however, is what we think of least; launched in the middle of a rapid stream, we obstinately fix our eyes on the ruins which may still be descried on the shore we have left, while the current sweeps us along and drives us backward toward the gulf. (De Tocqueville (1835) 1946, 7)

APPENDIX I
A note on sources and method

The basic approach we have used in this study, as in earlier research (Hood and Dunsire 1981), is one we call *bureaumetrics*, a term meant to indicate that what we do stands in relation to bureaucracy theory much as econometrics relates to economic theory, in trying to put actual values to the variables of a theoretical model. The scores of theories we surveyed in Chapter 2 and later make assertions about vulnerability to cuts that *ought* to be able to stand up to verification by numerical data, if appropriate data can be found. The attempt to put numbers on models sometimes also exposes problems of inadequate conceptualisation or classification, and of maintaining rigour and consistency, more sharply than alternative methods of discourse.

In all this research we have avoided the use of interviews and questionnaires as data collection methods, and relied as far as was feasible on 'unobtrusive measures' (Webb 1966) or *available data*: that is, milking already-published statistics for all they are worth, and, if we have to supplement these, asking only for sight of figures that have already been prepared for their own purposes by the people we approach. Unobtrusive measures are 'non-reactive' – that is, the data do not react to the questioner as does the respondent in an interview or a questionnaire; and access is either certain (in the case of published data) or considerably easier to obtain.

The method also has its drawbacks. The most obvious is that research questions tend to be limited to those that can be answered from available data. Sources tend to be 'low-grade ore' – a great deal of 'dross' for relatively few items of usable material. Statistical bases and categories keep changing even over quite short time periods. Data may be 'contaminated' in various ways, by deliberate 'dressing-up' of figures, by unappreciated ambiguity of category, by hidden 'loadings' of conventional understandings, and so on (see discussion in Hood and Dunsire 1981, 31–5). But with all these drawbacks the 'available data' method has one overriding virtue in a project such as ours: it is possible to encompass a larger number of units of analysis and a longer series of

218

observations with relatively small resources of people, money, and time, than by alternative methods. It is virtually unavoidable when dealing with a population of 36 organisations, a large number of variables, and a timespan of ten (or more) years.

There is a passage in McCloskey (1985, 182) which, with the substitution of 'bureaucratic' for 'economic' and 'bureaumetrics' for 'econometrics', sums up our own approach:

It is true . . . that no proposition about [bureaucratic] behaviour has yet been overturned by [bureaumetrics], at any rate not to the standard that the hypothetico-deductive model of science would demand . . . [Bureaumetrics] for adults claims merely to tell us how complicated life is, how few are the scientific matters that can be settled by the look-see of the crucial experiment, how we must look behind the appearance of the data.

As already indicated, the great bulk of the information used in this book is available to anyone from Her Majesty's Stationery Office, in such government publications as the *Annual Abstract of Statistics*; the Supply Estimates as presented annually to the House of Commons, along with the Chief Secretary to the Treasury's Memorandum; the *Appropriations Accounts* likewise; the annual White Paper on Public Expenditure; the Central Statistical Office monthly publication *Economic Trends*; the annual Blue Book (formerly entitled *National Income and Expenditure*, now called *The United Kingdom National Accounts*). On the staffing side: the annual *Civil Service Statistics* and the *Civil Service Yearbook*.

Some sources were at first published for sale, but then (although continued) became available only on request – as happened with the Reports on Manpower Reductions submitted by the Civil Service Department (later the Management and Personnel Office of the Cabinet Office) to the House of Commons' Treasury and Civil Service Committee. One or two sources were not generally available at all, and released to us only after suitable editing and under guarantees of confidentiality of detail: such were the government's periodical summary for internal use of *Staff in Post*, and extracts from the computer record named 'MANDATE'. Other sources of data (other government publications, published books, and articles in scholarly journals, etc.) are noted as they are used. No data at all for this research were collected by interview or by questionnaire.

We have not in the book mentioned the statistical problems in using such data – changes in categories or in basis of reporting information, differences in figures for what appears to be the same item between different sources, and the like – which are well known to anyone who uses government statistics for research purposes. For example, totals of civil service staff can be found in various places, and they seldom agree for any one year: one is an estimate made the previous year about numbers as at 1 April, another is a report of numbers as at 1 April, a third uses 1 January as base date, a fourth takes 1 January as base date but produces a different total, and so on. That is not too difficult to deal with. But one such matter which the reader will need to know about concerns the *unit of analysis*, the 'departments' or 'bureaus' into which the various 'Whitehall' totals (spending, staff, etc.) are disaggregated.

For consistency of comparison we wanted a constant set for all the variables we wished to use, from whatever source we were drawing the figures, and giving as near complete a coverage of the entire population (a 'census') as was compatible with that – and a set, moreover, which would persist throughout our period of analysis. It is not a simple matter even to list all the 'departments' there are in British central government (Hood, Dunsire and Thompson 1978; Hood and Dunsire 1981, chap. 3). Different lists are compiled for different purposes by different agencies. A list of all the departments accounting for a Vote in the Supply Estimates in 1976–7 contained 69 units; but some of these were minor departments (such as the several museums) which did not appear in, for example, *Civil Service Statistics*, and for which we would not, therefore, be able to collect data on a number of our variables. And ten years later the 'same' list would not be 69 items long.

Beginning from the list of departments accounting for a Vote in 1975/6, we first took account of mergers and splits between 1975 and 1985. For example, since the period began with a Civil Service Department which was later split between the Treasury and the Cabinet Office, we created a 'group' labelled TCC which for the earlier years aggregated the separate figures for the Treasury, the Cabinet Office, and the Civil Service Department, and for the later years aggregated Treasury and Cabinet Office figures, so that the content of the group was constant over the period. Similar aggregations were necessary in the Trade and Industry field, the Environment/Transport field, the Education/Arts and Libraries field, and in one or two minor areas.

Secondly, we surveyed the availability of data in all the principal series we would be using for each of the units on the list so created, and where there were large gaps for any unit, considered whether for the main purposes of the exercise that unit could be dispensed with. The outcome was a list of 36 'departments', comprising all the major and important ministries and omitting mainly minor units that are departments for some purposes but not for others. This list appears in Table A2, giving the

Table A1. *Conventional acronyms for central departments, in alphabetical order*

ACAS	Advisory, Conciliation, and Arbitration Service
CO	Cabinet Office
CIO	Central Office of Information
CC	Charity Commission
C&E	HM Customs and Excise
CEO	Crown Estate Office
DE	Department of Employment
DEn	Department of Energy
DES	Department of Education and Science
DHSS	Department of Health and Social Security
DNS	Department of National Savings
DOE	Department of the Environment
DTI	Department of Trade and Industry
DTp	Department of Transport
ECGD	Export Credits Guarantee Department
FCO	Foreign and Commonwealth Office
GA	Government Actuary's Department
HO	Home Office
HMT	Her Majesty's Treasury
HSC	Health and Safety Commission
IBAP	Intervention Board for Agricultural Produce
IND	Department of Industry
IR	Board of Inland Revenue
LCD	Lord Chancellor's Department
LR	HM Land Registry
MAFF	Ministry of Agriculture, Fisheries and Food
MOD	Ministry of Defence
MSC	Manpower Services Commission
NIO	Northern Ireland Office
ODA	Overseas Development Administration
OFT	Office of Fair Trading
OPCS	Office of Population Censuses and Surveys
OS	Ordnance Survey
PCO	Privy Council Office
PRO	Public Record Office
PSA	Property Services Agency
RFS	Registry of Friendly Societies
RGS	General Register Office (Scotland)
ROF	Royal Ordnance Factories
ROS	Department of the Registers of Scotland
SO	Scottish Office
SRO	Scottish Record Office
TCC	[Non-conventional] Treasury + Cabinet Office (+ Civil Service Department)
TS	Treasury Solicitor's Department
WO	Welsh Office

Table A2. *Selected departments and departmental groupings. Ranked by total staff (non-industrial and industrial) as at 1 January 1985 and giving total budget estimate 1985/6*

			Staff	Staff	£000
1	MOD	Defence Group	176,355		
		Ministry of Defence		195,322	16,564.508
		Royal Ordnance Factories	18,967	93,588	32,826.182
		Total Defence			
2	DHSS*	Department of Health and Social Security		69,175	975.815
3	IR	Inland Revenue			
4	DE	Employment Group	28,833		
		Employment	20,838		
		Manpower Services Commission	615		
		ACAS	3,582	53,868	2,668.170
		Health & Safety Commis/Exec			
		Total Employment Group			
5	DOE	Environment Group	6,566		
		Excluding PSA	27,405		
		Property Services Agency	14,297	48,268	16,828.451
		Transport			
		Total Environment Group			
6	HO	Home Office		36,584	3,420.375
7	C&E	Customs and Excise		25,535	354.925
8	DTI	Trade and Industry		12,460	1,648.076
9	MAFF	Ministry of Agriculture, Fisheries, and Food		11,219	496.983
10	LCD	Lord Chancellor's Department		10,093	474.399
11	SO	Scottish Office		9,849	5,155.182
12	FCO	Foreign and Commonwealth Office		8,247	604.791
13	DNS	National Savings Department		7,862	153.100
14	LR	Land Registry		6,792	79.143
15	TCC	Treasury Group	3,363		
		Treasury	1,659		
		Cabinet Office			
		Total TCC		5,022	2,316.606

16	OS	Ordnance Survey	2,959	17,445
17	DES	Department of Education and Science	2,485	3,376,054
18	WO	Welsh Office	2,269	2,240,537
19	OPCS	Office of Population Censuses and Surveys	2,076	26,520
20	ECGD	Export Credits Guarantee Department	1,779	666,629
21	ODA	Overseas Development Administration	1,573	1,195,884
22	DEn	Department of Energy	1,080	1,899,651
23	COI	Central Office of Information	925	67,200
24	ROS	Registers of Scotland	806	1
25	IBAP	Intervention Board for Agricultural Produce	720	305,716
26	TS	Treasury Solicitor	446	24,042
27	PRO	Public Record Office	403	10,821
28	CC	Charity Commission	321	4,861
29	OFT	Office of Fair Trading	303	7,479
30	RGS	General Register Office (Scotland)	258	3,079
31	NIO	Northern Ireland Office	171	1,315,854
32	SRO	Scottish Record Office	120	1,808
33	RFS	Registry of Friendly Societies	120	2,299
34	GA	Government Actuary	60	1,166
35	PCO	Privy Council Office	31	1,160
36	CEO	Crown Estate Office	28	574

Note:*In 1988, the Department of Health and Social Security was divided into two ministries, the Department of Health (DH) and the Department of Social Security (DSS). This change was, however, outside the period covered by this analysis, and references in the text to DHSS have for the most part been left as they were.

Sources: Supply Estimates (excluding Supplementaries); *Civil Service Statistics*, 1985

conventional acronyms, ranked by total staff size at 1 January 1985, and giving also figures for 1985/6 budget (the ranking by budget clearly is not the same).

For some purposes, a subset of the 36 was used, in order to eliminate distortions caused by small absolute numbers when using percentages in aggregate comparisons; this subset comprises all the departments with more than 1,000 staff, that is, excluding those at the bottom of the list in the table, Nos. 24 onwards – except for the Northern Ireland Office, No. 31. The figure of 171 staff at 1 January 1985 is of UK civil servants only; but for a true parallel with, for example, the Scottish Office or the Welsh Office, the Northern Ireland Civil Service, a separate body, ought to be included. In 1975, the beginning of our period, the NIO had on this basis 3,075 staff. We decided therefore to include NIO among the 'large departments' in aggregate calculations, giving a subset of 24 departments. Which set is being used is made clear at the head of each table in the main text.

Table A1 gives an alphabetical list of the commonly used acronyms for British central government departments, for easy reference.

APPENDIX II
Geographical dispersion

The annual compilation *Civil Service Statistics* has a table giving for each department the number of non-industrial ('white-collar') civil servants in each of the Standard Regions of the country (the same as the Economic Planning Regions). Table A3 shows the distribution of *all* white-collar civil servants among regions in each year 1977 to 1986, with the overall percentage change during this period. In order to present the data for individual departments succinctly, we devised a *concentration index* (of which the reciprocal becomes an index of *dispersion*).

The relevant data were available for only twenty departments over this period. For each department, the mean number of staff per region was calculated, together with the standard deviation. If the standard deviation is high in relation to the mean, this indicates that staff in that department are concentrated in one or a few regions. Conversely, if the standard deviation is low in relation to the mean, staff are highly dispersed – some in all or many regions. The index, therefore, is expressed by

$$\frac{\text{standard deviation}}{\text{mean}}$$

Table A4 shows twenty departments ranked in order of concentration index for the years 1976 and 1986. As might be predicted, the most concentrated departments (most staff in one or very few regions) were the territorial departments, Scottish Office and Welsh Office, followed by the group of central policy and control departments we labelled TCC (Treasury, Cabinet Office, and Civil Service Department while it existed). At the most highly dispersed end appeared the departments with extensive local office networks, the Department of Health and Social Security, the Department of Employment, and Inland Revenue.

The concentration/dispersion index for the white-collar civil service as a whole (all departments) fell between 1977 and 1986 from 1.27 to 1.15, meaning that the civil service became more dispersed. This effect, however, is heavily influenced by the fact that two out of the three *largest*

Table A3. *Non-industrial (white-collar) staff by standard region, 1977–86 (000s)*

Region	1977	1978	1979	1980	1981	1982	1983	1984	1985	1986	% change
South-East*	240.3	234.9	230.6	86.1	85.3	83.9	81.3	79.0	78.3	78.0	− 9.4
South-West	51.3	51.7	51.8	51.5	50.4	49.1	48.1	47.5	47.0	47.1	− 8.2
Greater London*				136.3	131.8	127.7	123.4	119.8	116.7	115.1	−15.6
East Anglia	10.8	11.3	13.2	12.4	12.3	12.2	12.1	12.2	12.6	13.1	+21.3
East Midlands	21.2	21.5	21.2	20.6	20.8	20.7	20.1	19.9	19.8	19.5	− 8.0
West Midlands	29.2	29.0	29.4	28.7	28.6	28.9	28.5	28.4	28.5	28.4	− 2.7
Yorkshire and Humberside	30.0	30.6	30.9	30.1	30.4	31.0	30.6	30.4	30.7	30.0	0
North-West	55.7	56.7	57.2	54.5	54.3	53.7	53.4	51.5	50.6	49.0	−12.0
Northern	35.4	35.6	36.6	34.9	35.6	34.6	33.5	32.1	31.3	30.6	−13.6
Scotland	51.4	51.6	52.2	50.8	50.8	50.3	49.2	48.9	48.9	48.4	− 5.8
Wales	30.9	31.5	31.5	30.4	30.2	29.7	29.5	28.6	28.4	27.5	−11.0
Northern Ireland	4.3	3.7	3.7	3.4	3.4	3.3	3.2	3.1	3.0	3.1	−27.9
Overseas, etc.	9.2	8.9	7.7	8.7	8.7	7.8	7.5	7.4	7.4	8.0	−13.0
All Regions	569.7	567.0	566.0	548.6	542.8	532.8	520.3	508.9	503.3	497.9	−12.6
Total†	560.5									489.8	
Mean	50.95									44.52	
St. dev.	64.89									51.38	
St. dev. Mean	1.27									1.15	

Note: * Separate figures for Greater London available only from 1980; included in South-East Region, 1977–9. Average change for both Greater London and South-East Region is from 1980 to 1986
† All UK regions (i.e. excluding Overseas etc.)

Table A4. *Twenty departments ranked by concentration/dispersion index, 1976 and 1986*

Department	1976	1986	
Scottish Office	3.28	3.31	most concentrated
Welsh Office	3.10	3.26	↑
Treasury/Cabinet Office	3.02	3.04	
Department of Energy	2.68	2.71	
Office of Population Censuses and Surveys	2.42	2.44	
Ordnance Survey	2.36	2.43	
Department of Industry	2.34	2.21	
Department of Education and Science	2.19	2.02	
HM Customs and Excise	1.76	1.67	
Department of the Environment	1.74	1.54	
HM Stationery Office	1.61	1.81	
Ministry of Defence	1.60	1.47*	
Home Office	1.58	1.38	
Department for National Savings	1.56	1.69	
Lord Chancellor's Department	1.51	1.54	
HM Land Registry	1.51	1.27	
Ministry of Agriculture, Fisheries, and Food	1.37	1.41	
Board of Inland Revenue	0.97	0.94	
Department of Employment	0.94	0.84	↓
Department of Health and Social Security	0.91	0.88	most dispersed

*Ministry of Defence included Royal Ordnance factories until 1986. The figure given is the Concentration/Dispersion Index for 1985

Concentration/Dispersion Index $\dfrac{\text{mean number of staff per standard region}}{\text{standard deviation}}$

Source: *Civil Service Statistics* (annually)

departments by staff count are also very highly dispersed. There was a tendency for highly concentrated departments to become more so over the period of cutbacks (the index of the top six departments went up), and for highly dispersed departments to become more so (the index for four out of the five bottom departments went down). Comparison with Table 5.4 (the distribution of cutbacks by frequency and severity) shows that the more highly dispersed departments suffered less that the more highly concentrated departments: six out of the ten lower-index departments were cut neither deeply nor continually in either spending or staffing, while none of the ten higher-index departments escaped in that way.

APPENDIX III
Functional analysis

There is a way of classifying the tasks of civil servants in and across departments which is called (by the civil service itself) 'functional analysis'. Staff of central government departments are apportioned to categories according to whether they are deemed to be engaged in 'central administration' or 'executive functions', and if the latter, whether in 'public services', 'trading and repayment services', or 'general support services'. These categories were defined (in *Civil Service Statistics*, 1973, p. 8) as follows:

Central administration
This column includes staff at headquarters concerned with:
    a. the introduction or development of policy and related matters;
    b. central services such as the provision of professional advice and support
        services e.g. finance, personnel, etc.

Executive functions
Public services include staff concerned with the application of policy, e.g. payment of sickness benefits, collection of taxes and contributions, staffing prisons and providing services to industry including research and development.

Trading and repayment services include staff engaged on activities which are largely financially self-supporting through sales, fees or charges for goods and service.

General support services include staff engaged in providing services for other departments. A department's own central services staff are included in the column headed *Central administration*.

The statistics relate to all industrial and non-industrial staff and include established and unestablished staff but exclude casual or seasonal staff. Two part-time staff are counted as one whole time staff.

This functional analysis of civil service work is not provided every year and the latest available to us was that in the Chief Secretary's Memorandum on the Estimates in 1980/1, table 6B. We have adapted this table to present the data for the 36 departmental groupings we are using in this survey, and calculated the percentage of the total staff of each department falling in each of the four classes, as in Table A5.

Partly because of the larger number of blanks in each of the 'trading and repayments' and 'general support' columns, and partly because of the broad similarity of these two functions as compared with either 'central administration' or 'public services' definitions, we found it convenient for present purposes to aggregate them under the label 'trading and support services', so as to produce only three categories. Nine departments are then found to have more than half of their staff engaged in 'central administration': NIO, CC, ECGD, and PCO (all 100 percent); FCO and DES (over 70 percent); and WO, OFT, and DEn (over 68 percent). Fifteen departments have more than half of their staff engaged in 'public services': SRO (100 percent), IR, C&E, DHSS, LCD, and RGS (over 90 percent); DE and HO (80–90 percent); OS, MAFF, PRO, RFS (70–80 percent); IBAP, ODA, and SO (50–70 percent). Nine departments have over half their staff in 'trading and support': LR, CEO, GA, and ROS (100 percent); DNS (98 percent); COI (81 percent); DOE and TS (70–80 percent), and TCC (52 percent). Two departments do not have as much as half their staff in any category, though the largest strength in each case is in 'public services' – IND and OPCS; and the information is not given for MOD.

Table A5. Functional analysis of staff by central administration, public services, and trading and support services, 1980/1. 36 departments. Numbers and percentages

| Department 1 | Central admini- stration 2 | Executive functions | | | Trading and support 6 (= 4 + 5) |
		Public services 3	Trading and repayment 4	General support 5	
Treasury and Cabinet Office	3,338	0	1,773	1,818	3,591
	48.2	0	25.6	26.2	51.3
Customs and Excise	1,769	25,881	0	0	0
	6.4	93.6	0	0	0
Department of Education and Science	1,837	788	0	0	0
	70.0	30.0	0	0	0
Department of Employment	5,997	45,614	792	0	792
	11.4	87.0	1.5	0	1.5
Department of Energy	897	248	160	0	160
	68.7	19.0	12.3	0	12.3
Department of the Environment	4,540	9,892	20,223	28,182	48,405
	7.2	15.7	32.2	44.8	77.0
Department of Health and Social Security	6,985	88,844	0	0	0
	7.3	92.7	0	0	0
Department for National Savings	202	0	10,240	0	10,240
	1.9	0	98.1	0	98.1
Export Credits Guarantee Department	2,040	0	0	0	0
	100.0	0	0	0	0
Foreign and Commonwealth Office	7,115	1,542	970	0	970
	73.9	16.0	10.1	0	10.1
Government Actuary's Department	0	0	0	62	62
	0	0	0	100.0	100.0
Home Office	5,307	29,419	0	0	0
	15.3	84.7	0	0	0

Department										
Industry and Trade	5,236	31.7	6,189	37.4	4,109	24.8	999	6.0	5,108	30.8
Inland Revenue	3,487	4.4	75,096	94.4	0	0	997	1.2	997	1.2
Intervention Board for Agricultural Produce	202	34.3	396	65.6	0	0	0	0	0	0
Land Registry	0	0	0	0	5,990	100.0	0	0	5,990	100.0
Lord Chancellor's Department	511	4.9	9,614	91.9	330	3.2	0	0	330	3.2
Ministry of Agriculture, Fisheries, and Food	3,270	23.7	10,550	76.3	0	0	0	0	0	0
Overseas Development Administration	980	43.5	1,273	56.5	0	0	0	0	0	0
Northern Ireland Office	258	100.0	0	0	0	0	0	0	0	0
Office of Fair Trading	241	69.0	0	0	108	30.9	0	0	108	30.9
Office of Population Censuses and Surveys	650	24.1	1,130	41.9	0	0	918	34.0	918	34.0
Ordnance Survey	240	6.8	2,740	77.2	570	16.1	0	0	570	16.1
Privy Council Office	40	100.0	0	0	0	0	0	0	0	0
Crown Estate Office	0	0	0	0	119	100.0	0	0	119	100.0
Public Record Office	36	8.4	326	75.8	68	15.8	0	0	68	15.8
Registry of Friendly Societies	30	25.0	85	70.8	5	4.3	0	0	5	4.3
Charity Commission	344	100.0	0	0	0	0	0	0	0	0
Scottish Office	5,162	47.1	5,727	52.3	64	0.6	0	0	64	0.6

Table A5. (cont.)

Department 1	Central administration 2	Executive functions				Trading and support 6 (=4+5)
		Public services 3	Trading and repayment 4	General support 5		
Department of the Registers of Scotland	0	0	476	0		476
			100.0	0		100.0
Scottish Record Office	0	139	0	0		0
		100.0	0	0		0
General Register Office (Scotland)	32	333	0	0		0
	8.7	91.2	0	0		0
Treasury Solicitor's Department	80	30	0	0		0
	17.5	6.5	0	0		0
Welsh Office	1,730	775	0	0		0
	69.1	30.9	0	0		0
Central Office of Information	227	0	236	0		236
	18.5	0	19.2	0		19.2

Source: Chief Secretary's Memorandum on the Estimates (Cmnd 7869) 1980/1, table 6B

APPENDIX IV
Cluster analysis

We noted in Chapter 6 that although departments differed greatly in the proportions of staff saving attributable to the several categories,[1] some departments *appeared* to adopt similar strategies in finding staff cuts. We applied techniques of cluster analysis to see whether, among departments of over 1,000 staff, groupings of departments emerged on the basis of (1), number of staff reductions, and (2), percentage of total staff reductions attributable to categories (a)(ii), (b), (c), (e), and (f)-with-(h). Category (g) was not used, being inappropriate to some departments; and, because of the 'distortion' caused by the large ROF transfer in 1984/5, only the first four years of the period were included.

Cluster analysis techniques find groupings of units that are highly similar to one another and very little similar to units not in the groupings. Three distinct techniques were used: single linkage, Ward's hierarchy, and relocation methods, used on matrices measuring departmental similarities and differences by product moment correlation coefficients, error sums of squares, and squared Euclidean distances. Both raw data and standardised data were analysed. Although minor differences appeared in the results, some departments were grouped together consistently by all hierarchical methods at the nine-group level, confirmed by the results of a Principal Components Analysis.

The following were the groupings that emerged:

C&E	MOD	OPCS	FCO	MAFF	SO
LR	DEn	COI	TCC	DES	IR
ECGD		DHSS	DTI	DE	HMSO
				NIO	LCD

[1] (a) decreases arising from change in workloads (including revised economic assumptions)
(b) carrying out work more efficiently by a major change in method
(c) general streamlining (including lower standards of service) and other minor changes
(e) dropping or materially curtailing a function
(f) privatisation, including contracting out
(g) hiving off to new or existing public body
(h) [from 1982/3] contracting out.

All these groupings appeared together regardless of the hierarchical method used. WO appeared with the MOD/DEn groupings more than once, and OS and DTp sometimes fell into one group, sometimes another. There were hints of affinity also between the MAFF-group and the SO-group. DOE, HO, and DNS were consistent outliers. (For a key to the initials, see Table A1 in Appendix I, or the Index.)

What a cluster analysis does not tell you is *why* these groupings form, what it is that makes the units within a group more like each other than they are like any other unit. You have to inspect the grouping for yourself, compare one with another, and see whether any 'principles' strike you. For some of these groups it is not too difficult to guess what the computer is picking up. FCO, TCC, and DTI, for instance, are in the top four departments by proportion of cuts in category (a), 'change in workload', over the four-year period – and the remaining one, OS, although probably excluded because its numbers are smaller, falls into the group on some analyses. C&E, LR, and ECGD are among the top four by proportion of cuts in category (b), 'change in methods'; and the remaining one, DNS, a consistent outlier, at least does not fall in any other group.

The link between MOD, DEn, and WO would appear to be that they are the top three departments in proportion of staff cuts in the (c), 'general streamlining and lowering of standards', category. OPCS, COI, and DHSS are the top three departments by proportion of cuts in the (e), 'dropping or curtailing functions', category.

The linkage between the remaining two groupings, the MAFF-group and the SO-group, is not quite so obvious, since neither group is in the 'top four' of any category; but MAFF, DES, DE, and NIO are in the top nine in (b), though also having notable proportions in other categories, while SO, IR, HMSO, and LCD are in the top seven in (e) but also high elsewhere – which would also explain the occasional clustering of both groups together.

So we can say with some confidence that, although the statistical appearance of a common 'strategy' is no guarantee that such a strategy was consciously adopted (let alone *concerted*), certain groups of departments were able to, or obliged to, or chose to, follow a similar course in meeting the government's demands for staff cuts over the period 1980–4. FCO, TCC, and DTI, we can say, seemed to be particularly susceptible to 'decreases arising from change in workloads (including revised economic assumptions)'; and similarly with the other groupings, as set out below:

(a)-dominated:	FCO, TCC, DT (OS)
(b)-dominated:	C&E, LR, ECGD
(c)-dominated:	MOD, DEn, WO
(e)-dominated:	OPCS, COI, DHSS
non-dominated:	MAFF, DES, DE, NIO
	SO, IR, HMSO, LCD
outliers:	DOE, HO, DNS, DTp

In an effort to 'tidy up' these last three categories we went back to the data and established a criterion for 'domination': more than 40 percent of savings in a particular category over the period (1980–4) would remove a department from the 'non-dominated' grouping (but we left DTI in the (a)-dominated group where the computer had put it, even though it had only 37.0 percent of (a) savings). Applying this criterion moved MAFF into the (b)-dominated grouping (along with DNS, at 55.0 percent), NIO into the (c)-dominated grouping, and IR and LCD into the (e)-dominated grouping. DOE became an (f)-dominated grouping on its own, and DTp the sole (g)-dominated department. That left a truly non-dominated grouping consisting of DES, DE, SO, HMSO, and HO, with a fairly even spread over at least four categories. The new groupings are (listed in order of domination):

1 (a)-dominated:	FCO, OS, TCC, DTI
2 (b)-dominated:	ECGD, LR, DNS, C&E, MAFF
3 (c)-dominated:	WO, DEn, MOD, NIO
4 (e)-dominated:	DHSS, OPCS, COI, LCD, IR
5 (f)-dominated:	DOE
6 (g)-dominated:	DTp
7 non-dominated:	DE(bcde), HMSO(ecba), DES(cbea), SO(geca), HO(bcfa).

These observations, of course, merely raise the further question 'Why?' – what it is about the Foreign Office, the Treasury and Cabinet Office, and the Department of Trade and Industry, for example, that makes them (and their occasional companion, the Ordnance Survey) particularly susceptible to that kind of cut? That question of underlying affinity, for all the groupings found, was explored in Chapter 6, section IV, and need not be repeated here.

References

Books and articles

Albrow, M. 1970. *Bureaucracy*. London, Pall Mall Press

Aristotle. 1932. *Rhetoric*, trans. and ed. L. Cooper. New York, Appleton-Century

Bagehot, W. 1867. *The English Constitution*, ed. R. H. S. Crossman, 1964. London, C. A. Watts

Barnard, C. I. 1938. *The Functions of the Executive*. Cambridge, Mass., Harvard University Press

Bray, A. J. M. 1987. The Clandestine Reformer: a Study of the Rayner Scrutinies. In *Strathclyde Papers on Government and Politics* No. 55. Glasgow, University of Strathclyde Politics Department

Breton, A. 1974. *The Economic Theory of Representative Government*. London, Macmillan

Bridges, Rt Hon. Lord. 1964. *The Treasury*. The New Whitehall Series, no. 12. London, George Allen & Unwin

Buchanan, J. M. 1967. *Public Finance in Democratic Process*. Chapel Hill, University of North Carolina Press

Buchanan, J. M. and Tullock, G. 1962. *The Calculus of Consent*. Ann Arbor, University of Michigan Press

Chapman, L. 1978. *Your Disobedient Servant: The Continuing Story of Whitehall's Overspending*. London, Chatto & Windus; Harmondsworth, Penguin, 1979

Crecine, J. P. 1969. *Governmental Problem Solving*. Chicago, Ill., Rand McNally

Crosland, C. A. R. 1956. *The Future of Socialism*. London, Cape

Dahl, R. and Lindblom, C. E. 1953. *Politics, Economics and Welfare*. New York, Harper & Row

Daly, M. and George, A. 1987. *Margaret Thatcher In Her Own Words*. Harmondsworth, Penguin

Downs, A. 1957. *An Economic Theory of Democracy*. New York, Harper & Row

Downs, A. 1960. Why the Government Budget Is Too Small in a Democracy. *World Politics*, 12, 541–63

Downs, A. 1967. *Inside Bureaucracy*. Boston, Little, Brown

Dunleavy, P. 1980. The Political Implications of Sectoral Cleavages and the Growth of State Employment. *Political Studies*, 28, 364–83 and 527–49

Dunleavy, P. 1985. Bureaucrats, Budgets and the Growth of the State. *British Journal of Political Science*, 15, 299–328

Dunleavy, P. and O'Leary, B. 1987. *Theories of the State*. London, Macmillan

Finer, S. 1975. *Adversary Politics and Electoral Reform*. London, Anthony Wigram

Fry, G. K. 1985. *The Changing Civil Service*. London, George Allen & Unwin

Fry, G. K. 1986. The British Career Civil Service under Challenge. *Political Studies*, 34(4), 533–55

Fry, G. K. 1988. The Thatcher Government, the Financial Management Initiative and the 'New Civil Service'. *Public Administration*, 66(1), 1–20

Gerth, H. H. and Mills, C. W. (eds.). 1948. *From Max Weber: Essays in Sociology*. New York, Oxford University Press; London, Routledge & Kegan Paul, 4th impr., 1961

Glassberg, A. 1978. Organizational Responses to Municipal Budget Decreases. *Public Administration Review*, 38(4), 325–32

Glennerster, H. 1981. Social Service Spending in a Hostile Environment. In Hood and Wright (1981), 174–96

Gray, A. and Jenkins, W. 1985. *Administrative Politics in British Government*. Brighton, Wheatsheaf Books

Griffin, T. (ed.). 1987. *Social Trends*, No. 17. London, HMSO

Griffith, J. A. G. 1966. *Central Departments and Local Authorities*. London, George Allen & Unwin

Grunow, D. 1986. Development of the Public Sector: Trends and Issues. In F.-X. Kaufman, G. Majone, and V. Ostrom (eds.). *Guidance, Control, and Evaluation in the Public Sector*. New York, de Gruyter, 25–58.

Halsey, A. H. 1987. Social Trends Since World War II. In T. Griffin (ed.) (1987), 11–19

Hanusch, H. (ed.). 1983. *Anatomy of Government Deficiencies*. Berlin, Springer-Verlag

Hartley, K. 1981. Defence: A Case Study of Spending Cuts. In Hood and Wright (1981), 125–51

Hartley, K. and Lynk, E. 1983. Budget Cuts and Public Sector Employment: The Case of Defence. *Applied Economics*, 15(4), 531–40

Heath, A., Jowell, R., and Curtice, J. 1985. *How Britain Votes*. Oxford, Pergamon

Heclo, H. and Wildavsky, A. 1974. *The Private Government of Public Money*. London, Macmillan

Hennessey, P., Morrison, S. and Townsend, R. 1984. *Routine Punctuated By Orgies: the CPRS 1970–83*. Glasgow, University of Strathclyde

Hogwood, B. and Peters, B. G. 1985. *The Pathology of Public Policy*. Oxford, Clarendon Press

Hood, C. 1981. Axeperson, Spare That Quango . . . In Hood and Wright (1981), 100–22

Hood, C. 1989. Rolling Back the State or Shifting to a Contract and Subsidiarity State? In Nethercote (ed.) (1989)

Hood, C. C. and Dunsire, A. 1981. *Bureaumetrics: The Quantitative Comparison of British Central Government Agencies*. Farnborough, Gower

Hood, C. C., Dunsire, A., and Thompson, K. S. 1978. So You Think You Know What Government Departments Are . . . *Public Administration Bulletin*, 27, 20–32

Hood, C. C., Huby, M., and Dunsire, A. 1984. Bureaucrats and Budgeting Benefits: How do British Central Government Departments Measure Up? *Journal of Public Policy*, 4(3), 163–79

Hood, C. C. and Wright, M. (eds.). 1981. *Big Government in Hard Times*. Oxford, Martin Robertson

Hotelling, H. 1929. Stability in Competition. *Economic Journal*, 39, 41–57

Illich, I. 1977. Disabling Professions: Notes for a Lecture. *Contemporary Crises*, 1(4), 359–70

Jackson, P. M. 1982. *The Political Economy of Bureaucracy*. Oxford, Philip Allan

Jenkins, K., Caines, K. and Jackson, A. 1988. *Improving Management in Government: The Next Steps*. Efficiency Unit Report to the Prime Minister. London, HMSO

Jessop, B., Bonnett, K., Bromley, S., and Ling, T. 1984. Authoritarian Populism, Two Nations and Thatcherism. *New Left Review*, 147, 32–60. September/October 1984

Jørgensen, T. Beck. 1982. Budget Making and Expenditure Control. Paper presented at OECD seminar on The Capacity to Budget, Paris

Jørgensen, T. Beck. 1985. The Management of Survival and Growth in Public Organizations. Paper presented at ECPR Joint Sessions, Barcelona

Jørgensen, T. Beck. 1987a. Models of Retrenchment Behavior. *Working Paper No 24*. Brussels, International Institute of Administrative Sciences

Jørgensen, T. Beck. 1987b. Financial Management in the Public Sector. In J. Kooiman and K. A. Eliassen (eds.). *Managing Public Organizations: Lessons from Contemporary European Experience*. London, SAGE

Kaufman, H. 1985. *Time, Chance and Organizations*. Chatham, NJ, Chatham House

Klein, R. 1976. The Politics of Public Expenditure: American Theory and British Practice. *British Journal of Political Science*, 6(4), 401–32

Kogan, M. 1973. *Comment on Niskanen's Bureaucracy, Servant or Master?* London, Institute of Economic Affairs

Lasswell, H. D. 1936. *Politics: Who Gets What, When, How*. Glencoe, Ill., Free Press. Reprinted 1951

Laver, M. 1984. On Party Policy, Polarization and the Breaking of Moulds: the 1983 British Party Manifestos in Context. *Parliamentary Affairs*, 37 (1), 33–9

Lee, M. 1981. Whitehall and Retrenchment. In Hood and Wright (1981), 35–55

Leibenstein, H. 1976. *Beyond Economic Man: A New Foundation for Microeconomics*. Cambridge, Mass., Harvard University Press

Levine, C. H. 1978. A Symposium: Organizational Decline and Cutback Management. *Public Administration Review*, 38(4), 316–25

Levine, C. H. 1979. More on Cutback Management: Hard Questions for Hard Times. *Public Administration Review*, 39(2), 179–83

Lynn, J. and Jay, A. 1981. *Yes Minister: The Diaries of a Cabinet Minister*, vol. 1. London, British Broadcasting Corporation (vol. 2, 1982)

Mackenzie, W J. M. and Grove, J. W. 1957. *Central Administration in Britain*. London, Longmans, Green & Co.

McCloskey, D. N. 1985. *The Rhetoric of Economics*. Madison, University of Wisconsin Press

March, J. G. and Simon, H. A. 1958. *Organizations*. New York, John Wiley

Marquand, D. 1987. The Literature on Thatcher. *Contemporary Record*, 1(3), 30–1

Martin, S. 1983. *Managing Without Managers*. Beverly Hills, Calif., SAGE

Meltzer, A. and Richard, S. F. 1978. Why Government Grows (And Grows) in a Democracy. *Public Interest*, 52, 111–18

Meriam, L. and Schmeckebier, L. F. 1939. *Reorganization of the National Government: What Does It Involve?* Washington, DC

Meyer, M. W. *et al.* 1985. *Limits to Bureaucratic Growth*. New York, de Gruyter

Midwinter, A. and Page, E. 1981. Cutting Local Spending – the Scottish Experience. In Hood and Wright (1981), 56–76

Mill, J. S. 1861. *Considerations on Representative Government*, ed. A. D. Lindsay (1910), London, Dent

Mowat, C. L. 1955. *Britain Between the Wars 1918–1940*. London, Methuen

Musgrave, R. A. 1969. *Fiscal Systems*. New Haven, Yale University Press

Musgrave, R. A. and Peacock, A. T. 1958. *Classics in the Theory of Public Finance*. London, Macmillan

Nethercote, J. (ed.). 1989. *Redefining the Role of Government*. Sydney, Hale & Iremonger

Niskanen, W. A. 1971. *Bureaucracy and Representative Government*. Chicago, Aldine

Nordhaus, W. D. 1975. The Political Business Cycle. *Review of Economic Studies*, 42, 169–90

Nutter, G. W. 1978. *The Growth of Government in the West*. Washington, DC, American Enterprise Institute

O'Connor, J. 1973. *The Fiscal Crisis of the State*. New York, St Martin's Press

Ostrom, V. 1974. *The Intellectual Crisis in American Public Administration*, rev. edn, Alabama, Ala., University of Alabama Press

Peacock, A. T. 1979. *The Economic Analysis of Government and Related Themes*. Oxford, Martin Robertson

Peacock, A. T. 1983. Public X-inefficiency: Informational and Constitutional Constraints. In H. Hanusch (ed.). *Anatomy of Government Deficiencies*. Berlin/Heidelberg, Springer-Verlag, 125–38

Peacock, A. T. and Wiseman, J. 1961/1967. *The Growth of Public Expenditure in the United Kingdom 1890–1955*, 2nd (1967) edn. London, George Allen & Unwin

Pommerehne, W. and Schneider, F. 1983. Does Government in a Representative Democracy Follow a Majority of Voters' Preferences? An Empirical Examination. In Hanusch (1983), 61–84

Posner, R. A. 1977. *Law and the Economy*, 2nd edn. Boston, Little, Brown

Punnett, R. M. 1968. *British Government and Politics*. London, Heinemann

Rose, R. 1976. On the Priorities of Government. *European Journal of Political Research*, 4, 247–89

Rose, R. 1984. *Understanding Big Government*. London, SAGE

Rose, R. 1985. *Public Employment in Western Nations.* Cambridge, Cambridge University Press

Rose, R. and Peters, B. G. 1978. *Can Government Go Bankrupt?* New York, Basic Books

Rourke, F. E. 1976. *Bureaucracy, Politics and Public Policy,* 2nd edn. Boston, Little, Brown

Schaffer, B. 1973. *The Administrative Factor.* London, Frank Cass

Schick, A. 1971. *Budget Innovation in the States.* Washington, DC, Brookings

Self, P. 1972. *Administrative Theories and Politics.* London, Allen & Unwin

Self, P. 1980. Public Expenditure and Welfare. In Wright (ed.) (1980), 120–41

Short, J. 1981. *Public Expenditure and Taxation in the UK Regions.* Aldershot, Gower

Smith, A. 1776/1812. *An Inquiry into the Nature and Causes of the Wealth of Nations.* 3 vol. edn, 1812. London, Ward, Lock

Tarschys, D. 1975. The Growth of Public Expenditures: Nine Modes of Explanation. *Scandinavian Political Studies Yearbook,* No. 10, 9–31

Taylor, Sir H. 1836. *The Statesman,* ed. Parkinson (1958). New York, Mentor Books

Thomas, R. M. 1984. The Politics of Efficiency and Effectiveness in the British Civil Service. *International Review of Administrative Sciences,* 50(3), 239–51

de Tocqueville, A. 1835. *De la démocratie en Amérique.* Part I (trans. H. Reeve, Oxford World Classics edn, 1946, reprinted 1965. Oxford, Oxford University Press)

de Tocqueville, A. 1850. *Recollections.* London, Anchor Books

Tullock, G. 1965. *The Politics of Bureaucracy.* Washington, Public Affairs Press

Wagner, A. 1877. *Finanzwissenschaft,* part I. Leipzig, C. F. Winter

Webb, E. J. *et al.* 1966. *Unobtrusive Measures: Nonreactive Research in the Social Sciences.* Chicago, Ill., McNally

Weber, M. 1921. *Wirtschaft und Gesellschaft.* Tübingen, J. C. B. Mohr

Wildavsky, A. 1964. *The Politics of the Budgetary Process.* Boston, Little, Brown

Wildavsky, A. 1980. *The Art and Craft of Policy Analysis.* London, Macmillan

Wilensky, H. L. 1975. *The Welfare State and Equality: Structural and Ideological Roots of Public Expenditure.* Berkeley, University of California Press

Williamson, O. E. 1975. *Markets and Hierarchies.* London, Collier-Macmillan

Wilson, H. 1976. *The Governance of Britain.* London, Sphere Books

Wright, M. 1977. Public Expenditure in Britain: The Crisis of Control. *Public Administration,* 55(2), 143–69

Wright, M. 1981. Big Government in Hard Times: The Restraint of Public Expenditure. In Hood and Wright (1981), 3–31

Wright, M. (ed.). 1980. *Public Spending Decisions: Growth and Restraint in the 1970s.* London, George Allen & Unwin

Young, R. G. 1974. The Administrative Process as Incrementalism. Part 3 of *Approaches to the Study of Public Administration.* In Public Administration. Block II D331, part of *Social Sciences: A Third Level Course.* Milton Keynes, Open University Press

Official publications

Report on the Organisation of the Permanent Civil Service (The Northcote–Trevelyan Report). C 1713. London, HMSO, 1854

First Report of the Committee on National Expenditure (Chairman: Sir Eric Geddes). Cmd 1581. London, HMSO, 1922

Second Report of the Committee on National Expenditure (Chairman: Sir Eric Geddes). Cmd 1582. London, HMSO, 1922

Third Report of the Committee on National Expenditure (Chairman: Sir Eric Geddes). Cmd 1589. London, HMSO, 1922

Report of the Committee on the Control of Public Expenditure (The Plowden Committee). Cmnd 4132. London, HMSO, 1961

Report of the Committee on the Civil Service (The Fulton Committee). Cmnd 3638. London, HMSO, 1968

Fourth Report from the Treasury and Civil Service Committee, Session 1979–80. HC 712

Civil Service Manpower Reductions. Seventh Report from the Treasury and Civil Service Committee, 1980–81. HC 423. 13 July 1981

Civil Service Manpower Reductions. First Special Report from the Treasury and Civil Service Committee, 1982–83. HC 46. 15 November 1982

Report on Manpower Reductions in 1982–83 to the Treasury and Civil Service Committee. Third Annual Report. Management and Personnel Office. 207. No date

Report on Manpower Reduction in 1983–84 to the Treasury and Civil Service Committee. Fourth Annual Report. Management and Personnel Office. 207. No date

Report on Manpower Reductions in 1984–85 to the Treasury and Civil Service Committee. Fifth Annual Report. Management and Personnel Office. 207. No date

Index

An entry in *italics* signifies *passim*

timing 35, 113, 115; customer waiting-
time 37, 111, 146, 171
Tocqueville, A. de 5, 6
top: brass 42, 103; civil servants 6, 43,
96–8, 103, 121, 140, 146, 195, 212–13;
-level staff, 26, 28, 72–3; -level
superiors 36; middle and bottom 95,
103, 199; people 34, 98, 134; ranks 21,
98, 100, 103, 108, 199
trade 27, 66; trading and repayment
services 126, 132, 162, 228–9; trading
and support services 54, 127, 133–5,
159, 159n, 160, 229; trade-offs 192
trade unions 12, 15, 35, 145, 203, 216;
public-sector 26
transaction, citizen/official 214
transaction costs 175–6, 184–5, 210, 214
transfer: of functions 167; payments 22,
26, 28, 31, 37–9, 45–7, 76–7, 85, 93–4,
113, 115, 179, 183
transferability 211
transferable ownership 40
transport 30, 209, 216, 220
Transport and Communications 113, 115,
117–18
Treasury, HM see HMT
Treasury and Civil Service Committee 18,
42, 148–9, 156, 219
trends: trend explanations 23–4, 28, 56,
77, 80, 86; trend variables 142;
demographic trends 31, 83, 86;
economic trends 85; employment
trends 31, 86; industrial trends 30–1,
85; long-term trends 211; socio-
economic trends 30–1, 85, 202, 206–7;
theories about trends 28–31
Trevelyan, Sir C. 32, 34
trough year analysis 179, 183–4
TS (Treasury Solicitor's Department) 133,
229
Tullock, G. 6, 33
types of explanation 23–4, 77, 104
types of work 54–5,126–8, 132–3, 160, 228

Under-Secretaries 97, 104
unemployment 1, 2, 4, 12–13, 30, 45, 84,
203, 206–7
Urban Programme Grants 84
urban renewal 30, 209
urban unrest 84, 209, 217
USA 13, 24–5, 41, 104–5, 170, 199
user charges 40, 165, 168
user pays principle 126
utility 41, 98, 100, 173; functions 41

value 173–4, 203, 210; value for money
40, 146–8, 150, 153, 158, 212–13
values: political 50; Victorian 190, 216
variables 138n, 142, 175, 218–20; clout
141; output 139
variance 130, 142
VFM see value for money
visibility 46, 47, 49, 50–1, 113, 120, 136,
137–9, 141, 144, 175
volatility 46, 113
Vote (in Estimates) 121, 137, 158–9, 220
voters 2, 24, 56, 69; marginal 24; payroll
62
votes 13, 24–6, 46, 145, 206
vote sensitivity 49
voting 52, 58; voting coalition 5
vulnerability 23, 38, 44–5, 48–9, 51, 53,
68, 71, 80, 95, 112, 120–1, 128, 130–1,
135–7, 138–9, 141–2, 144, 163, 175,
186, 191–2, 200, 215, 218:
vulnerability theory 144, 218;
allocational vulnerability 51, 139;
departmental vulnerability 68, 121,
130, 141–2; identificational
vulnerability 49; operational
vulnerability 50, 138–9; output efffects
vulnerability 49–51, 135, 138–9, 144;
political vulnerability 48–9, 52, 140;
programme vulnerability 69, 120–1,
142

wages and salaries 22, 25, 27, 43, 46, 48,
54–5, 72, 77, 93, 99, 100, 102, 113,
118–19, 121, 124–5, 149 (see also
salaries)
Wagner, A. 5
Wales 22, 26, 28, 217
War Office 44
Washington, Tyne and Wear 214
waste 3, 194; wastage rate 97;
wastefulness 171, 194, 203;
bureaucratic waste 212; natural
wastage 36, 38, 95
Wealth of Nations, The 3, 177
Weber, M. 33, 110, 196; Weberian
bureaucrat 36, 53, 87–8, 94, 97, 109,
121, 130, 145, 163, 186; Weberian
logic 38; Weberian model 36, 53, 88,
110; Weberian official 37–9, 90, 95
welfare 98, 203, 210; benefits 26, 29, 77;
economist 47; foods 63; gains 98, 100;
programmes 12, 31; spending 30, 83
welfarism 13
West Midlands 28